Frommer's®

irreverent guide to Manhattan

D1113091

other titles in the

irreverent guide

series

Frommer's®

irreverent guide to Manhattan

2nd Edition

**Second Edition by
Ian McMahan
and
Jordan Simon**

Based upon First Edition by
Susan Spano and Sherill Tippins

A BALLIETT & FITZGERALD BOOK
MACMILLAN • USA

about the authors

Ian McMahan lives in New York City and spends as much time as he can manage in rural France. In addition to travel journalism, he writes both fiction and nonfiction. His most recent book is *Get it Done! A Guide to Motivation, Determination, and Achievement*.

Jordan Simon (Dining, Nightlife, and Entertainment) is author of many travel books, including Frommer's *Irreverent Guide to the US Virgin Islands*, and also their *Madrid & Barcelona by Night*. He is co-author of the upcoming *Astronumerology: Your key to Empowerment through Stars and Numbers*, published by Avon Books. He is a regular contributor to scores of magazines, including *Travel & Leisure*, *Town & Country*, and *Elle*. Jordan lives in New York City.

Balliett & Fitzgerald, Inc.

Editorial director: Will Balliett / Line editor: Holly Hughes / Executive editor: Tom Dyja / Managing editor: Rachel Aydt / Production editor: Maria Fernandez / Associate editors: Vijay Balakrishnan, Mike Walters

MACMILLAN TRAVEL

A Simon & Schuster Macmillan Company
1633 Broadway
New York, NY 10019

Find us online at www.frommers.com

ISBN 0-02-862438-6
ISSN 1085-4835

Macmillan Travel Art director: Michele Laseau
Interior design contributed to by Tsang Seymour Design Studio

what's so irreverent?

It's up to you.

You can buy a traditional guidebook with its fluff, its promotional hype, its let's-find-something-nice-to-say-about-everything point of view. Or you can buy an Irreverent guide.

What the Irreverents give you is the lowdown, the inside story. They have nothing to sell but the truth, which includes a balance of good and bad. They praise, they trash, they weigh, and leave the final decisions up to you. No tourist board, no chamber of commerce will ever recommend them.

Our writers are insiders, who feel passionate about the cities they live in, and have strong opinions they want to share with you. They take a special pleasure leading you where other guides fear to tread.

How irreverent are they? One of our authors insisted on writing under a pseudonym. "I couldn't show my face in town again if I used my own name," she told me. "My friends would never speak to me." Such is the price of honesty. She, like you, should know she'll always have a friend at Frommer's.

Warm regards,

Michael Spring

Michael Spring
Publisher

contents

HOTLINES & OTHER BASICS 214

INDEX 224

introduction

Visitors, who glean their impressions of the city from movies or television shows like *NYPD Blue* and *Law and Order*, are in for a case of culture shock.

Cab drivers may not have the greatest command of the English language, but their taxicabs won't be smoke-filled anymore. Steve Post, the curmudgeonly classical music disk-jockey who is a local institution, pointed out that now when you enter a cab the worst you're going to be exposed to is an "unsanitary" recording of Eartha Kitt (or Judd Hirsch, or Joan Rivers, or Placido Domingo) asking you to buckle your seatbelt and take your receipt. You will still spot squatters sporting filthy jeans and stray dogs on ropes in Tompkins Square Park, but it is unlikely you will witness an eviction riot anytime soon (unless you manage to get tickets to witness the one depicted in *Rent*, the hit downtown musical which has transformed the East Village lifestyle into another Broadway attraction, in New York's newly manicured theater district). People now travel to 10th Street and First Avenue for sushi, not crack.

At the helm of the big clean-up has been Mayor Giuliani, who also seems to have a pretty tight reign on crime—which is down dramatically. There are cops everywhere, rolling through the cities' parks in golf cart-like vehicles... and on horses and on bikes.

So the city is cleaner, and safer, but is it a better place to visit? Most New Yorkers would say yes. How do we know? Because every New Yorker is a visitor here at one time or another. In fact, the ability to do this may be the strongest reason the city's residents put up with its noise and chaos. New Yorkers, with all of their daily rushing around, are adept at finding oases and retreats in unexpected places. But even they are surprised to rediscover the view of the Hudson River from the medieval portion of the Metropolitan Museum of Art—the Cloisters—in North Manhattan's Fort Tryon Park. Or the Hasidic Jewish neighborhood that borders it, complete with a knish factory. A day at the beach with a real-life freak show is only a token's distance away at Coney Island. I once spent a day on a Russian boardwalk in Sheepshead Bay, Brooklyn (also a token away) and then went night blue-fishing, two hours offshore, all without a car. It is impossible to be so knowledgeable about the city that you can't find a new place to go.

In one weekend you can hear Bobby Short sing "Manhattan" at the Carlyle Hotel and then live out a Nineties update of Cole Porter's famous song. You can walk across the Brooklyn Bridge or catch a Rangers game at Madison Square Garden. You can eat hot dogs and giant pretzels from Central Park vendors and wander through the park's zoo. And later, after seeing Van Gogh's sunflowers, Ming Dynasty ceramics, and a rooftop sculpture garden during the Metropolitan Museum of Art's evening hours, you can wind your way through Chinatown and pick out your favorite basement restaurant.

By the same token, newcomers can become New Yorkers in no time. Things change so fast around here, who would doubt you? As a transplant of five years, I can testify to that. And since I have lived here, New York's landscape— and my understanding of it—have changed dramatically. My neighborhood, Chelsea, has experienced a dramatic makeover by buff gay men, and the spillover from expensive SoHo galleries has settled comfortably on West 22nd Street. Then again, disorienting as it may seem, if I wanted to, I could walk about eight blocks from my apartment over to the new Chelsea Piers Sports Complex and ride a rent-a-horse at their equestrian center, or practice my swing at a driving range that takes up the length of an entire pier. I have seen lower Eighth Avenue take off, with some restaurants turning over two, even three times in five years. It seems to me that each generation gets better, *and* more expensive. The once needle-infested Lower East Side now has a new nickname from Realtors: LoHo. Why do the locals detest this gentrification indicator? Say goodbye to *another* bastion of cheap-rents, that's why. Cozy candlelit couch bars are littering the Lower East Side's Orchard Street, the pin that fastened together the "Bargain District." Even Hell's Kitchen, where my Long Island son-of-a-butcher grandfather begged me to never go alone because it was home to notorious gang wars, is up and coming. And right across the Manhattan Bridge going into Brooklyn there is a neighborhood filled with lofts and empty streets that somehow feel extra dark at night. But now DUMBO (Down Under the Manhattan Bridge) holds a new neighborhood festival, when artists who've relocated there to obtain larger spaces open up their splattered studios to serve cider to the curious.

Neighborhoods continue to melt together. Where does SoHo stop and TriBeCa begin? One can hardly tell apart their expensive French bistros. When exactly did David Bouley's culinary kingdom help transform anonymous TriBeCa (crammed between Canal Street, City Hall and the World Trade Center) into a pocket of hipness that is now home to De Niro, JFK, Jr. and a bevy of supermodels (and even the clandestine Manhattan police horse stables)? Chinatown continues to choke a very little Little Italy, and the Ukraine district of the East Village is now littered with Starbucks and—count them—three McDonald's.

The sky rocketing real-estate market has brought about perhaps the most often mentioned and locally detested changes: sky-high rents and corporate franchises. Disney has spearheaded both the rescue and the sterilization of Times Square, and the Reebok gym now resides in the same hood as Planet Hollywood (along with a new Crate and Barrel, Pottery Barn...). But while the corporations plow ahead, gobbling up storefront properties with their expensive brand names, the infamous New York attitude prevails, and never fails to surprise. Many New Yorkers don't actually mind this growth; indeed, it can be viewed as a shopping opportunity whose time has come. One friend, a dentist who has a Farrah Fawcett poster hanging in his office, said to me recently, "Why shouldn't we finally get a K-Mart? We've been punished with expensive everything for years just because we live in this city. Everyone seems like they're in a better mood now."

Alas, New York has said goodbye to a generation of beloved small businesses. Its old friend, a popular independent bookdealer Shakespeare and Company, created a stir when it closed down its flagship store on 83rd Street and Broadway. On my block, West 16th Street, a Starbucks now resides over the ghost of another local soldier–of–misfortune,Verso Books, whose walls were painted with the epitaphs of famous writers (the only evidence Starbucks allowed to remain). Barney's lost its Fashion Avenue lease and had to move uptown. Poor old Cafe 57 (on West 57th Street), where local gentlemen in dark glasses made film deals from the payphone in the foyer, has given way to the influx of cheesy theme restaurants. And back downtown again, the Lion's Head bar that resided in a wooden-panelled basement off of Sheridan Square, where hack writers once framed their trashy book covers (my favorite was Ed Koch's *Mayor*), had to move its rollicking Pete Hamill lifestyles over to 10th Street's Peter's Backyard bar. Sadly, now that too has gone the way of the El.

And it isn't just the residents and the shopowners who are affected by these changes: it is the visitors! Hotels are expensive and often at-capacity. But prices can't soar so high that *no one* can afford to visit, and so, instead, hotel entrepreneurs are doing what all the other New York entrepreneurs are doing to stay competitive: building, building, building. There are at least four new hotels opening in the next year or so. Hotels here get many of the best chefs in the world and their restaurants are often steadfast pinnacles of dining. The Mercer Hotel, coming soon to SoHo, is to open a restaurant where models and stars will clamor for a fresh taste of cool. Why? Because it's new. By nature, New Yorkers, even though they gripe about all these changes, love change, and *love* to be visitors. Perhaps that's one reason why this city continually rips itself down and builds itself up again.

The late photographer Berenice Abbott, a New Yorker who was herself a transplant, first from Ohio, and later from Paris, documented New York's architectural changes around the same time E.B. White was writing about the city. Her series of photographs, titled *Changing New York*, documented the amazing architectural boom that transformed the city as it tore down El platforms and built up the world-famous skyline. Abbott wrote of her series, "How shall the two-dimensional print in black and white suggest the flux of activity of the metropolis, the interaction of human beings and solid architectural constructions, all impinging upon each other in time?"

In these new boom times, you might ask the same question of the media's endless attempts to depict—and capitalize on—New York. And the only answer is that none of them really does it justice. You simply have to let yourself be a tourist. Ask any New Yorker.

—*Rachel Aydt, Managing Editor*

Manhattan Neighborhoods

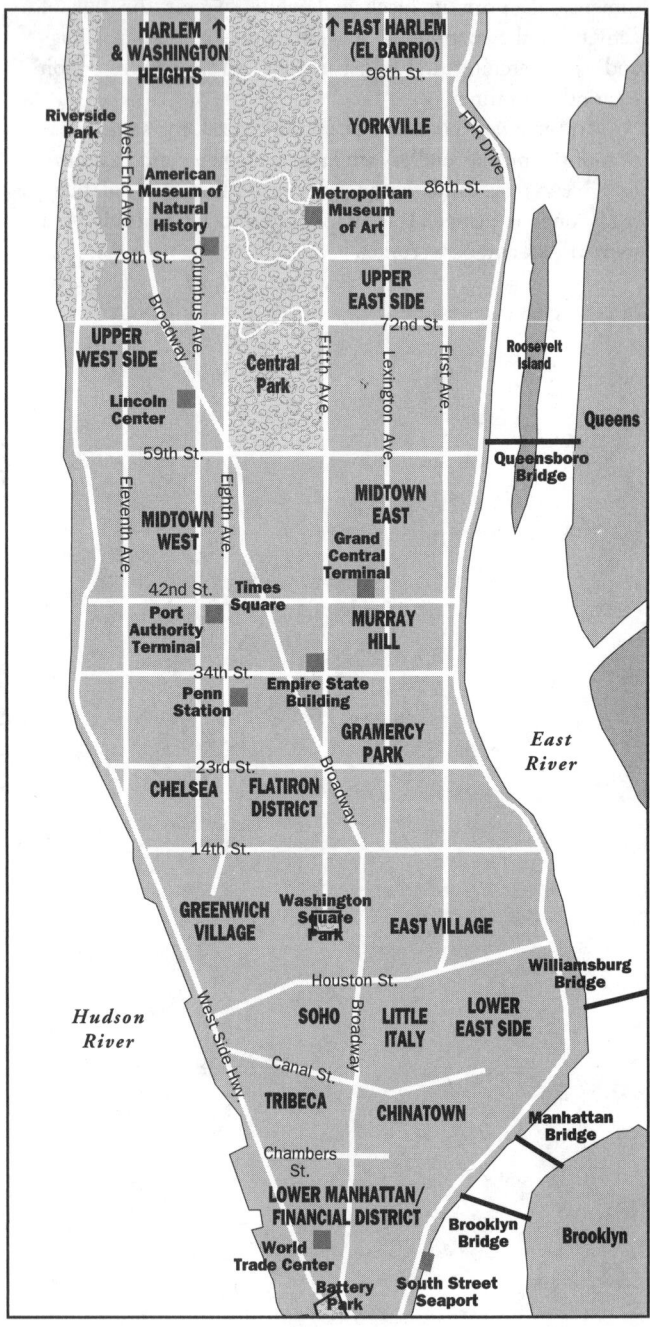

you probably didn't know

Where to find the best New York panorama... The **Empire State Building** and **World Trade Center** are summits worth conquering, but they're on very beaten-track. Many feel that the best view of New York is from the harbor, aboard the **Staten Island, Statue of Liberty**, or **Ellis Island ferries, Seaport Liberty cruise boats** embarking from the South Street Seaport, or the **Circle Line** (See Diversions). From a watery vantage point, you get to see the great skyscraper cliffs of New York, meeting in an awesome wedge at Battery Park, magnificently lit at sunset. But my favorite viewpoint is from the **Promenade** in Brooklyn Heights, cantilevered over the Brooklyn–Queens Expressway, providing nonpareil vistas of downtown and the Brooklyn Bridge. It's easy to get there; take the 2 or 3 train to Clark Street and walk toward the East River; then stroll back to Manhattan over the **Brooklyn Bridge**, with more magnificent views all the way.

How to see wildlife in the city (and not just cross-dressers and the extremely body-pierced)... Did you know that New York City is home to 70 percent of the state's breeding peregrine falcon population? They nest atop bridges and skyscrapers, in boxes placed there by officials hoping the falcons will keep down the local pigeon population; there's one pair that hunts pigeons and blue jays on the grounds of the New York Public Library on 42nd Street and Fifth Avenue. What's more, there have been reports of coyotes in the city, entering via the verges of highways leading south from Connecticut. And one day, I saw an opossum scrambling along Seventh Avenue in front of a jazz club—perhaps he'd just caught the show. Take that, Yellowstone.

How to stay out of trouble... Crime and big cities are firmly linked in many people's minds, and since New York is *the* big city, it must be Crime City too, right? Well, no. In fact, it doesn't even make the Top 100. Over the past few years, the major crime rate has fallen faster in New York than in any other U.S. city. It is now at its lowest point in decades. To help keep it that way, New York has 38,400 police, including 100 who patrol on horseback and a new unit of 120 on mountain bikes. Frankly, I've felt more nervous in Sofia and Marseilles, and found myself in riskier spots way out in the sticks. Most New Yorkers have cultivated a certain way of moving about the city that functions like a protective shield; they act as if they know where they're going, even when they don't, and rarely make eye contact with passers-by. (Remember that when you're tempted to brand all New Yorkers as rude.) The New York Police Department advises visitors not to flash their cash, credit cards, and expensive jewelry; men should keep their wallets in front pants pockets, and women shouldn't let their handbags dangle or hang from the backs of chairs; fasten all the locks on hotel room doors, and put your valuables in the safe. Other than that, use your common sense: Never, never walk down a street or enter a park if you see no one else around—whether it's light or dark outside. If you notice something out of line up ahead—like a gang of kids up to no good or a street person screaming obscenities—casually cross the street. Favorite spots for pickpockets include crowded buses, sardine-packed subway cars, and sidewalk crowds gathered around three-card monte games or street performers.

How to walk the walk... Sure, you know how to walk. But in New York, it helps to walk like a New Yorker. This is a matter of sheer practicality. Day or night, sidewalks in Midtown are jammed. In the rejuvenated Times Square area, as many as 8,500 people will pass a given point per hour. That's almost two and a half warm bodies *every second*. And research shows that New York pedestrians walk thirty percent faster than those in smaller cities. It's like driving the Interstate: keep up with the traffic, or else a hectic situation gets worse. When you line up your friends to take a souvenir snapshot, the ripples will be felt for 15 minutes. The natives won't deliberately bump you, but you might overhear a rude remark or two. Oh yes—and keep to the right when possible. The locals don't all follow this rule—some pride themselves on their skill at cutting in and out of slower–moving pedestrians, but if you keep right, you're more likely to avoid the Sidewalk Two–Step. One final note: All New Yorkers jaywalk but lately the NYPD has been given directions by the mayor to give out tickets for this (yes, crime *is* down). Unless you've had their years of experience, don't try it. New York drivers have as much sporting instinct as those in Mexico City or Karachi. If you step into the street against the light, they probably won't hit you, but they'll see how close they can come.

How to get about below... Paul Goldberger, architecture critic at the *New York Times*, once wrote, "There is no public environment in the United States as squalid as the New York City subway. It is dirty, cramped, smelly and altogether lacking in amenities as basic as a place to sit down." Lord knows, he's right; but, above all, what the New York subway system is, is old, some of it built almost a century ago. That it continues to get 3.4 million people around every day seems a miracle to me; and though it has frequently made me late and let me down, I stand behind it. Some 25 lines ply 238 miles of track under the city—for a map, ask at a token booth, or call the MTA at 718/330–1234, and also ask for the "Token Trips" brochure, describing how to visit 150 major attractions via the subway. Follow the color codes: red runs along Seventh Avenue and then Broadway, blue along Eighth Avenue and Central Park West, green along Lexington Avenue, orange on Central Park West and Sixth Avenue. (For more subway details, see Hotlines and Other Basics.) Once you're on the train, you'll notice many passengers burying their heads in books and newspapers (or surreptitiously reading their neighbors' books and newspapers over their shoulders). If you've forgotten to bring along reading material, look up at the ad posters above subway seats, like those that made a local celebrity out of a dermatologist named Dr. Jonathan Zizmor. Poetry Society of America posters raise the city's consciousnesses with often haunting lines of poetry by the likes of e.e. cummings and Walt Whitman. Sleek car-long advertisements for high-profile advertisers like Bell Atlantic's *Where the Wild Things Are* campaign have replaced some of the time-honored clutter of small ads, though—one more glossy improvement threatening New York's local color.

How to do lunch at an expensive restaurant and still have enough left over for dinner... Every year New York celebrates **Restaurant Week** (generally in June) with great bargains on lunches at many of the city's top restaurants. Amazing but true. In 1997, lunches at high-end eateries like Le Cirque, Lutèce, Jean–Georges, Montrachet, and the River Cafe cost just $19.97 (with some restaurants extending the program through Labor Day). Reservations made long in advance are generally required, because New Yorkers—who always know a good deal when they see one—don't mind snatching the goodies out of tourists' mouths. For information, contact the **New York Visitors and Convention Bureau** (tel 212/397–8222).

How to flag a taxi... The white lights on the roofs of yellow cabs indicate which ones are free; the yellow "Off Duty" light means the driver is on his way home—though he may still stop and ask whether your destination lies along his route. Look for people disembarking from a taxi, hold the door open for them, and then snag the cab. It is very bad form to plant yourself in front of someone else signaling for a taxi in order to get the next one first. That doesn't mean you won't see some New Yorkers doing it. Be aware that it can be hard to find cabs between 4 and 6pm, when drivers are changing shifts, and a pounding rainfall always make it doubly hard to catch a cab.

Where to smoke... Can you smoke in New York? Sure, if you're outdoors. Otherwise, it's problematic. New smoking regulations have made it illegal to light up in offices, restaurants seating more than 35 people, and other enclosed public places. You can smoke at a bar, providing it's at least 6 feet away from tables where people are eating. Restaurateurs hate the new rules, but they're the law. Four cafes with streetside tables (in fair weather) at the Greenwich Village intersection of Bleecker and McDougal streets—**McDougal**, **Borghia**, **Carpo's**, and **Le Figaro**—have become a mecca for visiting smokers. In hotels, make sure to ask for a smoking room if you're a nicotine fiend.

Where to find the facilities... There's an excellent public restroom in **Bryant Park**, on 42nd Street between Fifth and Sixth avenues, which even has attendants, and a good one on the ground floor of the **New York Public Library** next door. But beyond this, stay out of toilets in public buildings—they're filthy and potentially unsafe. Coffee shops and restaurants have bathrooms, though you should make a purchase before using them (even if it's only a cup of coffee to go); and of course, museums offer facilities, providing you buy an admission ticket first. I favor the restrooms in hotel lobbies, which are generally top-notch, though not always easy to find. The bathrooms at the rear of the second-floor lobby in the Grand Hyatt on 42nd Street between Park and Lexington avenues have never let me down. Or try the ladies and gents rooms in the Plaza Hotel or the Waldorf-Astoria. If a concierge stops you, just say you're meeting a friend in the bar for a drink.

How to get a theater ticket... If you didn't call Ticketmaster, Tele-Charge, Teletron, Hit-Tix, or the theaters themselves months ago, you may be out of luck, at least for Broadway blockbusters—you can bet they won't be offered at the day-of-performance discount **TKTS** booth. Ticket brokers and the concierges at hotels can help out in a pinch, providing seats for hot shows at the last minute—though always at a substantial premium. But if you're intent on seeing a particular show, try the theater box office about an hour before show time, where you may meet someone desperate to unload tickets for the evening's performance. As curtain time approaches, many box offices free up house seats (which are routinely saved for the theatrical elite) and sell them off, first-come-first-served, at full price; and some theaters sell standing-room tickets at the last minute, generally at half price, which can provide better views than seats way up near the rafters. For more details, see the Entertainment chapter.

The best art museum nights... Insiders take advantage of "pay what you wish nights" at the **Whitney Museum of American Art** and **Solomon R. Guggenheim Museum** (Fridays), and the **Cooper-Hewitt National Design Museum** (Tuesdays). These are three of the city's greatest museums; besides, the crowds often go off to dinner after about 5pm—leaving you free to wander in blissful solitude. On Friday and Saturday nights, the **Metropolitan Museum of Art** turns itself into a date venue, with drinks, music, and late closing.

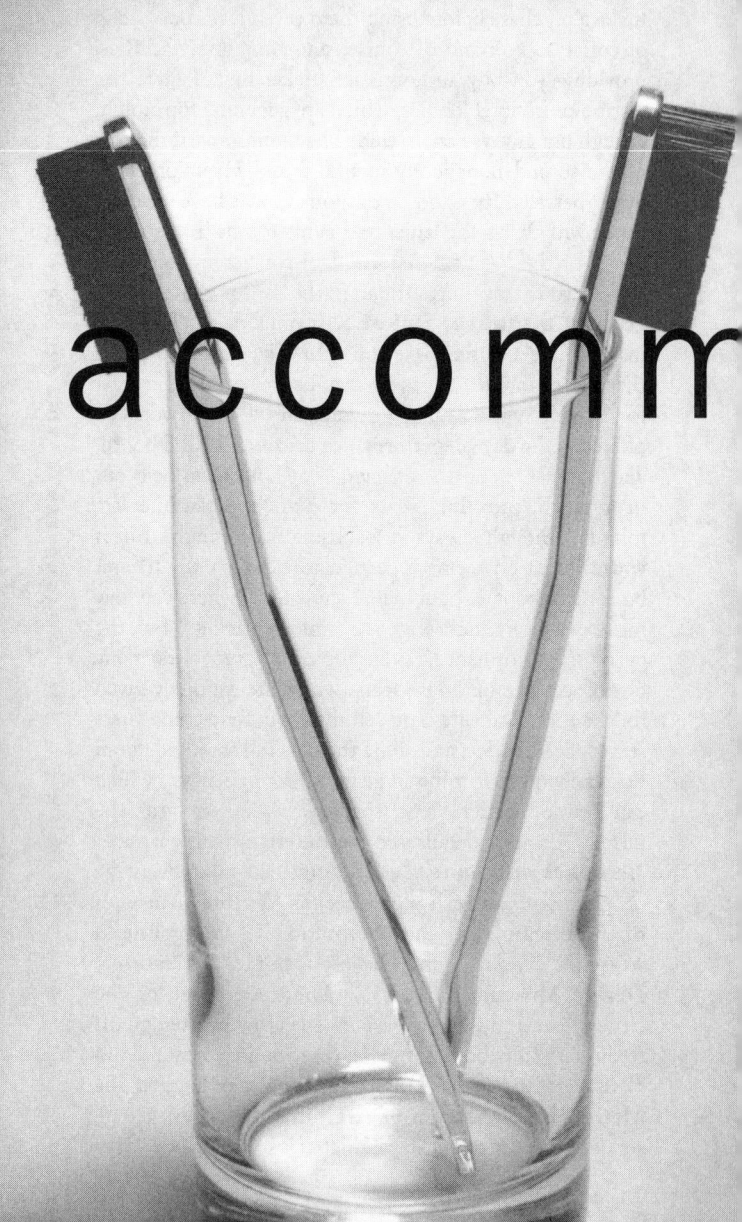

accomm

1

odations

You may enjoy
roaming the
streets of a new
town, luggage in
tow, letting fate
dictate where
you'll spend

the night. Listen up: New York is not the place for that. New York has 60,000 hotel rooms, enough to house the entire population of Laredo, Texas, and still they're in short supply. In 1997, some 32 million visitors pushed occupancy rates past 85 percent. That's including blizzards, heat spells, and slow periods. On ordinary days the figure was probably more like 105 percent. Planned conversions and new constructions costing one billion dollars will add another 5,000 rooms in the near future, but for now, things are *very* tight. So unless you want to spend your vacation in a motel off the turnpike in New Jersey, do your homework before you come: research the city, pick a neighborhood that suits your frame of mind, and then choose lodgings as close to it as possible—in your price range, if possible. Which isn't as impossible as it sounds. Behind the imposing facades of New York's luxury monoliths hover some perfectly charming and less expensive "boutique" hotels, where you're closer to the city's fascinating street life and yet often enjoy nicer furnishings and more attentive service. For an even more genuine taste of the real New York, consider going the bed-and-breakfast route, where accommodations range from penthouse apartments to walk-ups. We've listed one of the best B&B agencies below. Those who decide to stay in a mid-priced or luxury hotel should bear in mind that a hotel concierge can become more valuable in New York than your best friend. These miracle workers sit patiently behind their desks in the hotel lobby, ever-eager to locate last-minute theater tickets or recommend a little French restaurant that's perfect for popping the question (whatever that question may be).

Winning the Reservations Game

The standard recommendation in New York is to make reservations a month ahead—even longer if you plan to be here between Thanksgiving and Christmas. Don't accept the first room price offered, especially from the higher-priced hotels. There are nearly always discount packages to be had, from "summer holidays" to "Christmas getaways" to "romantic weekends." These packages are advertised in the free *Big Apple Visitors Guide* published by the New York Convention and Visitors Bureau (tel 800/NYC–VISIT, or pick it up in person at 810 7th Avenue). Keep in mind that at some hotels, children under 12 stay free with their parents. And be sure to ask for corporate rates, even if you aren't part of a corporation. Desk clerks rarely check your credentials—they just want to fill the room. If you're stuck, the **Hotel Hotline** (tel 800/846–7666, fax 800/511–5317) is usually able to track down a room. As a very last resort, start calling hotels just after 6pm on the day you need the room. Most places cancel non-guaranteed reservations—what the industry calls "timers"—at 6pm, so something just may turn up. Hotel tax in Manhattan is a stiff 13.25%, plus $2 per room per night. Taxes are not included in the price listings below.

Is There a Right Address?

There is a New York neighborhood for *every* personal philosophy and lifestyle, but traditionally the "right" residential address has been the East Sixties, Seventies, and Eighties—the white-glove **Upper East Side**. Here one finds the city's most elegant and snooty shops, townhouses, hotels, and nearly all the members of New York's upper crust. Come summer, the East Side's a ghost town as the wealthy flee the heat for the Hamptons. Head across Central Park for the **Upper West Side**, a funkier, more family-oriented scene of century-old townhouses and rambling vintage apartment buildings. Bounded on the north by Columbia University, by Lincoln Center on the south, and bracketed by Central Park and Hudson-hugging Riverside Park, this area's museums, theaters, affordable restaurants and

New York's celluloid alter-ego

If you want to prepare yourself for a visit to the Big Apple, rent a flick. The classics are: Miracle on 34th Street (1947) for sweetness and light at Christmastime; Breakfast at Tiffany's (1961) for bitter-sweetness à la Truman Capote, and Audrey Hepburn in Givenchy gowns; The Sweet Smell of Success (1957) with Tony Curtis and Burt Lancaster as two rats chasing celebrity and power; and Woody Allen's Annie Hall (1977), all about Upper East Side chic in the days before Woody and Mia's split revealed its seamy side. For a gritty taste of the city, try Serpico (1974) with Al Pacino, Greenwich Village, and corrupt factions in the NYPD; The Godfather (1971) and The Godfather Part II (1974) for the other side of the badge. If you want a love story, grab Cher's Moonstruck (1987) about a nice Brooklyn–Italian girl who wants something more from life than pasta. Midnight Cowboy (1969), perfectly perverse, sad, yet lovable, features Dustin Hoffman and Jon Voight as two New York losers.

INTRODUCTION | ACCOMMODATIONS

hotels, and boutique shopping make it a pleasant place to hang. **Midtown**, running from Central Park South to the Thirties, is Manhattan's central business district and the chief hotel zone, convenient for tony Fifth Avenue shopping, the theater district, and expense-account restaurants galore. The best and costliest hotels are on Central Park South; room rates generally descend as you work your way south. Head south on Fifth

Avenue and you'll bump into the triangular Flatiron Building at 23rd Street, which has lent its name to the very hot **Flatiron District**, where models and trendoids haunt a score of high-profile bars and restaurants. There are few hotels around the Flatiron, but you can enjoy the pulse of this happening area by staying in peaceful **Gramercy Park**, a few blocks to the east, or trendy **Chelsea** to the west, gentrified by an ambitious gay community. Downtown starts at 14th Street, the northern border of **Greenwich Village**. The home of New York University and vibrant Washington Square Park, this neighborhood of neat 19th-century brownstones is where generations of bohemians have made their mark. Jazz clubs, coffee shops, romantic restaurants, and proximity to Little Italy, Soho, the East Village (home of cutting-edge clubs and punky new bohemians), and the West Village (capital of gay America—with Chelsea coming in now as a close and younger-populated runner–up) should make this area ripe for hotels. Oddly enough, though, good hotels are hard to find here—unless you're willing to put up with tiny rooms, tenement housing, or a bed-and-breakfast room, you may have to commute to this playground. The southern tip of Manhattan—occupied by the **South Street Seaport** area to the east, the loft spaces of urban-hip **TriBeCa** to the northwest, **Battery Park City** to the west, and **Wall Street** at the very bottom—has only a few luxurious hotels, though more are in the works. Compellingly urgent during the work week, strangely empty on weekends, this neighborhood is an especially memorable place to stay; squeezed between financial-industry towers you'll find soot-blackened churches whose cemeteries contain crooked, worn tombstones. The streets can be deserted and sometimes dangerous late at night, especially near the water. Stick to your hotel at those times, or take a ride uptown.

The Lowdown

Old faithfuls... Always the first to come to mind is the venerable **Plaza**, a French-Renaissance pile docked at the southeast corner of Central Park. Frank Lloyd Wright once claimed this was one of the few buildings he liked that he hadn't designed himself. In the early 1900s, New York's high rollers kept suites there, and the Plaza's blinding gold-and-crimson lobby (courtesy of former doyenne Ivana Trump, though Fairmont Hotels now manages the pile) continues to celebrate the joys of extravagant consumerism. The recently refurbished **Waldorf-Astoria** presides over Park Avenue, its Art Deco lobbies returned to their past splendor, though its guest roster is no longer as grand. Happily, the **Algonquin** functions much as it did in the days of Dorothy Parker and the Round Table—in the wood-paneled lobby, at least, where graying authors of both sexes, ensconced in armchairs, ogle young women in leopardskin coats.

For travelers with old money... The **Pierre**'s romantically frescoed downstairs rooms teem with European film directors, as well as American heiresses; even Hollywood types turn up frequently, now that Barney's has set up shop next door. Miraculously, the staff is alert and deferential, no matter who you are—unlike the help at the **Plaza-Athénée**, where you get the feeling you should show proof of a high income before walking through the door. The **Carlyle** on Madison Avenue has long been a bastion of good taste, though its reputation has slipped a notch. If you dislike feeling forced to dress for dinner, you may prefer the gracious **Stanhope**, where the high tea is perfectly English, and you can people-watch like a Parisian on the Terrace, sipping an aperitif and overlooking the tourist frenzy at the Metropolitan Museum of Art across the street.

For travelers with new money... If your reason for being in New York is to spend cash, then the **Plaza**, at the top of the Fifth Avenue shopping district, in view of Bergdorf Goodman and FAO Schwartz, is the place to stay. Big hair, Midwest accents, and slack-jawed kids crowd the lobby, where plainsclothes security guards warily eye all but the wealthiest. Visitors bored with the Plaza might move up the ladder to the **New York Palace**, a modern black tower jammed behind the 100-year-old Villard House. Formerly owned by the infamous Leona Helmsley, The Palace lies in the shadow of St. Patrick's Cathedral, and its ornate public rooms put both the Plaza and St. Patrick's to shame—too bad the guest rooms don't live up to them. Visitors who've made their money in Hollywood would feel most at home at the **Mark**, a sleek East Sider where producers strike deals just crossing the lobby to the bar.

Places to misbehave... Just off Times Square, the **Paramount**, with its Whiskey Bar, whimsical acid-colored Philipe Starck furniture, and weirdly furnished (also very, very tiny) rooms, is the place to meet kindred souls if you work in advertising and are under 35. Media and show biz types prefer the **Royalton**'s Club 44, where you might catch a glimpse of Claudia Schiffer or Tina Brown before retreating to your higher-budget Starck bed upstairs. If your hypercool all–black outfit is by Yamamoto or Armani, you'll fit right in at the recently–built **SoHo Grand**. But if all this is too sophisticated-Disneyland for you, never fear: **Hotel 17**, a pensione for club-hoppers, just north of the East Village, may let you party in the dingy rooms where Madonna did her *Details* photo shoot.

Broadway bound... The **Millenium Broadway**'s 33 soundproof executive boardrooms and its sleek, black tower may be a corporate wet-dream to some, but at 44th Street off Broadway, it's a sexy place for a theater-and-dinner weekend as well. The lobby's leather lounge chairs and black marble floors give way to cream-colored upstairs rooms whose glass walls offer killer city views. The more relaxed, Italian-owned **Michelangelo**, 5 blocks up Broadway, offers a choice of room design: Empire, Art Deco, or French Provincial. **Ameritania**, a former SRO hotel nicely renovated by gentrification genius Hank "Location, Location, Location" Freid, sits next door to the Ed Sullivan Theater (home of "Late Night with David Letterman"): It offers decent rooms with marble bathrooms and the very same views for $200 less than the Michelangelo. Bottom-rung among the Broadway hotels is the 1,300-room **Milford Plaza**, which has much the same ambience as an airport terminal. Lines to the front desk form behind a velvet rope, and it's often necessary to wait 20 minutes just to pick up your room key. A prime destination for flight attendants and talk show guests, but at least there's *always* a room.

Park views to die for... A new company took over the Ritz–Carlton in late 1997 and promptly changed the name to **Luxury Collection Hotel**. This move does not bode well, but they can't ruin the location. Rooms at the Luxury Collection Hotel, from about the eighth floor up, offer the Central Park views people want on their honeymoons. Even the small fitness center lets you look at the trees while aerobicizing. Avoid the rear rooms—their windows face a wall. It's no surprise that the **Plaza**'s parkside vistas are as nice as the Hotel-Formerly–Known–As–Ritz's—it's just a block down the road. Over on Central Park West, the **Mayflower** offers less opulent rooms-with-a-view for substantially less. Then there's the **Stanhope**, whose best quarters reveal the park and the Metropolitan Museum of Art as you've never seen them before.

Eyepopping city views... Check in after dark at the **Regal U.N. Plaza**, and you'll open your curtains to a heart-stopping east-Midtown view of the city lights—guaranteed, since all rooms are on the 28th floor or above. The **Millenium**, across from the World Trade Center downtown, provides a New York Harbor panorama or skyline views from the higher rooms; take a dip in the pool overlooking St. Paul's Church. The **SoHo Grand** gives you both worlds; rooms on the north side face Midtown, dominated by the Empire State and Chrysler buildings, while those on the south offer up the twin towers of the World Trade Center and the lower but still stirring cluster of Wall Street skyscrapers. See how many buildings you can spot that were once the world's tallest. (Hint: at least five.)

Location, location, location... Best Western Seaport **Inn**, a fully restored, 19th-century, pink-brick building between the Brooklyn Bridge and South Street Seaport, provides an excellent departure point for walks around Old New York—and even delivers a bit of colonial sea-captain's ambience at a decent price, though the rooms are motel-like. The rooms at the **Washington Square Hotel** are disappointingly motel modern, too, but their mid-Greenwich Village location makes possible walks around NYU, Little Italy, Soho, and the East and West Villages. The **Larchmont Hotel** offers a quieter and more charming Village experience. The comfy dowager **Mayflower** is a good, mid-priced starting point for walks around Central Park and the Upper West Side.

For culture vultures... For a long time, the dingy Empire Hotel, directly across from Lincoln Center, was a prime piece of New York real estate going to waste. Then the Radisson chain took over, changed the hotel's name to the **Radisson Empire**, and transformed the joint. From designers' models of opera sets in the tony brass-and-mahogany lobby to the CD players in every (sometimes quite small) room, this hotel should make arts aficionados very happy. Way uptown and to the east, **Hotel Wales**, a renovated Victorian with banners flying, offers a sweet, intimate alternative to the larger and more expensive hotels near Museum Mile. Downtown devotees might try the dreary-but-cheap **Washington Square Hotel** for its dinner-and-jazz package, or the **Incentra Village House**, a small, antique-filled inn with turn-of-the-century Village bohemian aura. The **SoHo Grand** sets you down right at epicenter of Soho's galleries, clubs, restaurants, and cutting–edge boutiques. Come evening, the bar, lobby lounge, and 2-star restaurant fill up with a young, hipper–than–thou crowd. **Off Soho Suites**, a clean, bright, and inexpensive all-suite hotel in an unlikely Lower East Side neighborhood, is close to downtown plays, poetry readings, and galleries; many European and Australian travelers stay here, along with downtown musicians and those who write about them. Appropriately, a free *Village Voice* comes with your suite.

Endearingly eccentric... New York breeds rugged individualists of all types; among those who get off on sharing their life view with the world is James Knowles, the artist-owner of the **Roger Smith**, a lighthearted Midtown hotel decorated on the outside with a delightful, cartoon-like mural (inside it's jam-packed with an assortment of high-quality paintings and sculptures). Augustin Paege takes art one step farther at his wonderful little **Box Tree** hotel, where the walls, ceilings, and even the guest-room doors are playfully adorned. The **Inn at Irving Place**, just south of Gramercy Park, is so uncommercial it doesn't even have a sign; this luxuriously restored Victorian brownstone specializes in fashion models and celebrities who value their privacy.

Twilight zones... Even in New York there's eccentric, and then there's going too far. Lifetime Achievement Award goes to the **Chelsea Hotel**, where William Burroughs wrote *Naked Lunch* and Sid and Nancy nodded out. The scene is seedy, but the spacious renovated rooms with fireplaces can be a fun place to spend a night. The **Carlton Arms**, to the east, takes up where the Chelsea leaves off, letting young artists stay for free if they'll decorate their rooms; every surface, from the steps leading to the tiny second-floor lobby to hallways decked with "conceptual" clotheslines hung with lingerie and long johns, is an expression of what appears to be howling New-York-visitor angst (or plain psychosis). Less visually riveting, but still way out there, is **Hotel 17**, former stomping grounds for J.P. Morgan and, somewhat later, a bunch of winos. Young manager Billy Candis advertises the place as offering "four times the fun, five times the glamour, ten times the cool, yet half the price" of other trendy hotels, in his bid for the media/fashion trade and "Norman Bates."

Luscious love nests... The **Michelangelo**'s spacious rooms, king-sized beds, and marble-clad Italian charm lend themselves to a perfect weekend getaway. The **Lowell**, although prim-looking on the outside, coyly reveals fireplace-and-terrace suites designed to rekindle the coldest flame. If you and your lover share the same gender, try the gay-friendly **Incentra Village Inn**, a double-townhouse in the West Village, filled with antiques, or the gay-frequented **Chelsea Pines Inn**, a bed-and-breakfast where each room is dedicated to a faded movie star, and breakfast in the rear garden makes for a romantic morning-after.

For stargazing... Celebrity hounds must absolutely stop by the **Royalton**, not only to scope out the talent, but to try to find the stalls in the overdesigned restrooms downstairs. If you consider checking out fashion models "stargazing," dine al fresco across from Gramercy Park's The **Inn at Irving Place**, or book a room at the East Side's **Franklin** and spend a few hours lurking in the post-modern breakfast room off the lobby. **Morgans** is where celebrities go when they don't want to be seen, but keep your eyes open as you pass through the small black-and-white lobby with the checkerboard trim, and you might catch one slipping out the anonymous side entrance. The bar at the **Mark** is another good fishing spot.

Frumpy but lovable... So "Sin City" has lured you into naughty acts you regret the next morning? Come home to the **Mayflower**, a comfortable, somewhat frumpy establishment with paintings of clipper ships adorning a long lobby. Have a good dinner in the Conservatory Cafe, then go for a healthy jog across the street in Central Park, or to a chamber music recital at nearby Juilliard. Broadway performers and, for some reason, middle-aged British tourists seem to feel secure at the **Wyndham** on 58th Street, another matronly hotel, with its apartment-like rooms and small upholstered lobby.

Have I got a deal for you... Breaks on Manhattan hotel prices are urgently needed; fortunately, they're increasingly available. The clean, reasonably comfortable, no-frills **Malibu Studios Hotel** on the Upper West Side—farther up Broadway than some may want to go, in a cruddy though safe-enough neighborhood—caters to young Europeans and students with very limited budgets. The faded but surprisingly comfortable **Excelsior** offers reasonable rooms near Central Park for older fans of the Upper West Side. The **Ameritania** provides theater-district rooms with marble baths, a fitness room, and a waterfall in the lobby for around $200 per night. The smart, pretty **Mansfield** on 44th Street is in the same price range, and you can hang out in the lobbies of the **Royalton** and the **Algonquin** down the block. The **Larchmont**, in the center of Greenwich Village, is quiet, charming, and cheap. **Off Soho Suites** answers downtowners' needs for low prices and sane desk clerks. And **Urban Ventures** can provide you with a bed-and-breakfast room in someone's apartment for under $100 per night.

Suite deals... Especially popular with relocating corporate execs and families, suites are also taking hold among short-term visitors. Among the best suite hotels is the **Surrey** on the Upper East Side, with kitchenettes or full kitchens, spacious rooms, and somewhat lavish decor for this sort of hotel. Farther south, the **Shelburne Murray Hill** offers a more ornate lobby, with French antiques, but more anonymous-looking rooms; it also has a large basement gym that actually gets used. **Off Soho Suites**, in its funky Lower East Side location, is the best priced of the lot; the executive-class **RIHGA Royal**'s 600-square-foot suites with French doors and elaborate marble bathrooms should have most visitors feeling like kings, or at least like CEOs.

Taking care of business... The **Millenium Broadway**'s four-story Conference Center, state-of-the-art audiovisual facilities, and its own personal Broadway theater available for corporate presentations, make this an ideal venue for any kind of business activity. The staff are accustomed to serving business needs, and rooms feature dual-line telephones, interactive communication systems, and so on. **New York Hilton and Towers** serves mid-level business guests as efficiently here as the chain does elsewhere, though you shouldn't have to put up with the mass-market feel of the lobby and reproduction furniture in the rooms. The **Drake**, owned and operated by Swissotel, caters to no-nonsense types who want their suits back from the cleaners when promised; expect spruced, good–sized rooms in a prime Midtown location. Go up the price scale, and the clean-lined, Japanese-owned **RIHGA Royal** brings the corporate climber's ultimate fantasy to life, with its hierarchical room structure—"royal suites" have minimal luxury appointments, "imperial suites" are higher up, with city views, and "pinnacle suites" at the top offer chauffeured rides to and from the airport, personalized business cards, and private phone and fax numbers.

For the body beautiful... The **Peninsula** wins hands-down, with its 35,000-square-foot health club, glass-enclosed rooftop gym, 42-foot pool with a view of all Midtown, beauty salon, body and skin care, massage and facial service, sauna, and, finally, a sundeck. The **Regal U.N. Plaza** isn't bad, with its 27th-floor health club, indoor pool, tennis courts, sauna, and exercise room. The **Lowell** can provide you with a sumptuous "Gym Suite," which consists of your own private windowed-and-mirrored gym, in addition to the usual large fireplace, full kitchen, and outdoor terrace for dining. (The gym is rumored to have been installed at Madonna's request, and is priced accordingly.) More economical bodily treats are available at the **West Side** and **Vanderbilt YMCAs**: one near Lincoln Center, the other close to Grand Central, both offering cheap if spartan rooms, most without private baths, with full use of the gym, pool, and other Y facilities.

For shopoholics... The **Plaza** is best, within sight of Bergdorf Goodman, FAO Schwarz, and most other places visitors like to shop. If you prefer Bloomingdale's, try the **Barbizon**: Rates are low (that's because rooms can be snug), but tower suites have terraces and city views. The Italian-operated **Jolly Madison Towers** is popular among shoppers for its East Side location, efficient ser-

ACCOMMODATIONS | THE LOWDOWN

vice, predictable if standard-issue furnishings, and reasonable price. If the boutiques along Madison Avenue will be your destination, try the **Carlyle**, set amid Lauren, Versace, Armani, et al.

So very literary... The **Algonquin** is still the obvious choice, and it can be amusing to watch Matilda the Algonquin cat lick her privates while you trade *bon mots* in the cozy, antique-filled lobby, where the Round Table actually held court. Meanwhile, editors of *Vanity Fair* and *Vogue* settle into the sleek postmodern bar of the **Royalton** across the street, where they can gossip all night while *New Yorker* editors try to listen in. The **Lowell** actually equips its suites' bookshelves with interesting volumes, and claims a number of authors among its loyal clientele—though you'd have to be a Clancy, Collins, or King to afford this joint. And the **Chelsea Hotel** has a raffish literary past, numbering writers such as Dylan Thomas, William Burroughs, and Tennessee Williams among its former guests.

Money's too tight to mention... The **New York International American Youth Hostel** is the largest AYH in the U.S.; its freshly appointed Upper West Side landmark building takes up half a city block. Even if it didn't, you could easily spot it due to the crowds of Nordic backpackers converging on it from all directions. Rooms are dormitory-style and cost a pittance. The communal atmosphere in the roomy cafeteria, sunny library, pool hall, and large rear garden encourages interaction among the guests. Don't confuse the AYH with the privately owned **Chelsea International Hostel**—cramped quarters make this place a little too interactive. The **West Side** and **Vanderbilt YMCAs** do better, with private rooms, though there's still communal life in the bathrooms.

Drop–dead decor... The **Four Seasons**, for its sycamore-paneled dressing rooms and a columned Grand Foyer with a 33-foot onyx ceiling, conceived by architect I.M. Pei; the **Lowell** for its perfect mix of French antiques and modern accents; the **Box Tree** for best impersonation of a private home, complete with 17th-century oil paintings, Tiffany panels, and roaring fireplaces, all in a slender East Side double-brownstone; the **Pierre** for its frescoed Rotunda and mahogany-furnished rooms; and the

Peninsula, for the art nouveau staircase rising to the salmon-pink Adrienne restaurant.

Family values... The slightly shabby **Excelsior**, situated across the street from the American Museum of Natural History (and the New York Planetarium) and half a block from the playgrounds of Central Park, is perfect for little ones who love dinosaurs. In the morning, take the kids to the coffeeshop off the lobby for eggs and a visit to the serve-yourself candy stand. The upscale suites at the **Surrey** on the Upper East Side provide enough space for kids and enough comfort for parents, as well as kitchens for making peanut-butter-and-jelly sandwiches when the kids can't face another restaurant. Worn furnishings at the **Gramercy Park Hotel** can take your kids' abuse, and many rooms have handy kitchenettes and sofabeds; pets are allowed, too. But best of all, the hotel will hand over a key to private Gramercy Park, where you can stroll with your baby from spring through fall. **Urban Ventures, Inc.** (tel 212/594–5650) provides entire empty apartments, which can be a blessing if your children loathe hotels.

Elbow room... The **Drake**'s are spacious but disappointingly bland; the **Four Seasons**' are enormous but heartstoppingly priced; the **Michelangelo**'s are just right—especially on Valentine's Day and New Year's Eve weekends, when they're on sale.

Silent nights... Silence in New York sounds like an oxymoron, but there really are peaceful enclaves to settle into. Think of the faded Grand Hotel in the last small midwestern town you visited, put it in a turn-of-the-century New York neighborhood, and that's what the **Gramercy Park Hotel** is like. The antique-filled eight-room **Inn at Irving Place**, just a couple of blocks away, provides silence and privacy as well, but at a high price. **Morgans**, a cousin of the Royalton, insulates its reticent celebrity guests with blessed quiet, but the tradeoff is a room with no view, whose walls are the mottled gray-brown of the inside of a cardboard box.

Hotels with history... The **Algonquin** again, for its very well-preserved downstairs. The **Best Western Seaport Inn** sits in the perfect spot for those curious about New

York's early seafaring days, when Wall Street was a street with a wall and nothing more. The **Chelsea Hotel** will make you relive the Sixties, whether you want to or not—wall-to-wall paintings, piles of revolutionary tracts, tacky furniture, and a collection of dazed-looking residents and animals hanging out in the lobby help keep the Andy Warhol era going. You can dine and dance in the grand ballroom at the **Waldorf-Astoria** as if World War II never happened; if there's no event in the ballroom, just while away some time in the glorious main lobby, near the famed bronze and mahogany clock. The **Plaza**'s more spacious rooms and the restaurants downstairs will have you feeling like you're on an ocean liner. The virginal **Barbizon**, once a women's residence for such transients as Grace Kelly, Ali McGraw, and Candice Bergen, retains a cloisterlike quality with narrow corridors and tidy studio rooms. (You can loosen up a little in the Star Bar, with its zodiac-studded ceiling.) These days, both genders are allowed to stay here.

It's a small world... The **Holiday Inn Downtown** is not what you think it is—at least, not quite. Smack in the middle of Chinatown, the hotel hosts many Chinese guests, and its Pacifica Bar and Restaurant can cook up some excellent Cantonese cuisine. The **Fitzpatrick**, on Lexington Avenue in the East Fifties, is owned by an Irish company, which is obvious because *everything* in it is green. Irish lilts pour forth from the desk clerks' mouths, and Fitzer's, the hotel's Irish bar, is extremely popular among (largely Irish) guests and locals. The best time to stay at the **Quality Hotel and Suites** is during the Brazilian Street Festival in September, when this Midtown neighborhood comes alive with samba rhythms and Brazilian dancers. The hotel itself is nothing special, but if you like Brazilian food (and Brazilian tourists) this is the place to be. For those who like their ethnic culture world-transforming, the ambience at the **Regal U.N. Plaza Hyatt**, across from the U.N., is highly international, with a multilingual staff and exotic flavors proffered at the Ambassador Grill.

May I get that for you, sir?... The Upper East Side's **Stanhope** specializes in cherubic European clerks who contribute charm and a sense of humor as well as strictly professional service. The **Lowell**'s people are also young, and sweetly earnest about performing well. At **Incentra Village Inn**, you can cozy up in the hotel's small parlor and chat with the owner about places to see and things to do.

Ringing in the New Year... The stylish **Royalton**, near, but not in the center, of Times Square, is a great place to observe the crowds gathered to watch the ball fall; the comfortably priced **Ameritania** will put you at the hub of the action, right on Broadway's Great White Way. Downtown, the **Millenium** will make your heart stop with views of fireworks over New York Harbor. The **Plaza** often offers New Year's specials, as do many other New York hotels. Ask around.

Try these when there's no room... If you're desperate, try **Days Hotel Midtown** on Eighth Avenue. Its location is pretty dreary, and its rooms pure cheap-motel, but at least it has a rooftop swimming pool. **Quality Hotel & Suites Manhattan** on West 46th Street can usually offer Broadway theater-goers a last-minute room at a good price. The **Milford Plaza**, also in the theater district, is so enormous there's got to be space for you. Rooms are motel-like, but at least they have remote-control TV, in-room movies, individually controlled heat, and air conditioning.

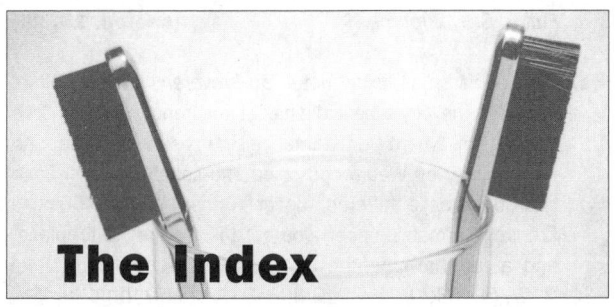

The Index

$$$$$	Over $450
$$$$	$350–$450
$$$	$250–$350
$$	$150–$250
$	under $150

Algonquin. A new owner has embarked on a big, expensive "historical restoration" of this classic New York literary landmark, guided by photos from its 1902 opening. Let's hope he has a light touch; museums are more interesting to visit than to stay in..... *Tel 212/840–6800, 800/548–0345, fax 212/ 555–8000. 59 W. 44th St., 10036, B/D/F train to 42nd St. 165 rooms. $$$* **(see pp. 17, 22, 24, 25)**

Ameritania. The lobby's silly imitation-Philipe Starck furniture (see Paramount below) fails to mar guests' satisfaction at getting a good deal. Some rooms have Broadway views. Two restaurants, a gift shop, and a lobby bar complete the picture—all done in an incongruous Caribbean style.... *Tel 212/247–5000, fax 212/247–3316. 1701 Broadway, 10019, B/D/E train to 7th Ave. 207 rooms. $$*
(see pp. 18, 22, 27)

The Barbizon Hotel. A $40–million restoration has contributed a pleasant-enough tan-and-pink decor, white tile bathrooms, and pedestal sinks. There's also a fitness center, bar, and pool.... *Tel 212/838–5700, 800/223–1020, fax 212/223–3287. 140 E. 63rd St., 10021, N/R train to Lexington Ave. 301 rooms. $$$* **(see pp. 23, 26)**

Best Western Seaport Inn. A chain mentality surfaces in the slightly cheesy reproduction furniture and the stiff, motelish bedding. Ask for a room with a view of the Brooklyn Bridge.... *Tel 212/766–6600, 800/HOTEL–NY, fax 212/766–6615. 33 Peck Slip, 10038, 2/3/4/5 train to Fulton St. 72 rooms. $* **(see pp. 19, 25)**

Box Tree. This small luxury hotel, an *Irreverent* favorite, offers some of the city's best dining, at the renowned Box Tree Restaurant, where Continental cuisine is served (jacket and tie required) on Wedgwood china and Lalique crystal. Each bedroom has a different decor (British Empire, Chinese Empire, German Empire—you get the picture), a fireplace, and a fur throw on the antique, queen-sized bed.... *Tel 212/758–8320, fax 212/308–3899. 250 E. 49th St., 10017, 6 train to 51st St. 13 rooms. DC not accepted. $$*
(see pp. 20, 24)

Carlton Arms. All the tenement-type rooms, decorated with wild murals, have sinks; some include a bathroom, while others use toilets and shower rooms down the hall (warning: though they're clean, the demon-head mosaics in the common bathrooms may make it difficult to concentrate). Outrageous ambience at a decent price (students and foreign tourists get a $10 discount).... *Tel 212/679–0680. 160 E. 25th St., 10010, 6 train to 23rd St. 54 rooms. AE, DC not accepted. $* **(see p. 20)**

Carlyle. An efficient staff extends every courtesy to movie stars and less-famous guests alike, and the large, private fitness center with sauna, steam room, and massage, is to die for. Downstairs are Bemelman's Bar, decorated with murals by he of the *Madeline* children's books fame; The Carlyle Restaurant, serving classic cuisine among the oil paintings and flower arrangements; and Cafe Carlyle, where Bobby Short still keeps the piano bench warm.... *Tel 212/744–1600, 800/227–5737, fax 212/717–4682. 35 E. 76th St., 10021, 6 train to 77th St. 190 rms. $$$$* **(see pp. 17, 24)**

Chelsea Hotel. The service here is friendly if lackadaisical, but a hotel with a history of violence, drug use, and a thousand scary New York stories is not for everyone, even if it has been renovated and the rooms are good-sized. The attached El Quixote restaurant serves okay Spanish cuisine.... *Tel 212/675–5531, fax 212/243-3700. 222 W. 23rd St., 10011, 1/9 train to 23rd St. 200 rooms. $$* **(see pp. 20, 24, 26)**

Chelsea International Hostel. A very small hostel with coed dorm rooms, a common kitchen, and a garden dining area. Breakfast and linens are provided, and there's a safe for valuables. The cheapest listing here.... *Tel 212/643–0214. 313 W. 29th St., 10001, A/C/E train to 34th St./Penn Sta. 2 dorms. No credit cards. $* **(see p. 24)**

Chelsea Pines Inn. A bed & breakfast catering exclusively to a gay clientele, located between the West Village and Chelsea. The 14th Street location is being gradually prettified, with trees and flowers. Breakfasts in the garden feature home–baked bread and Krispy Kreme doughnuts.... *Tel 212/929–1023, fax 212/620–5646. 317 W. 14th St., 10014–5001, A/C/E train to 14th St. 24 rooms. $* **(see p. 21)**

Days Hotel Midtown. What you'd expect from a motel chain— its one plus is the rooftop pool. Downstairs, the Metro Restaurant and bar serve those too timid to venture out among the sex shops on Eighth Avenue.... *Tel 212/581–7000, 800/572–6232, fax 212/974–0291. 790 8th Ave. at W. 48th St, 10019, C/E train to 50th St. 367 rooms. $$* **(see p. 27)**

The Drake Swissotel. Swiss-owned, it's efficient and impersonal. Every room has a color TV and refrigerator, plus a hair dryer in the beige marble bathrooms. Some offer fax service and voicemail, and there's a business center.... *Tel 212/ 421–0900, 800/63–SWISS, fax 312/565–9930. 440 Park Ave., 10022, E/F train to Lexington–3rd Ave. 600 rooms. $$$$* (see pp. 23, 25)

Excelsior Hotel. Spacious rooms and suites have been renovated just enough to be respectable, without removing the Art Deco tile in the bathrooms. Choose front rooms for a spectacular view of the American Museum of Natural History.... *Tel 212/362–9200, 800/368–4575, fax 212721–2994. 45 W. 81st St., 10024, B/C train to 81st St./American Museum of Natural History. 200 rooms. DC not accepted. $$* (see pp. 22, 25)

Fitzpatrick Manhattan Hotel. As Irish as its name. The rooms are large, with wet bars, trouser presses, and terrycloth robes. No fitness center, but free guest privileges at the nearby Excelsior Health Club are available.... *Tel 212/355–1371, 800/367–7701, fax 212/308–5166. 687 Lexington Ave., 10022, 4/5/6 train to 59th St. 92 rooms. $$$* (see p. 26)

Franklin. This very neat boutique hotel's pleasant rooms have white canopies over the beds, fresh flowers, VCRs, cedar closets, and European-style showers. Breakfast is served in a tiny room off the lobby, where the coffeepot operates around the clock. Good value for the neighborhood.... *Tel 212/369–1000, fax 212/369–8000. 164 E. 87th St., 10128, 4/5/6/ train to 86th St. 53 rooms. DC not accepted. $$$* (see p. 21)

Four Seasons. The huge guest rooms have elegant contemporary decor with art deco touches. The subdued Fifty Seven Fifty Seven Restaurant and Bar and the Armani-studded Lobby Lounge offer sustenance, a business center provides secretarial services, and, for the body, there's a fitness center and spa.... *Tel 212/758–5700, fax 212/758–5711. 57 E. 57th St., 10022, E/F trains to 5th Ave. 370 rooms. $$$$$* (see pp. 24, 25)

Gramercy Park Hotel. The rooms are decidedly worn-looking, with nylon bedspreads, a few chips on the furniture, and aged (but clean) bathroom fixtures. The downstairs restaurant is usually empty, and the crooner in the cocktail lounge sings off-key, but the place has a kind of run-down charm—maybe that's why the fashion set has recently moved in. Service is pleasant but slow.... *Tel 212/475–4320, 800/ 221–4083, fax 212/505–0535. 2 Lexington Ave., 10010, 6 train to 23rd St. 509 rooms. $$* **(see p. 25)**

Holiday Inn Downtown. Near Little Italy, SoHo, TriBeCa, and the Lower East Side, this chain hotel has standard-issue rooms and amenities. Fax machines are available in the lobby, where you can send messages while humming along to the Chinese Muzak—actually a relief from the subway noise.... *Tel 212/966–8898, 800/HOLIDAY, fax 212/966–3933. 138 Lafayette St., 10013, R train to Canal St. 227 rooms. $$* **(see p. 26)**

Hotel 17. Yes, the grimy old building has a certain sordid charm, but the rooms are small, dark, and hot in summer (at least the ceilings are high), with uneven floors and dingy wallpaper. All rooms have phones; most share toilets and tubs off the hall.... *Tel 212/475–2845, fax 212/677–8178. 225 E. 17th St., 10003, L train to 3rd Ave. 120 rooms. No credit cards. $* **(see pp. 18, 21)**

Hotel Wales. This attractive eight-story Victorian hotel's potted ivy, wing-backed chairs, and antique issues of *Country Life* all look very proper. Free breakfast is served in the antique filled Pied Piper Room, where at tea-time a harpist plays. Rear rooms can be dark and small—ask for a front view, unless you loathe street noise....*Tel 212/876–6000, fax 212/860–7000, 1295 Madison Ave., 10128, 4/5/6 train to 86th St. 86 rooms. DC not accepted. $$* **(see p. 20)**

Incentra Village House. This West Village guest house boasts working fireplaces and lovely antiques. Bathrooms are small and utilitarian; the galley kitchens in every room come with all utensils. Clientele is largely gay and lesbian, but all are welcomed.... *Tel 212/206–0007. 32 8th Ave., 10014, fax 212/604–0625, A/C/E train to 14th St. 12 rooms. DC not accepted. $* **(see pp. 20, 21, 27)**

Inn at Irving Place. A higher-budget version of the Incentra (see above), with exquisite antiques in every room, along with cable TV, VCRs, remote climate-control, and a very pleasant personal welcome (unless you are under 13, in which case you are not welcome at all). Continental breakfast is included, as well as services like in-room fax machines and laptop computers with Internet access.... *Tel 212/533–4600, 800/685–1447, fax 212/533–4611. 54 Irving Pl., 10003, 4/5/6/L/N/R train to Union Square. 12 rooms. $$$* **(see pp. 20, 21, 25)**

Jolly Madison Towers Hotel. Popular with Italian vacationers and corporate types, the Jolly, near Grand Central Terminal Station, offers standard amenities for a very fair price. The lobby is hotel modern, the furniture neo-colonial, and the bathrooms awfully small, but you get a minibar, air conditioner, and Italian stations on the cable TV. Health spa, bar, and coffeeshop on premises.... *Tel 212/802–0600, 800/225–4340, fax 212/447–0747. 22 E. 38th St., 10016, 4/5/6/7 train to Grand Central. 216 rooms. $$* **(see p. 23)**

Larchmont Hotel. Hidden on one of the most beautiful blocks in Greenwich Village, this small hotel has a European feeling, from the wire chairs in the breakfast room to the old floral and animal prints on the walls. The rooms are good–sized and comfortably furnished, with TVs, voicemail, and complimentary robes and slippers. Rooms have washbasins, but showers and toilets are down the hall. Some floors also have kitchen facilities for guests...*Tel 212/989–9333, fax 212/989–9496. 27 W. 11th St., 10011, B/F train to 14th St., L to 6th Ave. 55 rooms. $* **(see pp. 19, 22)**

Lowell Hotel. A small and unassuming lobby little prepares one for the wonders above, totally luxurious without ever being stuffy. Rooms have minibars with fridge, a writing desk, multiline phones with computer and fax hookup, home entertainment centers, even a complimentary umbrella; but if at all possible, choose a suite: They each have a fireplace, Scandinavian comforters, and a garden terrace. The Post House Restaurant is on the second floor; the antique-studded Pembroke Room serves breakfast and afternoon tea.... *Tel 212/838–1400, 800/221–4444, fax 212/319–4230. 28 E. 63rd St., 10021, B/Q train to Lexington Ave. 65 rooms. $$$* **(see pp. 21, 23, 24, 26)**

Luxury Collection Hotel New York. Until mid-1997, this was the Ritz–Carlton New York, one of the grand dowagers of Central Park South. The location and views are as splendid as ever, and the Fantino Bar and Restaurant is still there, but the jury is still out on what—aside from dreaming up clunky names—the new owners will do.... *Tel 212/757–1900, 800/325–3589, fax 212/757–9620. 112 Central Park South, 10019, Q train to 57th St. or 1/9/A/B/C/D to 59th St./Columbus Circle. 209 rooms. $$$$* **(see p. 18)**

Malibu Studios Hotel. In the small mirrored lobby, one flight up from the sidewalk, you'll usually find a few backpack–laden Europeans getting info from the patient, 24–hour-a-day desk clerks. The small, spartan rooms are freshly decorated and spotlessly clean but for now lack phones. Some come with TV and bath; others make do with a clock radio and sink in the room and a shared bathroom down the hall.... *Tel 212/222–2954, 800/647–2227, fax 212/678–6842. 2688 Broadway, 10025, 1/9 train to 103rd St. 150 rooms. No credit cards. $* **(see p. 22)**

Mansfield Hotel. Substantially lower-priced than the neighboring Royalton and the Algonquin, the Mansfield is the smart theater-goer's place to stay. The rooms are pleasant enough, with remote TV, VCRs, and hairdryers. Continental breakfast is free.... *Tel 212/944–6050, fax 212/764–4477. 12 W. 44th St., 10036, B/D/F train to 42nd St. 124 rooms. DC not accepted. $$* **(see p. 22)**

The Mark Hotel. Relax in the "neo-classical, English-Italian" lobby and watch Hollywood types make deals. Upstairs, rooms are sharp and elegant, with the usual luxury amenities, including marble bathrooms with large tubs and separate shower stalls. Some larger suites have libraries, terraces, and so on. Stop by the intimate Mark's Bar for a cocktail, or dine at the handsome (and expensive) two-tiered restaurant.... *Tel 212/744–4300, 800/THE–MARK, fax 744–2749. Madison Ave. at E. 77th St., 10021, 6 train to 77th St. 180 rooms. $$$$* **(see pp. 17, 21)**

Mayflower Hotel. The Mayflower remains a dependable hotel with a fair price, right on Central Park. Standard rooms have two closets and a kitchenette; there's a small fitness room upstairs. The decor may be early maiden-aunt, but the low-key atmosphere can be a lifesaver.... *Tel 212/ 265–0060, 800/223–4164, fax 212/265–5098. 15 Central Park West, 10023, 1/9 or A/B/C/D train to Columbus Circle. 365 rooms. $$* **(see pp. 19, 21)**

Michelangelo. Acres of Italian marble downstairs, and upstairs all the upper-crust amenities you'd expect—very large rooms with king-sized beds, stunning Times Square views, marble bathrooms. A small fitness room, lobby bar, and business facilities are on the premises.... *Tel 212/765–1900, 800/237–0990, fax 212/581–7618. 152 W. 51st St., 10019, N/R train to 49th St. 178 rooms. $$$$*
(see pp. 18, 21, 25)

Milford Plaza. With so much commotion on the enormous first floor, with its gift shops, hairdresser, ATM machine, fax- and copy service, you may wonder why people stay here. (It isn't for the motel-like rooms.) The answer: cheap package deals of Broadway tickets plus a room.... *Tel 212/869–3600, 800/221–2690, fax 212/944–8357. 270 W. 45th St., 10036, A/C/E trains to 42nd St. 1,300 rooms. $*
(see pp. 18, 27)

Millenium Broadway. Huge Art Deco frescoes adorn the lobby, while etched mirrors and chrome light the adjoining Restaurant Charlotte, a pleasant place to dine after a play. Sleek, modern rooms feature dual-line phones, TVs, and all the futuristic gadgets you might expect. Then there's that dynamite skyscraper-view of New York.... *Tel 212/768–4400, 800/622–5569, fax 212/768–0847. 145 W. 44th St., 10036, 1/2/3/7/9 and N/R trains to Times Square. 627 rooms. $$$* **(see pp. 18, 22)**

Millenium Hotel. High-octane Hilton, with tempting weekend rates. Modern furnishings combined with the usual business amenities, fitness room, computerized room service, mini-bars—and, from the higher floors, an absolutely spectacular view of New York Harbor.... *Tel 212/693–2001, 800/752–0014, ext. 25, fax 212/571–2317. 55 Church St., 10007, N/R train to Cortlandt St. 561 rooms. $$$*
(see pp. 19, 27)

Morgans Hotel. If you are tall, thin, overpaid, and wear only black, you'll fit in at this ultra-discreet little hotel. Rooms lack views but offer down comforters, fresh flowers, and some very high-tech communications capabilities. Room service 24 hours a day; Continental breakfast is free. There's a trendy bar and cafe downstairs.... *Tel 212/686–0300, 800/334–3408, fax 212/779–8352. 237 Madison Ave., 10016, 4/5/6/7 train to Grand Central Station. 154 rooms.* $$$ **(see pp. 21, 25)**

New York Hilton and Towers. Expect a standard-issue Hilton room (the glass outer walls are tinted blue), with modern decor; Tower rooms are larger and higher-priced. A multilingual staff, business center, and new exhibit complex keep the Hilton popular with corporate customers; for the rest of us, there's a fitness center, massages, two mediocre restaurants and a pair of lounges, and numerous shops in the lobby.... *Tel 212/586–7000, 800/HILTONS, fax 212/315–1374. 1335 Avenue of the Americas, 10019–6078, B/D/E/F/Q train to 47-50th St./Rockefeller Center. 2,042 rooms.* $$–$$$ **(see p. 23)**

New York International American Youth Hostel. The Hilton of hostels offers lodging to travelers of all ages (you have to be an AYH member, but you can join at nominal cost when you register). Most rooms are dormitory style, but some semi-private and family rooms are available. The community-college ambience extends to the dining area, library, laundry, meeting room, chapel, espresso bar, student travel offices, and sunny garden where a fountain plays. Much cheaper than the YMCA, and lacking only a swimming pool.... *Tel 212/932–2300, fax 212/932–2574. 891 Amsterdam Ave., 10025, 1/9 train to 103rd St. 480 beds. AE, DC not accepted.* $ **(see p. 24)**

New York Palace. Reproduction furniture and unexceptional (though luxurious) amenities hit one like a hangover after the glamour of the downstairs, which features one of New York's best restaurants, Le Cirque 2000. Non-smoking floors are offered, as well as 24-hour room service, and same-day laundry and valet. A business center, fitness center, and free limousine rides to Wall Street may mollify business travelers. You can dine al fresco in The Courtyard restaurant, in the shadows of St. Patrick's Cathedral.... *Tel 212/888–7000, 800/NY–PALACE, fax 212/644–5750. 455 Madison Ave., 10022, 6 train to 51st St. 900 rooms.* $$$$$ **(see p. 17)**

Off SoHo Suites. Though cheek to jowl with the grim Lower East Side, this place is clean, reasonably priced, and near downtown plays, poetry readings, music, and galleries. The apartment-like suites have phones, color TV, air conditioning, marble baths, and well-equipped eat-in kitchens are cheery in a Crate and Barrel way. Large basement fitness room and laundry—but maid service is an extra $10 per day.... *Tel 212/979–9651, 800/OFF–SOHO, fax 212/979–9801. 11 Rivington St., 10002, F train to 2nd Ave. 37 suites. DC not accepted. $$* **(see pp. 20, 22)**

Paramount Hotel. A happening place for the young—check out the very modern lobby, or the Whiskey Bar with its bright, cartoonlike furniture. Rooms are extremely cramped but very stylish. No views, lots of street noise, and a staff that believes looking good should be enough.... *Tel 212/764–5500, 800/225–7474, fax 212/354–5237. 235 W. 46th St., 10036, 1/9 train to 50th St., or 1/2/3/9 to Times Sq. 600 rooms. $$* **(see p. 18)**

The Peninsula Hotel. The bathrooms are to die for—giant marble tubs with plenty of thick, white towels—and the soothing, carpeted bedrooms with accents of peach, green, and gold match any other Manhattan hotel for luxury. And don't forget the 35,000-square-foot health spa, afternoon tea at the Gotham Lounge, meals at Le Bistro, and drinks way up in the Pen-Top Bar and Terrace. Closing for most of 1998 for major renovations.... *Tel 212/247–2200, 800/262–4967, fax 212/903–3949. 700 5th Ave., 10019, E/F train to 5th Ave. 242 rooms. $$$$$* **(see pp. 23, 25)**

Pierre Hotel. With an ambience more sophisticated than the Plaza's, yet livelier than the Plaza Athénée's, this is a place to come home to, assuming you have a few million in your pocket. If so, put dibs on a room with a Central Park view and make reservations at the sumptuous Cafe Pierre.... *Tel 212/838–8000, 800/332–3442, fax 212/940–8109. 2 E. 61st St., 10021, N/R train to 5th Ave. 202 rooms. $$$$$* **(see pp. 17, 24)**

Plaza. The ceilings here are high, the beds are firm, and the flowered duvets are actually pretty. Bathrooms have big, thick towels. Service is very casual, though—quick enough, but not particularly deferential.... *Tel 212/759–3000,*

800/759–3000, fax 212/759–3167. 768 5th Ave., 10019, N/R train to 5th Ave. 830 rooms. $$$–$$$$
(see pp. 16, 17, 19, 23, 26, 27)

Plaza Athénée. Rooms are very sophisticated and very French, with soft carpets and delicate antiques, marble baths with Frette robes, Belgian sheets, VCRs, and everything else top-level; the penthouses really let loose, with velvet upholstery, oil paintings, and terraces and glass solariums. Even the hotel's small fitness room has paintings on the walls, and La Régence restaurant, a Louis XV gem, resides downstairs.... *Tel 212/734–9100, 800/447–8800, fax 212/722–0958. 37 E. 64th St., 10021, B/Q train to Lexington Ave. 152 rooms. $$$$* **(see p. 17)**

Quality Hotel and Suites. The lobby is long, narrow, and often crowded with chattering Brazilian tourists. Murals depicting views of New York lighten up the place. Otherwise, this is your typical budget-priced hotel, handily near the jewelry district, Rockefeller Center, Midtown shopping, and Broadway.... *Tel 212/719–2300, 800/223–1900, fax 212/790–2760. 29 W. 46th St., 10036, B/D/F/Q trains to 47th-50th St./Rockefeller Center. 200 rooms. $$* **(see pp. 26, 27)**

Radisson Empire Hotel. The halls are narrow, but who cares when Lincoln Center is just across the way. Chintz is everywhere, the bathrooms compact but sweet. Service is very professional, polite, and alert but understated, not at all stuffy. A good hotel for the price.... *Tel 212/265–7400, 800/333–3333, fax 212/315–0349. 44 W. 63rd St., 10023, 1/9 train to 66th St./Lincoln Center. 376 rooms. $$* **(see p. 19)**

Regal U.N. Plaza. This sleek high-rise right near the U.N. gives movers and shakers a raft of furnishings so modern you hardly see them. The rooftop swimming pool, tennis courts, the banquettes in the lobby with custom telephones, and the super-alert desk clerks assure you that you're in the hands of experts.... *Tel 212/758–1234, 800/222–8888, fax 212/702–5051. 1 United Nations Plaza, 10017–3575, 4/5/6/7 train to Grand Central. 427 rooms. $$$*
(see pp. 19, 23, 26)

RIHGA Royal Hotel. A grand, mosaic-tiled and carpeted lobby, the sharp-looking Halcyon Lounge and Halcyon Restaurant, and comfortable beige suites with state-of-the-art business amenities make this a perfect place to meet your clients. Fabulous views of Central Park and the Hudson River, a business center, small fitness center with personal trainer, and—you guessed it—complimentary shoe shine.... *Tel 212/307–5000, 800/937–5454, fax 212/765–6530. 151 W. 54th St., 10019, B/D/E train to 7th Ave. 500 suites. $$$$–$$$$$* **(see pp. 22, 23)**

Roger Smith. Bright, amusing, and sophisticated, this hotel is a place people come back to. Ignore the colonial-style upstairs bedrooms and spend your time with the other guests in Lily's Restaurant and Bar. Even the clerks here have character, and breakfast is free.... *Tel 212/755–1400, 800/445–0277, fax 212/319–9130. 501 Lexington Ave., 10017, 4/5/6/7 train to Grand Central. 135 rooms. $$* **(see p. 20)**

Royalton. The Algonquin of the nineties, featuring the 44 Bar and Restaurant where you can study the lifestyles of the rich and famous. Upstairs, the post-modern style is almost scary at times, but fun, with designer Philipe Starck's stark velvet armchairs complementing cherry headboards, thick teal carpets and, in some cases, granite hearths with working fireplaces. There's a 24-hour fitness room, naturally.... *Tel 212/869–4400, 800/635–9013, fax 212/869–8965. 44 W. 44th St., 10036, B/D/F train to 42nd St. 205 rooms. $$$–$$$$* **(see pp. 18, 22, 24, 27)**

Shelburne Murray Hill. Most guests here are on long-term corporate stays, living in the workmanlike rooms with full kitchens. Amenities are pretty basic, but you can hook up your laptop and fax machine. Secretarial services are available downstairs, and there are gym and laundry facilities in the basement.... *Tel 212/689–5200, 800/ME–SUITE, fax 212/779–7068. 303 Lexington Ave., 10016–3104, 4/5/6/7 train to Grand Central. 257 rooms. $$* **(see p. 22)**

SoHo Grand. Since it opened in mid–1996, the SoHo Grand has been full practically every night, and for good reason. It is the only hotel in the hippest part of town; its Canal House restaurant got 2 stars from the picky *New York Times*. The rooms are tiny, but the views are fabulous, the sheets are Frette, and the toiletries are from Kiehl's (see Shopping).... *Tel 212/965–3000, 800/965–3000, fax 212/965–3244.*

310 W. Broadway, 10013, A/C/E train to Canal St. 369 rooms. $$$ **(see pp. 18, 19, 20)**

The Stanhope Hotel. Museum Mile gives the Stanhope an artistic flair, and the mood here is almost like a country estate—one where anything might happen. Newly renovated rooms feature Louis XV-style antiques with Asian accents. The perfect place for a mogul who wants out of Midtown.... *Tel 212/288–5800, 800/828–1123, fax 212/517–0088. 995 5th Ave., 10028, 6 train to 77th St. 150 rooms. $$$$* **(see pp. 17, 19, 26)**

Surrey Hotel. Half a block from the Whitney Museum, with large, comfortable, recently redecorated suites, this place has a lot to recommend it—including full kitchens with surprisingly attractive dining areas. Fitness center, secretarial services, and room service (from Restaurant Daniel, one of the city's best, downstairs) available.... *Tel 212/288–3700, 800/ME–SUITE, fax 212/628–1549. 20 E. 76th St., 10018–1103, 6 train to 77th St. 133 rooms. $$$* **(see pp. 22, 25)**

Urban Ventures, Inc. Mary McAulay and Frances Tesser started this bed-and-breakfast concern in 1979 with only four rooms to offer. They now command 900, nearly all in Manhattan. You'll have a choice of rooms with breakfast or empty apartments without—quality varies wildly, but the two owners have checked out each home and interviewed the hosts. "Comfort Range" rooms (most with private bath) run $85–95, "Budget Range" (most with shared bath) at $65–80, and entire apartments begin at $105/night.... *Tel 212/594–5650. Box 426, 10024. DC not accepted. $* **(see pp. 22, 25)**

Vanderbilt YMCA. The rooms are YMCA quality, but you still get a lot for your buck: the use of the recently renovated fitness club, two pools, and a sauna, plus an excellent and safe East Side location. The suites have private bathrooms.... *Tel 212/756–9600, fax 212/752–0210. 224 E. 47th St., 10017, 4/5/6/7 train to Grand Central. 400 rooms. AE, DC not accepted. $* **(see pp. 23, 24)**

Waldorf-Astoria. Owned by the Hilton chain, the lobby areas bring back New York's best old days. Upstairs, furniture is Hilton reproduction colonial, but the peach carpets are thick and the baths are marble. Some suites have fireplaces. There's a fitness center, a business center, four restaurants, and four lounges.... *Tel 212/355–3000, 800/WALDORF, fax 212/421–8103. 301 Park Ave., 10022, 6 train to 51st St. 1,215 rooms. $$$–$$$$* **(see pp. 17, 26)**

Washington Square Hotel. The Spanish-style lobby is nice enough, with its wrought-iron gate and tile floors, but the rooms are deadly dreary. Front rooms are supposed to be better, but they're noisy. Continental breakfast included, but the basement restaurant smells like goulash. Cheap, but worth no more than what you're paying. Still, what a location.... *Tel 212/777–9515, 800/222–0418, fax 212/ 979–8373. 103 Waverly Place, 10011–9194, A/B/C/ D/E/F/Q train to W. 4th St. 160 rooms. DC not accepted. $* **(see pp. 19, 20)**

West Side YMCA. Steps from Lincoln Center and Central Park, the bustling lobby rings with several languages, and there are plenty of opportunities to converse—in the gym, at the pool, the espresso bar, or in the new restaurant (with room service!). Rooms are very basic. They come as singles or doubles, with or without private bath. (Showers are down the hall.)... *Tel 212/787–4400, fax 212/496–7789. 5 W. 63rd St., 10023, 1/9 train to 66th St./Lincoln Center. 530 rooms. AE, DC not accepted. $* **(see pp. 23, 24)**

Wyndham. Personal attention from the staff gives this modest place an edge. Smaller than the roughly equivalent May-flower, the Wyndham has large, apartment-like rooms and suites (some guests are long-term residents), most with modern decor.... *Tel 212/753–3500, 800/257–1111, fax 212/754–5638. 42 W. 58th St., Q train to 57th St. 200 rooms. $* **(see p. 22)**

Uptown Accommodations

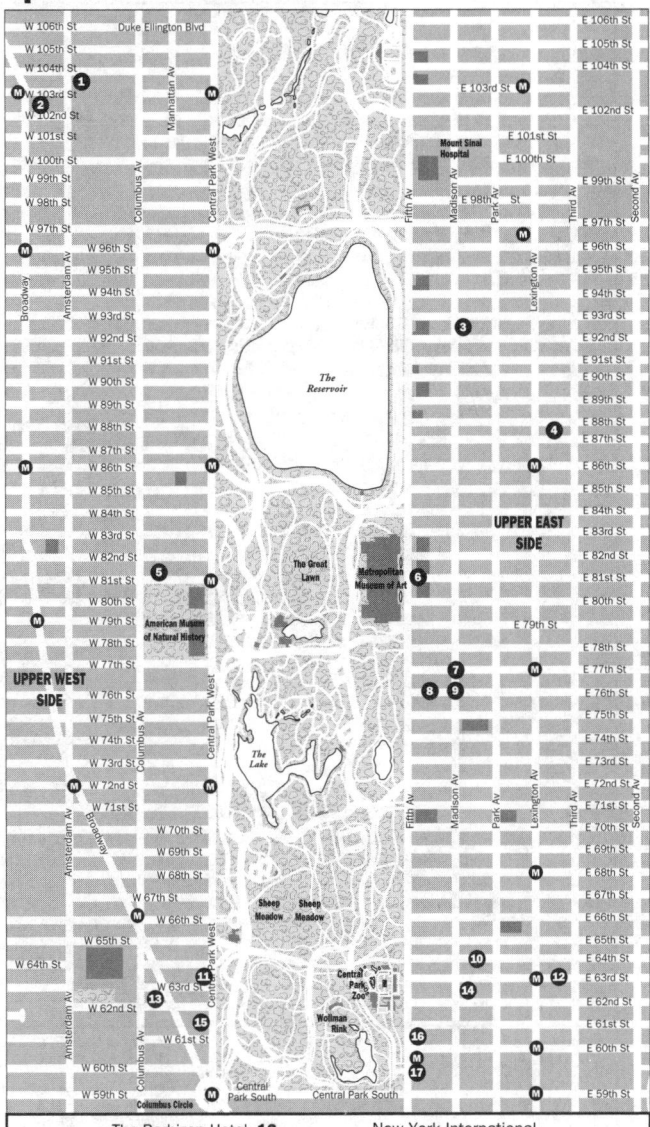

The Barbizon Hotel **12**
The Carlyle Hotel **9**
Excelsior Hotel **5**
The Franklin **4**
Hotel Wales **3**
Lowell Hotel **14**
Malibu Studios Hotel **2**
The Mark Hotel **7**
Mayflower Hotel **15**

New York International
 AYH Hostel **1**
Pierre Hotel **16**
Plaza Athenee **10**
Radisson Empire Hotel **13**
Sherry Netherland Hotel **17**
The Stanhope Hotel **6**
Surrey Hotel **8**
West Side YMCA **11**

Midtown Accommodations

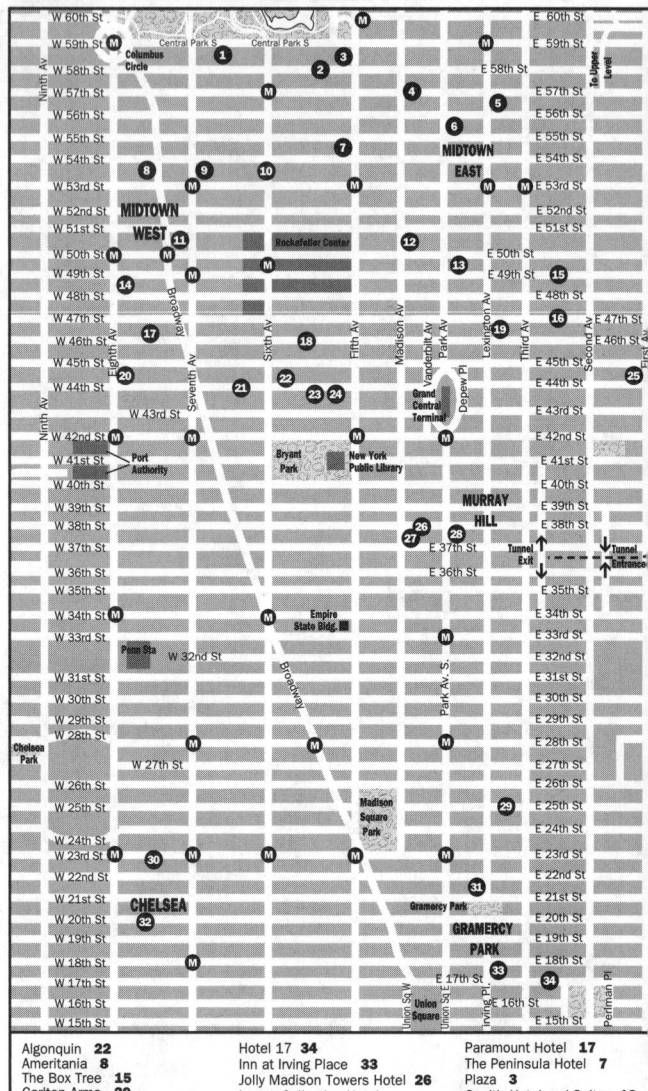

Algonquin **22**
Ameritania **8**
The Box Tree **15**
Carlton Arms **29**
Chelsea Hotel **30**
Chelsea International
  Hostel **32**
Days Hotel Midtown **14**
The Drake Swissotel **6**
Fitzpatrick Manhattan
  Hotel **5**
Four Seaons **4**
Gramercy Park Hotel **31**

Hotel 17 **34**
Inn at Irving Place **33**
Jolly Madison Towers Hotel **26**
Luxury Collection Hotel
  New York **1**
Mansfield Hotel **24**
The Michelangelo **11**
Milford Plaza **20**
Milleniom Broadway **21**
Morgans Hotel **27**
New York Hilton and Towers **10**
New York Palace **12**

Paramount Hotel **17**
The Peninsula Hotel **7**
Plaza **3**
Qualtiy Hotel and Suites **18**
RIHGA Royal Hotel **9**
Roger Smith **19**
Royalton **23**
Shelburne Murray Hill **28**
Regal UN Plaza **25**
Vanderbilt YMCA **16**
Waldorf-Astoria **13**
Wyndham **2**

Downtown Accommodations

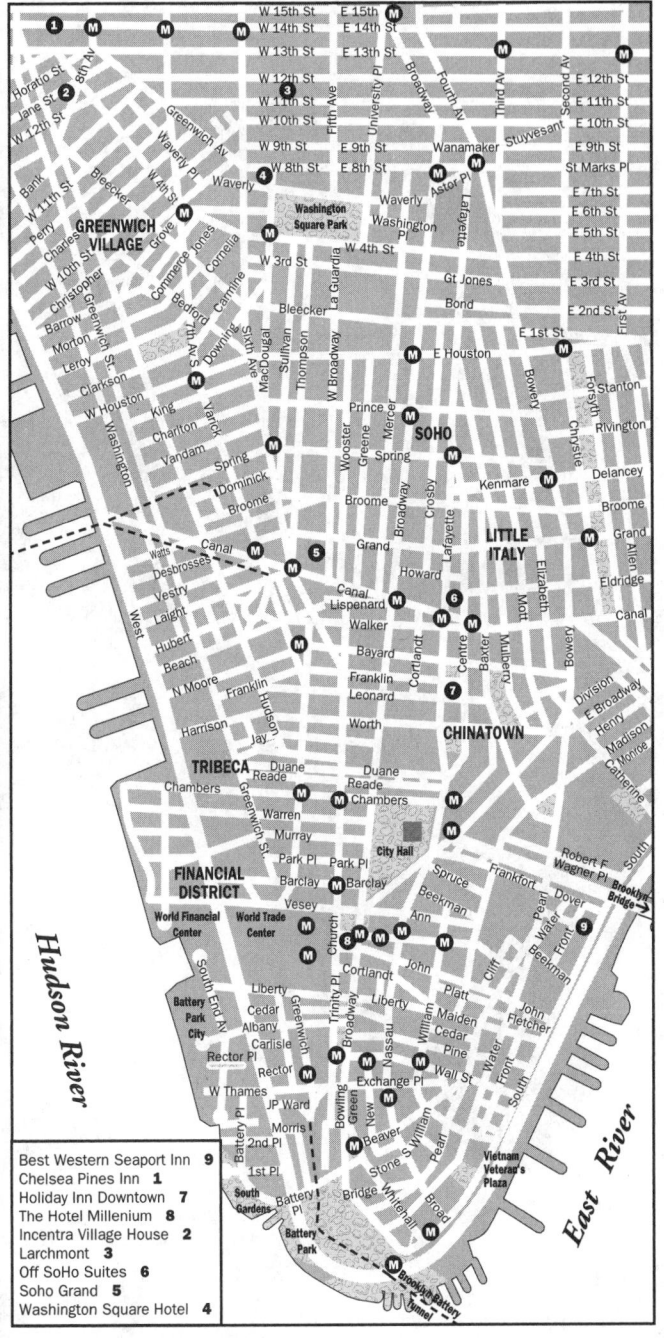

Best Western Seaport Inn **9**
Chelsea Pines Inn **1**
Holiday Inn Downtown **7**
The Hotel Millenium **8**
Incentra Village House **2**
Larchmont **3**
Off SoHo Suites **6**
Soho Grand **5**
Washington Square Hotel **4**

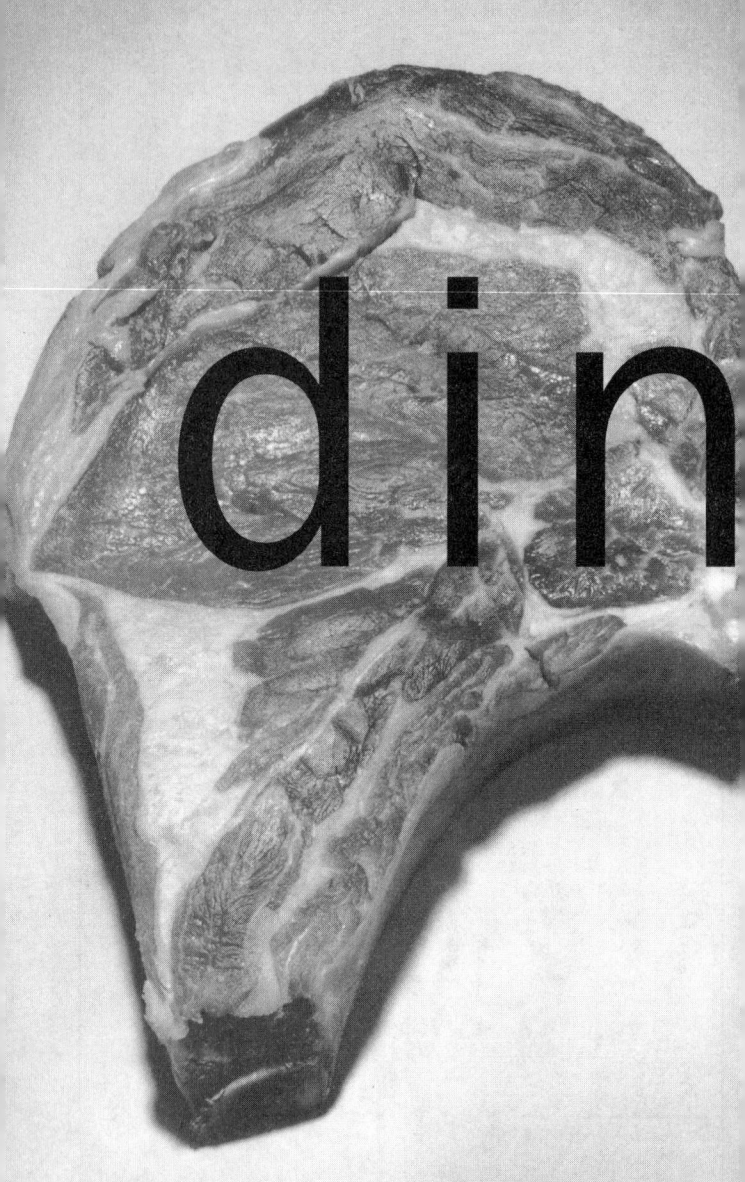

2

ing

Manhattan
invented the
concept of
dining out as
performance art.
It isn't just the
extravagant decor

of many top restaurants (interior design as artwork), or exquisite presentation of the dishes (pastry chefs vie to produce extravagant structures worthy of *Architectural Digest*). It's the hushed buzz as yet another celebrity walks in. It's the high-powered deals shouted at top volume. It's the sheer exuberance of people-watching, wondering if that really IS a man in drag, or an adulterous liaison being played out.

The minimalist trend of the 90s has already passed; big, bold, brash, and expensive seems in again. Nothing succeeds like excess. Size is prized: To top them all, a vast 50,000-square-foot space is expected to open by 1999 in the World Trade Center (dining out as amusement park?). Another trend still surging is theme restaurants, most of them found within a few-block radius in the West 50s. These high-concept spots masquerade as real restaurants, only not nearly as much fun: Hard Rock Cafe, Planet Hollywood, All Star Sports Cafe, Harley Davidson Cafe, Jekyll and Hyde (the interior is a museum of the macabre), Television City, and the Fashion Cafe, which reportedly paid $50,000 apiece to Claudia Schiffer, Elle MacPherson, Naomi Campbell, and Christy Turlington to lend their names to the joint (of course, they haven't been caught dead there since its flashbulb-popping opening). Even McDonalds goes for the glitz in this town: The Wall Street branch features a pianist tinkling the ivories.

Manhattan strives to do it better than anywhere else—be it blini, sushi, California health-nut food, skyscraping appetizers and desserts, or the thinnest tuna carpaccio. You can get anything from reindeer in lingonberry sauce to Lake Michigan perch with fiddlehead ferns. You can pay up at such gastronomic shrines as La Côte Basque, Aureole, and Lespinasse, or nibble your way through the city's countless ethnic neighborhoods.

Manhattan is heaven for grazers, too. The coffee and bagel carts stationed at corners during the morning rush hour get replaced around noon with stands selling those quintessential New York comfort foods: pretzels and hot dogs. At the ubiquitous Korean salad bars, the term salad is so broadly defined as to include pasta, sushi, spring rolls, and fried chicken, all sold by the pound. You'll also find a few bona fide American food courts, like the fine one at South Street Seaport; and, of course, the onslaught of designer coffee bars purveying cappuccino, latte, and espresso, and muffins heavy enough to serve as ballast.

Only in New York

The hot haute places get all the press, but to truly eat like a New Yorker, go to the neighborhoods and eat ethnic. East Sixth Street is Little India, the rest of the Lower East Side a slice of the Ukraine; venturing farther afield, you can coo over couscous on Brooklyn's Atlantic Avenue, or chow down on churrasco (mixed grill) in authentic South American restaurants in Jackson Heights. Chinese food is such a staple in the Manhattan diet, you'll find good candidates all over the island—but mind, it's come a long way from tired old General Tso's chicken, incorporating the flavors of Thailand, Viet Nam, Burma, and Malaysia in an *au courant* Asian cuisine. Hispanic storefront cafes crop up everywhere, too; the accent may be Cuban, Dominican, or Bahamian, but so long as the menu in the window features rice and beans, it's bound to be cheap, filling, and flavorful. Perhaps the quintessential Noo Yawk food is pizza: For atmosphere and authenticity, go to **Lombardi's** (32 Spring St., tel 212/941–7994), a Little Italy fixture since 1905, or the original **John's Pizzeria** (278 Bleecker St., tel 212/243–1680) in the West Village. The word "deli" is practically synonymous with New York: The classic counter culture is dished up at **Katz's Deli** (205 E. Houston St., tel 212/254–2246) on the Lower East side; Midtown's ever-crowded **Carnegie Deli** (854 Seventh Ave., tel. 212/757–2245), renowned for its borscht; or the glitzier **Stage Deli** (834 Seventh Avenue, tel 212/245–7850), where the overstuffed sandwiches are named after stars.

What Will It Cost?

A multi-course dinner at one of the city's fanciest eating establishments, including drinks, freely flowing wine, and a tip, can set you back over $100 per person. Lunches at places like **The Four Seasons** and the **Union Square Cafe** are somewhat less expensive, and occasionally you'll find prix fixe options—though these seldom include specialty dishes with exotic ingredients. Careful ordering (a glass of wine and an entree, or two appetizers instead of an entree) can help keep the tab down. You can dine at the bar in the swankier joints, where lower-priced menus are sometimes available. In the summer, keep your eye open for special lunch deals (costing the same as the year, for instance $19.98 in 1998) offered as part of a city-wide promotion at some of Manhattan's top restaurants. But you also really can find great meals for under $20 at places with character rather than class, and intensely flavored food rather than subtle haute cuisine. New Yorkers certainly don't spend $100 every time they dine out—and they do so often.

Tipping

Contrary to reports, service in top New York extablishments is usually exemplorary, and always at least professional (no "Hi, *my* name is Judy, and I'll be your singing waitress."). Of course, you get several actors betweeen jobs, posing and dishing when they should be more attentive, but it's all part of the New York vibe. Service compris is not a concept understood in New York, where restaurant salaries are woefully low and most waiters are only working tables as a means to some other end. (The classic cliche overheard at a restaurant table: "Oh actor, actor..."). Dollar bills for coat checkers are standard. When calculating a waiter's tip, many New Yorkers simply double the tax amount on their check (2 x 8.25% = 16.5 %, a reasonable tip). But New York waitpeople work hard for their money, so round it up to 20 percent if you can, unless the service is wretched.

Getting the Right Table

Perhaps some high-rollers tip maitre d's to get see-and-be-seen tables. Since money talks in New York, it can work, but the practice strikes many as more than a little gauche. After all, the real way to get a great table is by being a regular. If you're from out of town, a good hotel concierge should have some pull—make your reservations through him or her if you plan to dine at any exclusive restaurants. If you know that you prefer one room in a restaurant over another (for instance, the clubby Grill Room versus the romantic Pool Room at The Four Seasons), ask for it specifically when you make your reservations. Barring that, once you're at the restaurant don't be too timid to request a change if you get put in a spot you don't like and you see better tables empty. Most maître d's will accommodate you, when at all possible. If not, and your assigned seat is simply too miserable, the answer's simple: just get up and go.

When to Eat and How to Dress

Manhattan Island runs on the office clock, lunching from noon to 2, and dining from around 7:30 to 9:30. Unless you just happen to strike it lucky, reservations are required at the kinds of places where they sweep the crumbs off the tablecloth with a little brush; a good general policy is to make a reservation at any place that accepts them, and check on the dress policy when you call. Don't be surprised—or offended—to be offered a table at 6 or 10:30 pm. (Listings below note any restrictions that apply at these restaurants.) These days, even top-of-the-line New York restaurateurs recognize the chilling effects of a room full of suits and ties, but the light sure comes to their eyes when hip-looking customers arrive. So if it's a dinner to remember you have in mind, celebrate the occasion by dressing with style.

Where the Chefs Are

In Manhattan's revolving culinary scene, top restaurateurs often must grind their teeth at the success of former apprentices— many remain with the restaurants they open, but others start their own, still others diversify and train new generations. And most are impossibly young (and usually svelte). **David Bouley** is notoriously imperious, but his former restaurant (the epony- mous Bouley) annually ranked atop the Zagat survey and is reopening in a new space in 1998; meanwhile his informal Bouley Bakery has become one of the most chic spots to break bread. **Daniel Boulud**, once of Le Cirque, sets the standard for classic French cooking at Daniel; others holding down the bastion of haute cuisine include **Eric Ripert** at Le Bernardin, **Jean-Jacques Rachou** at La Côte Basque, and **Bernhard Mueller**, who amazingly replaced the irreplaceable Andre Soltner at legendary Lutece. Of course, New York boasts sev- eral chefs so cutting edge, they draw blood: **Jean-Georges Vongerichten** (Vong, Jean-Georges), **Gray Kunz** (Lespinasse), and **Sottha Khunn** (Le Cirque 2000) are widely admired for their dazzling Asian-French fusion food. **Nobu Matsuhisa** has reinvented Japanese cuisine at Nobu. **Charles Palmer** (Aureole) is beloved in the food industry for both his cooking and I'm-no-star manner; his apprentices are already becoming New York's next wave. If your standard of fame is having your own best-selling cookbook, how about **Alfred Portale** (Gotham Bar & Grill), **Michael Romano** (Union Square Cafe), and **Bobby Flay** (Mesa Grill)? Other New York fixtures in the foodie firmament include **Wayne Nish** (March), **David Waltuck** (Chanterelle), **Tom Colicchio** (Gramercy Tavern)... oh, the list could go on and on.

The Lowdown

New York classics... The architect Philip Johnson designed the airy Pool Room and dark, woody Grill Room at **The Four Seasons**, where the service is impeccable and the tables so far apart that the Macy's Thanksgiving Day Parade could almost be routed between them. Dover sole, steak tartare, and tuna carpaccio head up the menu, but people have been known to rhapsodize even over The Four Seasons' baked potato, doused in Lungarotti olive oil. **Peter Luger** remains the steakhouse where the well-bred cut their chops on prime beef. Despite the untimely death of owner/chef Gilbert Le Coze, **Le Bernardin** remains New York's finest seafood restaurant, with faultless service and memorable dishes such as roast lobster tail on asparagus with risotto crepes or a simple pan-seared sea bass. The husband/wife team of David (chef) and Karen (hostess) Waltuck make **Chanterelle** the consummate Manhattan fine dining experience, where you can feast on gossamer-light potato ravioli in vegetable crepes or meltingly tender braised free-range chicken. Everything from the towering floral arrangements to the artfully arranged desserts is impeccable. Trademark miniature jockeys still line up outside the **'21' Club**, while heavy hitters jockey for position inside this oh-so-masculine enclave. The new American menu has been reinvigorated, and where else can you brag about paying $24 for a burger? **Tavern on the Green** is set in a Central Park bower haunted by topiary beasts, lit up like a diamond tiara at night. The beauty of the site still draws out-of-towners, but locals know the American food's not the same since Patrick Clark left the kitchen. The soufflés and cassoulet at **La Côte Basque** prove that French cuisine doesn't have to be stuffy to be exquisite. And if the French fare isn't quite as distinguished at the **Café des Artistes**, the setting is to die for, in the lobby of a grand old Upper West Side apartment building, with murals of naked maidens painted by Howard Chandler Christy. At the newly refurbished **Windows on the World** on the 107th floor of the World Trade Center what you get is, above all, a soaring Manhattan view; the Continental menu has been revamped too, with sophisitcated entrees such as grilled venison chops or seared sea scallops with truffle vinaigrette. I'd sell the family jewels for the view of downtown Manhattan from the windows at **The River Cafe**, tucked beneath the eastern end of the Brooklyn Bridge. Chef Rick Laakkonen's menu features such delicacies as cod-and-lobster risotto and pan-seared baby chicken stuffed with smoked bacon. At **One if by Land, Two if by Sea**, strings of white lights twinkle in the garden and four fire-places glow warm and mellow. The restaurant occupies a historic carriage house in the West Village, once owned by Aaron Burr, who might have been convinced to quit dueling with Alexander Hamilton had he sampled chef David McInerney's beef Wellington or Cornish game hen in honey-lavender glaze.

Feeling their hautes... They're the celeb haunts of the moment, and act accordingly. At **Asia de Cuba**, in the boutique hotel Morgan's, the air is heavy with knowing winks and whispers about the latest in social and political gossip. JFK Jr., Denzel Washington, Annette Bening, and Michael Jordan have stopped in. **Clementine**, featuring John Schenk's superlative new American food, is the latest hot spot for the younger performing set, whether it's Mary J. Blige, Mark Wahlberg, Leonardo di Caprio, Matthew Perry, Ewan MacGregor, or Tori Spelling; more mature regulars include Joan Rivers, Alec Baldwin, Debbie Harry, and David Lee Roth. Sundays are like a star-gazing zoo. **Le Cirque 2000** is still the benchmark for snootiness and I-can-get-us-a-table braggadocio, with Sirio Maccione running the show as smoothly as ever; heads still swivel whenever someone new walks in. Even though **Vong** has been open forever in New York terms, its sublime Asian-French food is still described reverently by its regulars (including the likes of Woody Allen, Christie Todd Whitman, Donatella Versace, Bono, and Shimon Peres—how's that for a cross-section of power types?). Needless to say, they all followed Vong's owner, Jean Georges Vongerichten, to his latest establishment, **Jean Georges**, this one a truly gourmet but healthful French restaurant, where such delicately flavored dreams as the garlic soup with frogs' legs or the artic char with sorrel, potatoes, and horseradish are true revelations. At **Moomba** the emotionless waitstaff serves rich preppies and such celebs as Oliver Stone, Harrison Ford, and the ubiquitous Madonna. **Bouley Bakery** is master-chef David Bouley's interim eatery before reopening his gourmet palace Bouley; the foodies clamor to get in, because they know the menu will nearly double in price once Bouley is back. Though the surroundings and service try to be unpretentious, the crowd is just too knowing about its gastronomy and viticulture. Specials to watch for include asparagus-roasted monkfish, honey-and-thyme glazed duck, and shrimp in phyllo with sweet corn and Thai curry paste. **Balthazar** makes big noise about recreating a plain old Paris bistro, but it's filled with the kind of trend-setters whose bitchy hauteur, chiseled cheekbones, and laser-beam stares could cut glass.

Hot spots that won't die... In TriBeCa, there's **Odeon**, encamped in a postmodern stripped-down cafeteria, which provides cassoulet, seafood chowder, roast lamb, and sorbet to the contemporary art crowd; opened in 1980, it's lasted long enough to prove that if you wait long enough anything will make a style comeback. It's upper West Side sibling, **Cafe Luxembourg**, is still the Lincoln Center restaurant of choice for literati, glitterati, and hangers-on who like hanger steak and cassoulet. Then there's **TriBeCa Grill**, where the trendy crowd was first lured by the star power of owner Robert DeNiro and then kept on coming for the inventive cooking of chef Don Pintabona. **Aureole**, in a pretty town house on the East Side with a massive two-story front window, has perfected the art of the dessert, like bittersweet chocolate timbale and crème brûlée. **March**, in another East Side town house, tucks diners away in peaceful little flower-decked nooks, then woos them with chef Wayne Nish's carefully reduced sauces and intriguing pre-appetizer "treats." Can't make up your mind? Try the clever "tasting menus"—four or seven small portions of various exquisite entrees. The menu at the stylish **Union Square Cafe** has been turned into a cookbook—which is only appropriate since this place is a favorite publishing-industry lunch spot. Try the tuna carpaccio in the sunken dining room lined with cherrywood and forest-green wainscoting, followed up with a plate of delectable cookies, or just grab a seat at the bar for oyster slurping and wine sipping. Union Square Cafe's Danny Meyer also runs **Gramercy Tavern**, which has become a designer-watering hole for trendoids and foodies alike: choices from the prix fixe three-course menu might include roast rabbit with black olives and sherry vinaigrette or seared tuna with white beans, and arugula. **Mesa Grill** is brash, colorful, loud (accentuated by cathedral ceilings), and swimming with yuppie sharks-in-training, thanks to its inventive, exuberant owner/chef Bobby Flay. The subtle Asian/French flavors, bold colors, and sheer energy of **Vong** continue to draw New Yorkers in the know. **Indochine** has remained a see-and-be-scene; it's a riot of palm trees, real, painted, and artificial, which also describes the moneyed, rail-thin clientele. **Nobu** has become the latest trend-setter for high-priced, high-quality melt-in-your-mouth food; it may be the only Japanese restaurant where the service borders on haughty. And folks still flock to Tribeca's **Montrachet**, which set the standard for minimalist design and maximum emphasis on flavor and presentation, with a killer wine list. At lower Fifth Avenue's **Gotham Bar and Grill**, the decor and crowds are sleekly handsome, but upstaged by the designer-chic cuisine—salads springing off the plate and desserts that could double as Easter hats.

We never close.... You'd be surprised how many people, from club kids emerging from their lairs to attorneys on deadlines, stuff themselves around 4am with the heavy-duty pierogis, blinis, and potato pancakes at the East Village's venerable Ukrainian institutions: **Veselka** wins top nod for its gorgeous mural-rich makeover and quintessentially indifferent service. The classic Manhattan all-nighter is **Empire Diner**, an art deco marvel way west in Chelsea, with live music during the wee hours and sublime people-watching from the sidewalk tables. Midtown's **Brasserie** caters to stuffed shirt workaholics rather than club rats, but its eggs Florentine are the perfect antidote to an expense-account drinking binge; avoid the pathetic excuse for "authentic" French onion soup. **Florent** is the delightful equivalent of a French greasy spoon—so real you feel like ordering a pastis with your steak frites. The bizarre decor includes ugly brick-red banquettes and weird pop art paintings of cartoon-colored circles; the people who stagger in as the night wears on match the setting—hip but definitely odd.

Bangs for your buck... You can dine at any of the following spots for under $20, easy. What's more, the food is pretty darned good and the atmosphere cheerful. **Aggie's**, a bustling, converted diner on Houston Street, brings home the good-deal honors by dint of its fresh, interesting seafood menu, listed on a blackboard above the counter. **Fanelli** predates most of the other restaurants in SoHo, and never could be called trendy—still, this old–New York tavern packs in the crowds for simple dinners and Sunday brunch. **Eddie's**, in the New York University neighborhood, starts you off with popcorn, followed by delicious burgers and salads; while you eat, listen in as Village scholars deconstruct *Moby Dick*. Just off Sheridan Square, twenty-somethings from Wall Street loosen their ties over thick club sandwiches and omelettes at **Boxers,** ogling the cute waitresses and knocking back a few beers. Then there's the **Cornelia Street Cafe**, which serves very reasonably priced, tasty meals in unpretentiously stylish surroundings, with live jazz or poetry readings often thrown in as well. This cafe has been part of the Village scene for ages, and there are always companionable fellow travelers at the bar, not to mention bartenders happy to treat you to a drink if you have the look of a potential regular. The too-hip-for-words **Republic** makes communism seem like a good thing, with chummy family-style seating and impossibly low prices mated to high Southeast Asian culinary standards. **Miracle Grill** earns its name for its charming atmosphere, delightful postage-stamp garden, trendy but not overbearing crowd, and creative takes on Southwestern food. The always chic, always bustling **Florent** offers the likes of lentil salad with feta and roasted red peppers, mussels in white wine and garlic, or *boudin noir* (black sausage) with apples and onions—all at coffee shop prices, along with a well-considered list of French country wines.

Just how big is your limo?... New York has no shortage of expense account restaurants combining superlative food, elegant ambience, and sterling service—restaurants that seem designed exclusively to show off for your client, mate, or fill-in-the-blank companion. The Laura Ashley-on-acid decor of **Le Cirque 2000** never fails to impress, especially if you can actually catch owner Sirio Maccione's eye and nab a prize table in full view of prying eyes. Then savor the subtle flavors of Cambodian-born chef Sottha Khunn's menu: white truffle risotto, foie gras ravioli with black truffles, and duck breast with fried lotus root are among the standouts. In marked contrast is the quiet refined elegance of **Daniel**, whose chef/owner Daniel Boulud was Maccione's right hand at the old Le Cirque. Daniel's food ranks at the zenith of French country and haute cuisine—dishes like nine-herb ravioli with chanterelles, ricotta, and tomato coulis, or wild hare braised in red wine with bitter chocolate. Even the fattest fat cats discreetly tuck away their cell phones here, rather than wield them ostentatiously as they do at most Manhattan restaurants. The glittering Versailles-like interior of **Lespinasse** would dazzle anyone, but A-list foodies make a beeline here; Grey Kunz is widely admired for his fusion of French and Asian cuisines.

The pre-theater scene... Let's hope you've got tickets to a great show, because the theater district's restaurants don't earn many standing ovations. There are plenty of eating spots in the neighborhood, of course, and the whole block of W. 46th Street between Seventh and Eighth avenues has come to be called Restaurant Row. **Orso** occupies stylish digs there, and is a notable exception, offering smashing cuisine from the north of Italy, plus famous faces and power-brokers among the clientele. On the east side of Times Square there's an inviting bistro called **Café Un Deux Trois**, situated in the airy lobby of an old hotel, with columns and endlessly high ceilings, paper tablecloths and crayons; the menu tends toward unremarkably prepared international standards like salads, steak, fish, and fries, but the place is mobbed before and after the theater. The late Frank Zappa started it and used to be a familiar fixture at the bar. Right in the middle of W. 44th Street's gaudy marquees and at the back door of the *New York Times*, wood-trimmed **Carmine's** is the nineties version of Mamma Leone's, that massive stage-set cliché of a New York Italian restaurant (which, perhaps not coincidentally, closed its doors after this place opened). The difference here is that the food is the real thing, and it's not just for tourists—everybody comes for straightforward, delicious southern Italian fare (between this and the Upper West Side branch, Carmine's reportedly goes through 13 *tons* of garlic a year). **Jezebel** offers upscale soul food in plush, red velour surroundings that scream New Orleans bordello. **Firebird** offers haute Tsarist decor, all velvet settees, Ballet Russes costumes, and gilt chandeliers; the food (try the grilled quail, blinis, sturgeon roe, or the borscht with smoked pork loin, braised duck, beef brisket, and pirjok) is served on sterling (with equally sterling service). Best way to avoid the imperial prices here is the excellent prix-fixe pre-theater. A fashionable buppie crowd frequents **B. Smith's**, a large, handsome space with granite floors and lots of bronze and mahogany run by ex-model Barbara Smith. The menu (pretentiously eclectic Southern with international touches) is almost as vast as a Greek diner's, but surprisingly well-prepared and fairly priced.

Bistros with cachet... Oysters on the half shell and chardonnay go down smoothly at **Le Pescadou**, where you can sit by the open French doors fronting lower Sixth Avenue, communing with the potted geraniums. Don't count on a bargain meal, but you can be fairly certain of a nice bowl of lobster bisque or bouillabaisse. Small, romantic **Dix et Sept** occupies the ground floor of a West Village town house, where candles flicker on white-clothed tables and Piaf croons. The menu leans towards well-prepared Gallic standards, like good old-fashioned onion soup. **Tartine**, more a closet than a restaurant, is on one of the prettiest blocks in the Village, with an inevitable line outside the door and tables squeezed so close together that by dessert you're generally good friends with the people at the next table (unless you're seated next to a would-be supermodel and her agent). The food's tasty but simple, the service rushed and rude—all authentically Parisian, at prices cheaper than you'd find on the Left Bank. The small lace-curtained bar at **Café de Bruxelle**—not French, obviously, but a kissing cousin—is an absolute joy, with a long list of Belgian beers, perfect pommes frites, and ever-appealing specialty wines. One of the latest hot spots, **Balthazar** is a totally new space decked out to resemble a fin-de-siecle Paris bistro, with huge mirrors on mustard walls and lots of brass trim. The decor may be faux, but the cuisine, including staples such as sauteed skate and country rillette of rabbit, is comme il faut. **Provence** seems transported from Aix, with overflowing flower pots, dim lighting, an old grandfather clock, an exquisite tiled garden, and yummy regional fare (near-classic variations on fish soup and the wonderful onion/anchovy/tomato/yeast tart called *pissaladière*). **Ici** is a tiny jewel opened by Eric Clapton on the Upper East Side, with equally gorgeous food and clientele; alas, you could be put off by the 'tude du jour, not to mention the Gauloise fog. And try to overlook the nicotine-stained Eurotrash at **Raoul's**, because when this dimly-lit Left-Bankish place does escargots, they do them right. **Park Bistro** has the look and feel down pat: dark wood paneling, zinc bar, leather banquettes, swirls of smoke, 1950s black-and-white photos; there's red, white, and rosé Bandol on the wine list, delicious tomato tart and skate sauteed in port on the menu, and waiters who even tolerate your feeble French.

Like Mama used to make... Down Bleecker Street is a plain man's Italian eatery, the **Trattoria Pesce Pasta**, with its antipasto beckoning from the front window; order the linguine with clams or the seafood risotto, and you won't be disappointed—though you'll reek of garlic for hours after. **Mappamondo** and its bambino, **Mappamondo Due**, do Italian food the same way, though the clientele tends to be younger and hipper, thanks to the Hudson Street address. Ditto for the East Village's **Cucina di Pesce**, in its cozy basement dining room. Little Italy is the tourist thing—unabashedly tacky, but fun. You've got to be careful about where you stop, though, because the restaurants along Mulberry Street aren't uniformly good. Try **Benito's I** (not II) for simple pasta dishes and delectable fried calamari, or **Puglia**, a real party scene, where you get crammed into long tables with strangers, the plates are passed down to you from the end, and an accordionist squeezes the life out of his instrument. It may not be the best Italian food in town, but if you're out for a rowdy good time, who cares?

Ciao, baby... La cucina classica is raised to brave new heights at **Remi**, in a deliciously airy Midtown dining room lined by Venice's Grand Canal in murals; the risotto takes a while but is marvelously worth the wait, and the ravioli is stuffed with nouvelle sorts of ingredients that would put mama in shock. **Da Umberto** is arguably Manhattan's finest Tuscan; the only problem is the snooty staff. Still, its handsome wood-trimmed men's-club setting, handsome big biz clientele, and handsome plates of luscious wild game place it atop the short list of great Italians. For sheer fun, you can't beat the circus theme and revelries at **Osteria del Circo**, complete with Harlequin-patterned chairs and bronze clowns. The food's no joke, though, as the risotti and roasted rosemary leg of lamb amply prove. Warm, welcoming Lydia Bastianich presides over Manhattan's most sumptuous Italian, **Felidia** a feast for the eye and palate. The room is exquisite, from the lovely tapestries and murals of the Adriatic to the gorgeous handpainted china; the food is orgasmic, including definitive venison with white truffles and grilled polenta with warm octopus. **Coco Pazzo** means "crazy chef," but the food (simple, elegant Tuscan grills served family-style to a big celeb crowd) is thoroughly sane and memorable. The quail over soft polenta and mushroom ragu is to die for. **Campagna** looks for all the world like a country house in the Tuscan hills, with muted earth tones and baskets of dried flowers; here Mark Straussman caters cannily to his powerful, moneyed clientele with such sublime dishes as seafood stew on bruschetta or gnocchi with truffle oil and wild mushrooms. **I Trulli** is the ultimate in romantic rustic Italians, with an enchanting garden and roaring glass-enclosed fireplace. The specialties, via Abruzzi, are unusual and delicious; try the game sausages or chickpea fritters with wild mushrooms over prosciutto. Next door, the bustling Enoteca I Trulli serves 50 Italian wines by the glass. In the Village, the luscious Italian fare at **Il Mulino** hails from the Abruzzi; the coiffed clientele looks like they hail from Greenwich and the Hamptons. **Bar Pitti** is Florentine all the way, with rustic pastas and sandwiches on hearty country bread—simple fare to keep the arty crowd from starving. **Po**, a classy Italian eatery hidden away on little Cornelia Street, has a long narrow dining room, postage-stamp-sized bar, and a menu that plays inventive games with tried-and-true favorites. And then there's the **Grotta Azzurra**, in a Little Italy cellar that evokes Rome's Trastevere, where the waiters warm up to a little good-natured sass. Great quantities of Chianti should be consumed, and it's utterly absurd to ask them to hold the garlic.

China chic... At the swish **China Grill**, East and West meet right on the plate with dishes like oriental antipasto and grilled beef in soy-cilantro sauce. Jimmy and Wally Chin do nouvelle Chinese (boneless duckling à l'orange, Chinese-Indian lamb stew, and pecan pie) with the spirit of true global villagers at **Chin Chin**, where the walls are lined with pages from the Chin family album. **Chiam** is about as fancy schmancy as Chinese gets: track-lighting, painted black-and-white high-gloss walls, black lacquer ceiling. But the nouvelle Cantonese fare is magnificent, beautifully presented, and best of all, low-sodium without sacrificing a bit of flavor. It also has the most comprehensive, intelligent wine list of any Chinese restaurant in the city. **Shun Lee Palace** is the dowager empress, with expensive but superbly turned-out standbys such as Hunan lamb and prawns in black bean sauce. Adam Tihany's design is sexy for a Chinese eatery, replete with a stunning glass dragon light running along the entire ceiling.

And tell me what street compares with Mott Street?... For gustatory adventure, wander down to Chinatown, jammed around the western ramparts of the Manhattan Bridge. Canal Street, a non-stop produce bazaar, is the neighborhood's center; the precariously narrow side streets hold Asian treasures, even if their names (Mott, Hester, Elizabeth, Oliver) bespeak the district's earlier Irish and Italian immigrant days. Restaurant decor tends toward velvet pictures of tigers, formica tables, and bare bulbs, while ordering from untranslated menus and non-English-speaking waiters can pose challenges. But what's a meal without a little suspense? Try dunking raw beef, giant clams, un-beheaded shrimp, bean curd, enoki mushrooms, and spinach greens into a bubbling broth hot-pot at the **Triple Eight Palace**, where even the simplest meal turns into a chaotic banquet. The **Oriental Pearl** puts on a splendid, all-you-can-eat dinner buffet for $17.95 per person, featuring over 50 different occasionally hard-to-identify options. **Joe's Shanghai** is worth it for its *World of Susie Wong* name alone, but it's also the best noodle shop east of the China Sea. Asian appetizers go on parade at Chinatown dim sum restaurants like **Tai Hong Lau**, where you fill out your own orders and then settle in for a taste-fest, starting perhaps with shrimp-filled noodle crêpes, steamed sausage rolls, or perfect pork and sesame pastries. **Jing Fong** is a virtual dim sum packing house, with a walkie-talkie toting hostess and enough room to accommodate 800.

Good for the soul... **Sylvia's** of Harlem and the funky little **Pink Teacup** in the West Village used to be the first and last words in Manhattan soul food. Both remain the city's chief suppliers of artery-clogging standards like Crisco-fried chicken, barbecued ribs, and candied sweet potatoes, but a raft of new southern-style restaurants have opened their doors, rewriting Granny's recipe book. **Jezebel**, an elegant theater-district spot, has white porch swings, glittering chandeliers, fine napery, and a racially mixed clientele with at least one thing in common—pockets deep enough to afford the seductive entrees on owner Alberta

Wright's menu. Alexander Smalls, a former opera singer who's become the genius behind **Cafe Beulah**, says that his menu is all about "southern revival cuisine based on traditional low-country cooking." Which is what has made this Flatiron spot one of the most chic places in town, with white wainscoting, a long wooden bar, black-eyed pea and arugula salads, Creole steak au poivre, and side orders of lemon candied yams. **B. Smith's** throws in some upmarket curves: crab-and-corn chowder and fried oysters with wasabi soy sauce rub shoulders with such dishes as duck breast with duck sausage in cabernet reduction. Still, it's stylish and a great theater district option. Last but not least, a real finger-lickin' barbecue place right in Midtown: **Virgil's Real Barbecue**, which could almost be a clone of Kansas City's fabled Arthur Bryant's and is just about as good as Gotham can do when it comes to smokin' pork. The place does charge a bit steeply to pig out, though—the gargantuan "Rock 'n' Ribs" combo will set you back $37.95—but you get two sides with each entree (dirty rice, mashed potatoes, pickled beets, or collards and rice). Wash it all down with a Rolling Rock and some of Virgil's piquant sauce.

Kitchens to a salsa beat... Latino cuisine is sizzling hot in Manhattan. The parade is led by **Asia de Cuba**, the super-chic Cuban-Chinese (and then some) in Morgan's Hotel. There's nothing timid about this place: a loud thrum of salsa and merengue on the sound system, a boisterous 50-seat marble communal table set dead center, holograms of waterfalls, walls of billowing white curtains, bizarrely mismatched chairs. But the food is never upstaged by the scene: It's a seamless fusion of tropical cultures, such as tuna tartare on wonton crisps, orange-pineapple ribs with Japanese jasmine-infused dashi, yucca-crusted grouper with red wine miso sauce. An amazing rum selection keeps things lively if they threaten to flag. **Boca Chica**, with its Afro/Brazilian food (savory rice and beans and Bahian dishes like shrimp in spicy coconut sauce) and decor (dig the zebra-striped fabrics) is just as energetic, at half the price and attitude—if you've ever longed to see bankers samba with bikers, stop by. At swank **Patria**, with its dramatic bi-level space of mosaics and exposed piping, the Nuevo Latino food creates quite a buzz: sample plantain-coated mahi mahi with fufu and lily salad or boneless braised short ribs with Paraguayan chipa guasu. New York is not noted for its cactus cuisine, but old standbys **Rosa Mexicano** and **Zarela** offer the closest thing to bona fide Mexican food to a lively young professional clientele that digs margaritas and great guacamole. If you're just looking for a quick salsa fix, scarf down the quesadillas, tacos, and chimichangas at **Benny's Burritos**, where the tab stays low, Coronas come with lime slices, and the food's, well, filling. The slightly more authentic Mexican menu at **Mary Ann's** has more variety, including spicy fish dishes and chicken mole. It's a loud, boisterous outpost where pitchers of margaritas fuel many a pick-up. Bobby Flay's inventive **Bolo** delivers equally high-octane crowds and margaritas, along with clever takes on traditional Spanish dishes (curried shellfish and chicken paella, baked eggplant with manchego cheese). Flay made his reputation at the still-bustling **Mesa Grill**, which remains the last word in innovative Southwestern cuisine; his first effort, **Miracle Grill**, offers similarly striking fare with somewhat less flair but at far lower prices. **Tasco Porto** does grills, tapas, and sangria the way they make them in Portugal and Brazil (and yes, Spain), and has a beguiling selection of ports, aromatic Spanish brandies, and *vinho verdes*, tangy white Portuguese wines redolent of green apples.

Assimilated Asian... **Vong** offers its upscale crowd an amazing hybrid of French and Thai food (rare Muscovy duck breast with tamarind-sesame sauce, anyone?), as well as jaw-dropping, art-filled decor. **Republic** is the Marxist version, with community seating and low prices. The decor is austerely chic, with grey walls, blond woods, a long sushi bar fronting the open kitchen, and Third World photos of women in burnooses and men in turbans. **Asia de Cuba** is a chic refuge for everyone from Michael Jordan to Annette Bening to Cuban emigres (of the type who run Miami), but the food is spiced with Asian flair—the Cubano sandwich is filled not with pork and pickles but flank steak and Chinese broccoli. At Midtown's Maugham-esque **Le Colonial** you half expect a whiff of opium in the air: It's dark and elegant, with sepia-toned photographs and bamboo and wicker up the yin yang. The food is genuinely good—try the roast duck marinated in ginger or the soft salad rolls in rice paper with shrimp. Catherine Deneuve has waltzed in the door, along with such habituels as Kevin Costner, Madonna, Woody Allen,

Calvin Klein, and Sarah Ferguson. **Indochine** could well be its downtown outpost, with French-tinged Vietnamese food and a beautiful-in-black celeb clientele. For Thai food there's **Kin Khao**, sensuously draped with loads of soft fabrics, right out of the *Story of O;* expect delectable curries, spiced with cilantro, and wonderful prawn dishes. **Rain** doesn't even resemble an Asian joint, with its deep buff walls and minimalist decor, but it's the happening Upper West Side spot for creative pan-Indochinese fare; order the stir-fried Chinese eggplant in yellow bean sauce or Vietnamese charred beef. **Dawat** is Manhattan's toniest Indian dining experience (50 blocks and several light years removed from East Sixth Street's Little India). The digs are coolly stylish, hardly exotic at all, but the tandoori grilled items and creative specials, courtesy of owner/celebrated cookbook author/Indian film star Madhur Jaffrey, are worthy of a Rajah. And if you stretch the term "Asian" to include the entire Pacific Rim, consider **Moomba** (the name means "Let's get together and have fun" in Aborigine). A wild hybrid of influences, Moomba's fare runs the gamut from lemongrass smoked salmon to country herb and foie gras roasted Amish chicken.

Mediterraneo... Manhattan boasts a wide variety of Middle Eastern/Greek/North African restaurants. **Layla** marries classic Moroccan with Mediterranean culinary traditions. Standout dishes include a couscous royale (with shellfish and merguez sausage), herb-crusted halibut wrapped in arugula, and cinnamon-glazed lamb shank with harissa bean stew. Soak in the sexy souk-like ambience of **Casa la Femme**, its low cushioned seats swaddled in colorful curtains. Supermodels and their dates imperiously ignore the fab *tajines* and even Monday's belly dancers. Manhattan's top Greek restaurant is **Periyali**, decorated to resemble an Attic farmhouse, with a pricy menu featuring such intriguing dishes as octopus in red wine and cinnamon ice cream, both pure ambrosia.

If you knew sushi, like I knew sushi... Nobu has redefined the sushi experience for Manhattan diners-out, who never again can order a simple *tekke maki* (tuna roll) or even *uni* (sea urchin), after sampling Nobu Matsuhisa's food; just order the *omikase*–chef's special–and be transported. **Blue Ribbon Sushi** is a foodie favorite for such creative American variations as dragon roll (tuna wrapped in avocado cut to resemble scales) and fried oyster roll. **Yama** is depressingly lit and the lines are legendary, but aficionados swear by its enormous slabs of fresh tender sushi. **Tomoe Sushi** has glaring lighting and utterly surly waiters that look like they'd like to use a Ginzu knife on you, but you won't mind when the fish melts in your mouth. And if noodles are more your thing, the food, service, and tranquil atmosphere at **Honmura An** are quite simply on another plane from your standard noodle shop. The slight, soothing whiff of cedar wafts through the space, which is all clean lines, soft lighting, and blond wood, and the sake selection rivals any in Japan.

Olde New York... Reconstructed Colonial-era **Fraunces Tavern** remains, chiefly as a watering hole for Wall Street types. It was on this site that General George Washington bade farewell to his troops at the end of the Revolutionary War, and the second floor tavern room has been decorated to commemorate that event. The ground-level restaurant serves solid if uninspiring American standards like steaks, pies, and chops. The **Bridge Cafe**, tucked between South Street Seaport and the entry ramp of the Brooklyn Bridge, evokes the mid-to-late 1800s; fresh seafood specialties are prepared with imagination and there's a tonic selection of wines by the glass. The Village has a few old-style eateries, like the **Minetta Tavern**, woody, dark, and favored by off-Broadway playgoers. It's been dishing out Italian food since 1937, and has a long bar perfect for drowning your sorrows in scotch. Manhattan's longest-lived speakeasy remains almost impossible to find, signless and secreted away among 19th-century row houses on Bedford Street in the West Village: To reach **Chumley's**, take the narrow walkway off Barrow Street into Pamela Court, sit yourself down at a table carved with guests' initials, and then order a burger and a draft New Amsterdam. It still looks like a speakeasy, but speaking isn't so easy anymore above the blaring jukebox. When it's cold outside there's generally a fire in the hearth at **Ye Waverly Inn**, down a flight of brownstone steps on Bank Street, with deep booths and chicken pot pie. And near Macy's, there's **Keen's Steakhouse**, famous for mutton chops since its founding in 1878; the restaurant, where you'll find a vast collection of antique clay pipes, is fancy, with prices to match, but at the bar you can get a good deal on a burger, beer, and oysters on the half shell. And then there's Brooklyn's restaurant gem: **Peter Luger** in Williamsburg. Ten tons of beef shortloins pass through this unreconstructed beer hall every week, dry-aged on the premises, cooked to order, and then served au jus. You'll need to take a cab, but after feasting on a huge slab of steak, German fried potatoes, creamed spinach, and cheesecake, you won't need to eat again for a week. Down by South Street Seaport, the seafood classic **Sloppy Louie's** occupies a landmark Federal building; no amount of scrubbing could take the stench of shellfish and garlic from the walls.

Over the top... Designer Adam Tihany went all out to make **Le Cirque 2000** an extravaganza: the sedate, ornate 19th-century Villard House (gleaming with gilt and mahogany and oak wainscoting) now includes oversized highback velvet chairs, wire loops, jugglers' balls. Figs are served solemnly in eye-catching Venetian glass goblets almost as big as your head. **Le Regence** and **Lespinasse**, with angels, gold gilt, and blue blue blue everywhere, are what Louis XIV could have done if he'd really had the bucks. **Osteria del Circo** actually employs circus acrobats, fire-eaters, and mimes to entertain its terrace diners, while monkeys cavort through the wacky interior, with dangling Calderesque mobiles and orange silk tents. Fortunately the kitchen, though exuberant, is more restrained than the decor. **Layla**'s architectural space is wittily design-infected, neo-Moorish meets Byzantine. There are Mexican pinatas, basketry, grass mats, lifesize porcelain dolls, an entire mini-wall of broken ceramicware, and multi-textural fabrics, all contrasting brilliantly with the turn-of-the-century pressed tin ceilings and brickwork. The menu is equally clever and eclectic. **Moomba**'s environmental-chic look is too too P.C.: the wood floors were recycled from discarded two-by-four ends, the flowered sconces are empty Clorox containers, even the bar and tables are fashioned from synthetic concrete. **Clementine** went all out with its nautical decor, which includes portholes and a bar salvaged from a scuttled ship. The back room features an enormous fountain.

Vegging out... Go vegetarian at **Pita Cuisine**, an NYU hangout with a pleasant deck overlooking the surprising sights and sounds of LaGuardia Place and marvelous prices on specialties like meatless chili and pita pockets stuffed with what you will. SoHo eats healthy at the **Spring Street Natural**, but the noise level there can be annoying. The funky **Life Cafe**, an East Village stalwart that has also branched out west, is cozier, serving Tex-Mex veggie specialties while the jukebox spins tunes. Real health-food freaks light up at the chance to sup at the elegantly subdued **Zen Palate**, with branches in the theater district and alongside Union Square. The food is Asian and gorgeous (they do wondrous things with tofu), but there's one drawback—the no-drinks policy means no accompanying goblet of wine. **Angelica Kitchen** is another out-of-body experience for those who go organic vegetarian; the crowd is militantly tattoos/grunge/piercings/torn jeans, and the attitude's slightly smug. Still, the macrobiotic menu may be Manhattan's finest and certainly most varied; the vegetable juices and fruit smoothies are pure velvet and surprisingly decadent-tasting.

Something fishy... The bivalves are bi-coastal at the freshly remodeled **Oyster Bar** in Grand Central Station Terminal—hailing all the way from the Olympic Peninsula to Long Island and Chincoteague. But the belly-of-the-train-station setting remains homely and purely functional, despite some new splashes of color. It's a similar sea of suits at **Dock's**, with two branches on the Upper West Side and Midtown, both equally commendable for polished brass fittings, woody bars, and all the ocean's bounty; try the fried seafood platter, with shrimp, scallops, and sole, a steamed lobster, or the New England clambake offered on Sunday and Monday nights. At little **Sloppy Louie's**, an old seamen's cafe in spitting distance from the Fulton Fish Market, you'll have no second thoughts about the bouillabaisse and clam chowder—and since you're here, please order it Manhattan-style (that is, red rather than white). Regulars at **Sea Grill** are hooked on the freshness of the fish; served with a minimum of flourishes and singing with flavor; the setting is ultra-romantic, by the Rockefeller Center ice rink. **Oceana's** Art Deco cruise ship decor could be patterned after the *QE2*, but the mouth-watering, knee-buckling ("please, can I have some more portions") seafood is what makes you woozy with delight. Swim straight for chef Rick Moonen's mussels, fragrant with ginger, garlic, cilantro, and Thai basil, or poached sea scallops with the smoky edge of black truffles. **Union Pacific** occupies a smashing space, with a soothing water curtain splashing peacefully into a pool. Chef Rocco di Spirito is spirited indeed; his seafood is a dazzling juxtaposition of tastes and textures, and artfully presented as well—witness pale white cod couterpointed by jungle green peppers and kimchi, or a single bay scallop swimming in a sea of bright orange sea-urchin roe.

Where's the beef?... **The Palm** is almost a parody of a classic steakhouse, from the celebrity caricatures to the ancient waiters (actually they're only pretending to be deaf). It's a toss-up as to which is higher, the beef quality or the prices, but $80 nets you melt-in-your-mouth filet or lobster. **Peter Luger** is reputed to serve New York's best porterhouse, but it may not be worth the trek to Brooklyn, the rude (not cutesy) service, and the oompah bierkeller atmosphere. **Smith & Wollensky** char-grills to perfection. The only thing to change in the 113 years **Keen's Steakhouse** has been in business is the name (originally Keen's Chop House, in deference to the signature dish, mutton chops, which are even better still than the steaks). The marvelous Old New York ambience and extensive selection of single malt scotches help make it Nirvana for carnivorous types.

For preppies only... **J.G. Melon** is where the rich kids hang out for burgers once they graduate from college and the 'rents are paying the rent on their first digs. When they make their first million, they go to **Mortimer's**, which ought to have been the sole setting for *The First Wives' Club*—it's where the ladies who lunch plot behind their husbands' thrones. Regulars include Brooke Astor, Happy Rockefeller, Blaine Trump, Lee Radziwill, and Princess Margaret, and obviously the designers follow suit: Oscar de la Renta, Mary McFadden, Bill Blass, and Caroline Herrera are frequently sighted. Stick to the lobster, filet mignon, and Dover sole and you'll do well. The **'21' Club** is so clichéd as a power spot, it's neo-hip. While it's been rediscovered by certain foodies, thanks to chef Eric Blauberg (heavenly wild mushroom-and-truffle risotto), the bulk of the menu still caters to the meat-and-potatoes tastes of Fortune 500 CEOs. Frederic Remington artworks, framed cartoons, and toy trucks and sports memorabilia adorn every nook and cranny of the brass, bronze, and hardwood interior. **Main Street** defines yuppieteria—an unending, high-ceilinged space echoing with raucous laughter and clattering dishes—but it's the Upper West Side's pitstop for the professional crowd, especially for weekend brunch, when the entrance is lined with designer strollers.

Rudest waitstaff... **Ici** redefines French arrogance. Even if you have a reservation, you may be forced to wedge in at the tiny bar for over an hour, while no one even offers to take your coat or your drink order. The food and setting are lovely, the prices surprisingly affordable given the neighborhood, but if you want warm service, don't go to icy Ici. The service at **Florent** is authentically Gallic (read: surly) and the hostess can be remarkably accommodating or haughty, depending on how she sizes you up. Are you Harrison Ford, Jodie Foster, or Tom Brokaw? If not, then the dapper black-clad bouncers at **Moomba**, impassive as Beefeaters, are unlikely to part the velvet rope for you.

May I get that for you, sir?... The hostesses at **Union Square Cafe** and **Gramercy Tavern** sound genuinely apologetic when they can't fit you in at 10:30 that night (or three weeks later)—just another reason why diners still *want* to patronize these Flatiron favorites. The service at **March** is almost miraculous, with the waitstaff anticipating your needs without ever seeming to hover. No matter what, they treat you as if you were a true connoisseur. You could complain in a loud New Yawk accent, sport an even louder plaid sportcoat, and the unruffled waitstaff at **Le Bernardin** wouldn't bat an eye. **Smith & Wollensky's** corps of veteran—and we do mean veteran—waiters show their professional mettle night after night. But the staff at **The Four Seasons** may well be the city's best waiters: they deliver attentive, intelligent, discreet service as fluid and well-timed as a ballet.

The caffeine scene... Arguably the city's best regular coffee, croissants, brioches, tartlettes, and quichettes are made at **Patisserie Claude**—just ask the folks who drive from Connecticut in their limos (yes, just like the Grey Poupon commercial) solely to visit this shoebox-sized bit of Gaul in the West Village. **Lanciani** is another West Village institution that puts the rush in espresso and the sugar high in its delectable flaky pastries. Looking for cannolis? Look no further than the Little Italy standby **Ferrara** or the East Village's almost as venerable **Veniero's**, which has marvelous biscotti to boot. **DT.UT** means Downtown Uptown, a commentary on the ambience at this Upper East Side lounge with plush chairs, marvy coffees (strong enough to give you the DTs) and desserts, and zilch attitude. If it's tea you crave, Greenwich Village's, **Tea & Sympathy** is like a Manchester middle-class tea shop, the menu full of bangers and mash, too many tables, and not a spot of sherry to be had. Far prettier is the West Village's **Anglers and Writers**, with Victoria's Secret decor, charming mismatched china, and buttery cakes, pies, and cookies. In the Flatiron District, the cozy, countrified **T Salon and T Emporium** serves up everything from proper cucumber sandwiches and scones with clotted cream to curried chicken salad delicately infused with tea.

The Index

$$$$	over $50
$$$	$35–$50
$$	$20–$35
$	under $20

Per person for a three-course meal, not including drinks, tax, or tip.

Aggie's. Big dinners, tangy recipes, and reasonable prices in a bustling converted coffee shop.... *Tel 212/673–8994. 146 W. Houston St., B/D/Q/F train to Broadway/Lafayette.* $
(see p. 53)

Angelica Kitchen. Uber-macrobiotic restaurant with classic neo-hippie Bohemian look and feel.... *Tel 212/228–2909.*

300 East 12th St., 4/5/6 train to 14th St. No credit cards.
$ **(see p. 65)**

Anglers and Writers. Victoria's Secret decor, high tea, and happy brunches.... *Tel 212/675–0810. 420 Hudson St., 1/9 train to Houston St. No credit cards. $* **(see p. 68)**

Asia de Cuba. From Owner Ian Schrager, designer Philippe Starck, chef Robert Trainor, top spot for a steamy wok-and-roll evening out.... *Tel 212/726–7755. 237 Madison Ave., 4/5/6/S/N/R trains to Grand Central. Reservations required.* $$$ **(see pp. 51, 60, 61)**

Aureole. Fancy French-inspired food in a romantically decorated East Side town house.... *Tel 212/319–1660. 34 E. 61st St., N/R train to Fifth Ave. Jacket and reservations required.* $$$$ **(see p. 52)**

B. Smith's. Ex-model Barbara Smith's sexy, contemporary soul food restaurant....*Tel 212/247–2222. 771 Eighth Ave., N/R to 47th St. $$* **(see pp. 55, 60)**

Balthazar. Bistro with capital A attitude yet admittedly capital food.... *Tel 212/965–1414. 80 Spring St., 6 train to Spring St. Reservations required. $$$* **(see pp. 52, 56)**

Bar Pitti. Italian chic with streetside tables in the lower Village.... *Tel 212/982–3300. 268 Sixth Ave., A/C/E or B/D/Q/F train to W. 4th St. $$* **(see p. 58)**

Benito's I. Pictures of Vesuvius on the wall, and good old-fashioned Southern Italian fare.... *Tel 212/226–9171. 174 Mulberry St., J/M/Z, N/R, or 6 train to Canal St. or B/D/Q to Grand St. $$–$$$* **(see p. 57)**

Benny's Burritos. Mass-produced Mexican basics in two locations, noisy and fun.... *Tel 212/633–9210. 112 Greenwich Ave., 1/2/3/9 to 14th St.; tel 212/254–3286. 93 Avenue A, F train to Second Ave. No credit cards. $* **(see p. 61)**

Le Bernardin. Sublime seafood, but just try and fish for a weekend reservation.... *Tel 212/489–1515. 155 W. 51st St., 1/9 train to 50th St. Jacket and reservations required. $$$$*
(see pp. 50, 67)

Blue Ribbon Sushi. You order the fish according to ocean at this ultra-trendy spot.... *Tel 212/343–0404. 119 Sullivan St., 6 train to Spring St. Closed Mon. $$* **(see p. 62)**

Boca Chica. Fun Latin and Caribbean eating, drinking, and making merry.... *Tel 212/473–0108. 13 First Ave., B/D/Q/F train to Broadway/Lafayette. $$* **(see p. 60)**

Bolo. Bobby Flay's flamboyant Flatiron tapas hangout.... *Tel 212/228–2000. 23 E. 22nd St., 6 train to 23rd St. Reservations required. $$$* **(see p. 61)**

Bouley Bakery. Chic New Yorkers descend in droves upon this deceptively simple spot run by star-chef/owner David Bouley.... *Tel 212/964–2525. 120 West Broadway, 1/9 train to Canal St. Reservations required. $$$* **(see p. 51)**

Boxers. Lively hetero Village bar scene; hearty salads, sandwiches, and fries.... *Tel 212/633–2275. 186 W. 4th St., A/C/E or B/D/Q/F train to W. 4th St. or 1/9 to Christopher St. $* **(see p. 54)**

Brasserie. Open 24 hours in the heart of Midtown; pretty bar, filling food.... *Tel 212/751–4840. 100 E. 53rd St., 6 train to 51st St. $$$* **(see p. 53)**

Bridge Cafe. Charming, old-fashioned, tucked alongside the Brooklyn Bridge; seafood prevails.... *Tel 212/227–3344. 279 Water St., J/M/Z, 2/3, or 4/5 train to Fulton St. $$–$$$* **(see p. 63)**

Cafe Beulah. Nouvelle soul food in elegant digs.... *Tel 212/777–9700. 39 E. 19th St., N/R, 4/5/6, or L train to Union Sq. $$$* **(see p. 60)**

Café de Bruxelle. Belgian beer, mussels, salads, and seafood stews, with a stylish dining room and comfortable pocket bar.... *Tel 212/206–1830. 118 Greenwich Ave., A/C/E or 1/2/3/9 train to 14th St. $$–$$$* **(see p. 56)**

Café des Artistes. Intensely lovely and romantic, serving adequate French cuisine.... *Tel 212/877–3500. 1 W. 67th St., B/C or 1/2/3/9 train to 72nd St. Jacket and reservations required. $$$$* **(see p. 50)**

Cafe Luxembourg. The Upper West Side's premier power spot's bistro menu has been recently reinvigorated (try the amazing cassoulet).... *Tel 212/873–7411. 200 W. 70th St., 1/2/3/9 train to 72nd St. Reservations required. $$$* **(see p. 52)**

Cafe Un Deux Trois. Cool, cavernous room; reasonably tasty pre- and post-theater fare.... *Tel 212/354–4148. 123 W. 44th St., N/R, 1/2/3/9, or 7 train to Times Sq. $$$*
(see p. 55)

Campagna. Splendid country Italian, with city prices and attitude.... *Tel 212/460–0900. 24 E. 21st St., 6 train to 23rd St. Reservations required. $$$–$$$$* **(see p. 58)**

Carmine's. Hearty Southern Italian—a good theater district choice. Go for family-style dining—the portions are immense.... *Tel 212/221–3800. 200 W. 44th St., N/R, 1/2/3/9, or 7 train to Times Sq.; tel 212/362–2200. 2450 Broadway, 1/9 train to 86th St. AE only. $$* **(see p. 55)**

Casa la Femme. Excellent Moroccan food in swank, romantic, chic Sheik space.... *Tel 212/505–0005. 150 Wooster St., 6 train to Spring St. $$–$$$.* **(see p. 62)**

Chanterelle. David and Karen Waltuck provide a flawless dining experience in a pristine space.... *Tel 212/966–6960. 2 Harrison St., 6 train to Canal St. Jacket suggested. Reservations required. $$$$* **(see p. 50)**

Chiam. Posh streamlined Chinese.... *Tel 212/371–2323. 160 E. 48th St., 6 train to 51st St. Reservations required. $$–$$$* **(see p. 58)**

China Grill. Chinese with Midtown class.... *Tel 212/333–7788. 60 W. 53rd St., B/D/Q/F train to Rockefeller Center. $$$*
(see p. 58)

Chin Chin. Elegant nouvelle Chinese.... *Tel 212/888–4555. 216 E. 49th St., E/F train to Lexington Ave. or 6 to 51st St. $$$* **(see p. 58)**

Le Cirque 2000. Top-notch and over-the-top, but a definitive dining experience, thanks to owner Sirio Maccione's flair.... *Tel 212/794–9292. New York Palace Hotel, 455 Madison*

DINING | THE INDEX

Ave., *6 train to 51st St. Jacket and tie required; reservations required. $$$$* **(see pp. 51, 54, 64)**

Chumley's. An old speakeasy catering to the beer-and-burger college crowd.... *Tel 212/675–4449. 86 Bedford St., 1/9 train to Christopher St. $* **(see p. 63)**

Clementine. This replica of an ocean liner sails along with superb new American food.... *Tel 212/253–0003. One Fifth Ave., 6 train to Astor Place. Reservations required. $$$–$$$$.* **(see pp. 51, 64)**

Coco Pazzo. The ultimate celebrity-watching Italian, with superlative Tuscan grilled meats.... *Tel 212/794–0205. 23 E. 74th St., 6 train to 77th St. Reservations required. $$$–$$$$* **(see p. 58)**

Le Colonial. Ultra-chic, swooningly romantic Asian..... *Tel 212/752–0808. 149 E. 57th St., 4/5/6/N/R train to 59th St. Reservations required. $$–$$$* **(see p. 61)**

Cornelia Street Cafe. Laid-back in the Village; well-prepared Continental specialties and a convivial bar.... *Tel 212/989–9318. 29 Cornelia St., A/C/E or B/D/Q/F train to W. 4th St. $$* **(see p. 54)**

La Côte Basque. Lots of stars, attitude, and splendid classic French fare.... *Tel 212/688–6525. 60 W. 55th St., E/F train to Fifth Ave. Jacket, tie, and reservations required. $$$$* **(see p. 50)**

Cucina di Pesce. East Village cellar that does garlicky Italian.... *Tel 212/260–6800. 87 E. 4th St., 6 train to Bleecker St. $–$$* **(see p. 57)**

Da Umberto. Now that's Italian, albeit with clubby interior and clientele.... *Tel 212/989–0303. 107 W. 17th St., 1/9 to 18th St. Jacket suggested. Reservations required. $$$–$$$$* **(see p. 57)**

Daniel. Pure heaven on every level, and worth every franc.... *Tel 212/288–0499. 20 E. 76th St., 6 train to 77th St. Jacket and reservations required. $$$$* **(see p. 54)**

DINING | THE INDEX

Dawat. Northern Indian cuisine, upscale atmosphere.... *Tel 212/355–7555. 210 E. 58th St., 4/5/6 train to 59th St. or N/R to Lexington Ave. $$$* **(see p. 62)**

Dix et Sept. A town house in the Village devoted to all things Parisian.... *Tel 212/645–8023. 181 W. 10th St., 1/9 train to Christopher St. $$$* **(see p. 56)**

Dock's. Seafood in two spiffy settings.... *Tel 212/986–8080. 633 Third Ave., 4/5/6 or 7 train to Grand Central; tel 212/ 724–5588. 2427 Broadway, 1/9 train to 86th St. $$$* **(see p. 65)**

DT.UT. Great little coffee lounge in an unexpected nabe (the Upper East Side).... *Tel 212/327–1327. 1626 Second Ave., 4/5/6 train to 86th St. No credit cards. $* **(see p. 68)**

Eddie's. Great big burgers, omelettes, and salads among NYU coeds.... *Tel 212/420–0919. 14 Waverly Place, N/R train to 8th St. AE only. $* **(see p. 53)**

Empire Diner. An art-deco standby that never closes and never fails.... *Tel 212/243–2736. 210 Tenth Ave., A/C/E train to 23rd St. $$* **(see p. 53)**

Fanelli. Clubby, pubby, pastas, steaks, and burgers, and nice Sunday morning reading-the-newspaper atmosphere.... *Tel 212/226–9412. 94 Prince St., N/R train to Prince St. $* **(see p. 53)**

Felidia. Unparallelled Italian, so good and so charming no one puts on airs–successfully.... *Tel 212/758–1479. 243 E. 58th St., 4/5/6/N/R train to 59th St. Jacket suggested. Reservations required. $$$–$$$$* **(see p. 57)**

Ferrara. The original Little Italy branch (opened 1892) is a cannoli and cappuccino institution.... *Tel 212/226–6150. 195 Grand St., 6 train to Canal St. $* **(see p. 68)**

Firebird. Fairy-tale spot with fabulous blinis and a knockout selection of vodkas (and champagnes).... *Tel 212/586–0244. 365 W. 46th St., 1/2 /3/9/A/C/E/S train to Times Square. $$$–$$$$* **(see p. 55)**

DINING | THE INDEX

Florent. A hip after-hours haunt in the unprepossessing meat district.... *Tel 212/989–5779. 69 Gansevoort St., A/C/E train to 14th St. No credit cards. $–$$* **(see pp. 53, 54, 67)**

The Four Seasons. About as elegant as New York gets, with great attention to both diners and food.... *Tel 212/754–9495. 99 E. 52nd St., 6 train to 51st Street. Jacket and reservations required. $$$$* **(see pp. 47, 50, 67)**

Fraunces Tavern. The oldest pub in New York.... *Tel 212/269–0144. 54 Pearl St., 1/9 train to South Ferry. $$–$$$* **(see p. 63)**

Gotham Bar & Grill. Swank setting, inventive American cuisine.... *Tel 212/620–4020. 12 E. 12th St., N/R, 4/5/6, or L train to Union Sq. $$$$* **(see p. 53)**

Gramercy Tavern. Impeccable nouvelle American cuisine courtesy of Danny Meyer (owner) and Tom Colicchio (chef) for $58 prix fixe, or à la carte in the less formal Tavern Room (i.e., the bar)....*Tel 212/477–0777. 42 E. 20th St., 6 train to 23rd St. Reservations required. $$$–$$$$* **(see pp. 52, 67)**

Grotta Azzurra. No reservations and long lines at this top spot for garlicky Neapolitan cuisine.... *Tel 212/925–8775. 387 Broome St., B/D/Q train to Grand St. No credit cards. $$* **(see p. 58)**

Honmura An. Delicately flavored noodles, noodles, and more noodles.... *Tel 212/334–5253. 170 Mercer St., 6 train to Bleecker St. Reservations required. $$$* **(see p. 63)**

Ici. Cash and cachet at an upscale address with downhome prices, haughty service.... *Tel 212/794–6419. 19 E. 69th St., 6 train to 68th St. Reservations required. $$$* **(see p. 56)**

Indochine. Perennially posh colonial-meets-downtown-chic spot with appetizing French/Vietnamese fusion fare.... *Tel 212/505–5111. 430 Lafayette St., 6 train to Astor Place. Reservations required. $$–$$$* **(see pp. 52, 62)**

J.G. Melon. Old school and red tie WASPy, this burger spot goes on and on like the Energizer Bunny.... *Tel 212/744–0585. 1291 Third Ave., 6 train to 77th St. $* **(see p. 66)**

Jean Georges. Wildly inventive chef/restarateur Jean Georges Vongerichten wows even his fellow chefs—this subtly elegant restaurant is considered New York's finest by many.... *Tel 212/299–3900. Trump International Hotel, 1 Central Park West, A/B/C/D/1/9 train to Columbus Circle. Jacket and reservations required. $$$$* **(see p. 51)**

Jezebel. Pork chops and collard greens as if at the Ritz.... *Tel 212/582–1045. 630 Ninth Ave., A/C/E train to 42nd St. AE only. $$$$* **(see pp. 55, 59)**

Jing Fong. Dim sum reigns.... *Tel 212/964–5256. 20 Elizabeth St., J/M/Z, N/R or 6 train to Canal St. or B/D/Q to Grand St. $* **(see p. 59)**

Joe's Shanghai. Zippo atmosphere and decor, but oh what sublime soups and dumplings.... *Tel 212/233–8888. 8 Pell St., 6 train to Canal St. No credit cards. $* **(see p. 59)**

Keen's Steakhouse. Old-style New York, old recipes, mutton chops.... *Tel 212/947–3636. 72 W. 36th St., A/C/E or 1/2/3/9 to 34th St. $$$* **(see pp. 63, 66)**

Kin Khao. Haute Thai for those who understand funky elegance.... *Tel 212/966–3939. 171 Spring St., C/E train to Spring St. $$* **(see p. 62)**

Lanciani. West Village cafe, excellent pastries.... *Tel 212/929–0739. 271 W. 4th St., 1/9 train to Christopher St. AE only. $* **(see p. 67)**

Layla. Scintillating, festive nouvelle North African restaurant.... *Tel 212/431–0700. 211 W. Broadway, 1/9 train to Franklin St. $$–$$$* **(see pp. 62, 64)**

Lespinasse. Peerless Asian-tinged French expense-account breaker.... *Tel 212/339–6719. St. Regis Hotel, 2 E. 55th St., N/R to Fifth Avenue. Jacket and reservations required. $$$$* **(see pp. 55, 64)**

Life Cafe. Tex-Mex vegetarian in the Village.... *Tel 212/477–8791. 343 E. 10th St., L train to First Ave. or 6 to Astor Place; tel 212/929–7344. 1 Sheridan Sq., 1/9 train to Christopher St. AE not accepted. $* **(see p. 65)**

Main Street. Classic American comfort food in a vast, soulless space.... Tel 212/873–5025. 446 Columbus Ave., 1/9 train to 79th St. $$ **(see p. 67)**

Mappamondo and Mappamondo Due. West Village pasta places, with fair prices and a neighborhoody feeling.... Tel 212/675–3100. 11 Abingdon Sq.; tel 212/675–7474. 581 Hudson St. 1/9 train to Christopher St. $–$$
(see p. 57)

March. Innovative French cuisine by master chef Wayne Nish, in a romantic East Side town house.... Tel 212/838–9393. 405 E. 58th St., N/R train to Lexington Ave. or 4/5/6 to 59th St. $$$$ **(see pp. 52, 67)**

Mary Ann's. Hearty Mexican in three locations.... Tel 212/633–0877. 116 Eighth Ave., A/C/E train to 14th St.; tel 212/249–6165. 1503 Second Ave., 6 train to 77th St.; tel 212/877–0132. 2452 Broadway, 1/9 train to 86th St. AE, D, DC not accepted. $–$$ **(see p. 61)**

Mesa Grill. Noisy, energetic, split-level hip Southwestern.... Tel 212/807–7400. 102 Fifth Ave., 4/5/6/N/R/L train to Union Square. $$$ **(see pp. 52, 61)**

Minetta Tavern. Southern Italian cuisine in an old-fashioned pub setting.... Tel 212/475–3850. 113 MacDougal St., A/C/E or B/D/Q/F train to W. 4th St. $$ **(see p. 63)**

Miracle Grill. Fine Southwestern food and an amazing value, especially in summer when you can sit in the garden.... Tel 212/254–2353. 112 First Ave., 6 to Astor Place. $–$$
(see pp. 54, 61)

Montrachet. A TriBeCa classic, with severe spotlit decor and impeccable culinary standards.... Tel 212/219–2777. 219 W. Broadway, 1/9 train to Franklin St. Reservations required. $$$–$$$$ **(see p. 53)**

Moomba. A provocative mambo of flavors, rain-forest chic decor, and oh-so-cool attitude have made this a hot spot.... Tel 212/989–1414. 133 Seventh Ave. S., 1/9 to Christopher St. Reservations required. $$$
(see pp. 51, 62, 64, 67)

Mortimer's. As white-bread and deliciously toadying a restaurant as you'll find in Manhattan.... *Tel 212/517–6400. 1057 Lexington Ave., 6 train to 77th St. Reservations required. $$$* **(see p. 66)**

Il Mulino. Top-flight Italian, via Abruzzi.... *Tel 212/673–3783. 86 W. 3rd St., B/D/Q/F train to Broadway/Lafayette. $$$$* **(see p. 58)**

Nobu. Gastronomic sushi temple where all the major celebs and power players worship.... *Tel 212/219–0500. 105 Hudson St., 1/9 train to Franklin St. Reservations required. $$$$* **(see pp. 53, 62)**

Oceana. Glorious recreation of an Art Deco ocean liner with well-nigh perfect seafood.... *Tel 212/759–5941. 55 East 54th St., 6 train to 51st St. Reservations required. $$$–$$$$* **(see p. 65)**

Odeon. By now an institution in chic; delicious American cuisine.... *Tel 212/233–0507. 145 W. Broadway, 1/9 train to Franklin St. $$$* **(see p. 52)**

One if by Land, Two if by Sea. Continental cuisine served with many flourishes in a historic Greenwich Village carriage house.... *Tel 212/228–0822. 17 Barrow St., A/C/E or B/D/Q/F train to W. 4th St. Jacket and tie advised. Reservations required. $$$$* **(see p. 50)**

Oriental Pearl. Where all the world's a Chinese banquet.... *Tel 212/219–8388. 103 Mott St., J/M/Z, N/R, or 6 train to Canal St. or B/D/Q to Grand St. $–$$* **(see p. 59)**

Orso. Very Tuscan, very good; an oasis in the theater district.... *Tel 212/489–7212. 322 W. 46th St., N/R, 1/2/3/9, or 7 train to Times Sq. Reservations required. $$$* **(see p. 55)**

Osteria del Circo. Three-ring circus act, with decor, Italian food, and extras all competing for attention.... *Tel 212/265–3636. 120 W. 55th St., B/D/E train to Seventh Ave. Reservations required. $$$–$$$$* **(see pp. 57, 64)**

Oyster Bar. Oysters from everywhere ordered from a chalkboard; basement train-station setting; whopping wine list....

Tel 212/490–6650. Grand Central Terminal, 4/5/6 or 7 train to Grand Central. $$$–$$$$ (see p. 65)

The Palm. Rude waitstaff, sawdust, caricatures, huge slabs of perfectly charred steak: the quintessential steakhouse.... *Tel 212/687–2953. 837 Second Ave., 4/5/6/S to Grand Central. $$$$* (see p. 66)

Park Bistro. Big publishing hangout that's dark, woody, and redolent of Paris.... *Tel 212/689–1360. 414 Park Ave. S., 6 train to 28th St. $$$* (see p. 56)

Patisserie Claude. Fabulous French pastries and cakes, for eating in or taking out.... *Tel 212/255–5911. 187 W. 4th St., A/C/E or B/D/Q/F train to W. 4th St. No credit cards. $* (see p. 67)

Patria. Latin at its most chic.... *Tel 212/777–6211. 250 Park Ave. S., N/R, 4/5/6, or L train to Union Sq. $$$–$$$$* (see p. 60)

Periyali. Chic Greek.... *Tel 212/463–7890. 35 W. 20th St., F train to 23rd St. $$$* (see p. 62)

Le Pescadou. Sweet setting, succulent French seafood.... *Tel 212/924–3434. 18 King St., 1/9 train to Houston St. $$$* (see p. 56)

Peter Luger. The best steaks in town—way out in Brooklyn.... *Tel 718/387–7400. 178 Broadway, J train to Marcy Ave. House credit card only. $$$$* (see pp. 50, 64, 66)

Pink Teacup. Little Village cafe that specializes in down-home cookin'.... *Tel 212/807–6755. 42 Grove St., 1/9 train to Christopher St. No credit cards. $* (see p. 59)

Pita Cuisine. Where NYU eats healthy.... *Tel 212/254–1417. 535 LaGuardia Place. B/D/Q/F train to Broadway/Lafayette. $* (see p. 64)

Po. Inventive Italian in a handsome but unpretentious Village dining room.... *Tel 212/645–2189. 31 Cornelia St., A/C/E or B/D/Q/F train to W. 4th St. $$$* (see p. 58)

Provence. This charming bistro sings with the colors and flavors of sunny Provence.... *Tel 212/475–7500. 38 MacDougal St., 1/9 train to Houston St. $$$* **(see p. 56)**

Puglia. Garlicky Italian in loud, lusty, close quarters.... *Tel 212/966–6006. 189 Hester St., 6 train to Spring St. $–$$* **(see p. 57)**

Rain. Super-cool Asian on the Upper West side.... *Tel 212/501–0776. 100 W. 82nd St., 1/9 train to 79th St. $$* **(see p. 62)**

Raoul's. Dimly lit and hip, with a lovely wine list, garden, and New York's best sweetbreads.... *Tel 212/966–3518. 180 Prince St., 6 train to Spring St. Reservations required. $$$* **(see p. 56)**

Le Regence. Sumptuous classic French cuisine in a recreation of the Trianon.... *Tel 212/606–4647. Hotel Plaza Athénée, 37 E. 64th St., 6 train to 68th St. Jacket and reservations required. $$$$* **(see p. 64)**

Remi. Homage to Venice in the form of risotto and pasta.... *Tel 212/581–4242. 145 W. 53rd St., B/D/Q/F train to Rockefeller Center. $$$–$$$$* **(see p. 57)**

Republic. Where a virtual U.N. of diners scarf down excellent udons (noodle broths) and sates.... *Tel 212/627–7172. 37 Union Square West, 4/5/6/N/R/L train to Union Square. $* **(see pp. 54, 61)**

The River Cafe. Christmas lights on the East River, stellar kitchen, companionable bar.... *Tel 718/522–5200. Fulton St. Landing, 2/3 train to Clark St. $$$$* **(see p. 50)**

Rosa Mexicano. Closest thing to genuine top-level Mexican food you'll find in New York, with guacamole prepared table-side.... *Tel 212/753–7407. 1063 First Ave., 4/5/6/N/R to 59th St. $$–$$$* **(see p. 61)**

Sea Grill. Rockefeller Center power spot with celestial seafood, including horseradish-striped bass.... *Tel 212/332–7610. 19 West 49th St., N/R to 49th St. Reservations required. $$$–$$$$* **(see p. 65)**

Shun Lee Palace. Where bluebloods have cut their teeth on elegant Szechuan fare since the seventies.... *Tel 212/ 371–8844. 155 E. 55th St., E/F train to Lexington/Third Ave. Reservations required. $$$* **(see p. 58)**

Sloppy Louie's. Seafood by the docks.... *Tel 212/509–9694. 92 South St., J/M/Z, 2/3, or 4/5 train to Fulton St. $$* **(see p. 65)**

Smith & Wollensky's. Bankers go bonkers for the superlative dry-aged rib-eyes at this marvelous upscale steakhouse.... *Tel 212/753–1530. 707 Third Avenue, 6 train to 51st St. Reservations required. $$$–$$$$* **(see pp. 66, 67)**

Spring Street Natural. SoHo on tofu.... *Tel 212/966–0290. 62 Spring St., 6 train to Spring St. $$* **(see p. 65)**

Sylvia's. The Harlem soul food standard.... *Tel 212/996–2669. 328 Lenox Ave., 2/3 train to 125th St. No credit cards. $$* **(see p. 59)**

T Salon & T Emporium. Delectable finger sandwiches, intensely flavored global selection of teas, and tea bric-a-brac on sale in a cozy cottage-like atmosphere.... *Tel 212/358–0506. 11 E. 20th St., 6 train to 23rd St. $* **(see p. 68)**

Tai Hong Lau. Dandy Chinatown dim sum.... *Tel 212/219–1431. 70 Mott St., J/M/Z, N/R, or 6 train to Canal St. or B/D/Q to Grand St. $* **(see p. 59)**

Tartine. Pretty West Village spot for French cuisine.... *Tel 212/ 229–2611. 253 W. 11th St., 1/9 train to Christopher St. $$* **(see p. 56)**

Tasco Porto. Brazilian steaks, port wine, sangria.... *Tel 212/ 343–2321. 535 Broome St., C/E train to Spring St. $–$$* **(see p. 61)**

Tavern on the Green. The Central Park classic.... *Tel 212/ 873–3200. Central Park W. at W. 67th St., 1/9 train to 66th St./Lincoln Center. Jacket advised. Reservations required. $$$–$$$$* **(see p. 50)**

Tea & Sympathy. Tea shop, Manchester-style.... *Tel 212/807–8329. 108 Greenwich Ave., 1/2/3/9 train to 14th St. No credit cards. $* **(see p. 68)**

Tomoe Sushi. Crowded, noisy, and unwelcoming, but the sushi is as good as it gets.... *Tel 212/777–9346. 172 Thompson St., 6 train to Bleecker St. $$* **(see p. 63)**

Trattoria Pesce Pasta. Very garlicky southern Italian, West Village neighborhoody.... *Tel 212/645–2993. 262 Bleecker St., A/C/E or B/D/Q/F train to W. 4th St. $$* **(see p. 57)**

TriBeCa Grill. Robert DeNiro's place, and très chic.... *Tel 212/941–3900. 375 Greenwich St., 1/9 train to Franklin St. Reservations required. $$$* **(see p. 52)**

Triple Eight Palace. Bustling joint, splendid Chinatown Chinese.... *Tel 212/941–8886. 78 E. Broadway, F train to E. Broadway. $$* **(see p. 59)**

I Trulli. Nouvelle Italian with a lovely tiled patio out back.... *Tel 212/481–7372. 122 E. 27th St., 6 train to 28th St. $$$* **(see p. 58)**

'21' Club. Ultimate bastion of testosterone, with a few surprising culinary innovations, perfect martinis, and a fine wine list.... *Tel 212/582–7200. 21 W. 52nd St., 1/9 train to 50th St. Jacket and tie required. Reservations required. $$$–$$$$* **(see p. 50)**

Union Pacific. Ultra-contemporary space with remarkably inventive global fusion cuisine.... *Tel 212/995–8500. 111 East 22nd St., 6 train to 23rd St. Reservations required. $$$* **(see p. 66)**

Union Square Cafe. Knock-out American cuisine, with French and Italian flourishes.... *Tel 212/243–4020. 21 E. 16th St., N/R, 4/5/6, or L train to Union Sq. Reservations required. $$$–$$$$* **(see pp. 47, 52, 67)**

Veniero's. Heavenly, flaky, delicate, delectable pastries.... *Tel 212/674–7070. 342 E. 11th St., 6 train to Astor Place. $* **(see p. 68)**

DINING | THE INDEX

Veselka. Your basic Ukrainian coffee shop, with remodeled hipster cachet. Fab pierogis and stuffed cabbage.... *Tel 212/228–9682. 144 Second Ave., 6 train to Astor Place. No credit cards. $* **(see p. 53)**

Virgil's Real Barbecue. Ribs, sausage, and chicken accompanied by stuffed jalapeño peppers, mashed potatoes, kale, corn relish, and subs in Bubba-sized portions.... *Tel 212/921–9494. 152 W. 44th St., N/R, 1/2/3/9, or 7 train to Times Sq. $$* **(see p. 60)**

Vong. French-tinged Asian stunner.... *Tel 212/486–9592. 200 E. 54th St., E/F to Lexington/Third Ave. Jacket suggested. Reservations required. $$$–$$$$* **(see pp. 51, 52, 61)**

Windows on the World. The last word in view restaurants, reopened with great fanfare and new panache in both food and decor. Still the world's greatest wine cellar.... *Tel 212/938–1111. 1 World Trade Center, N/R or 1/9 train to Cortlandt St., 2/3 to Park Place, or C/E to World Trade Center. Jacket, tie, and reservations required. $$$$* **(see p. 50)**

Yama. Sushi stalwart for savvy New Yorkers.... *Tel 212/475–0969. 122 East 17th St., 4/5/6/N/R/L train to Union Square. $$* **(see p. 63)**

Ye Waverly Inn. Colonial-style eatery in the West Village.... *Tel 212/929–4377. 16 Bank St., 1/2/3/9 to 14th St. $$* **(see p. 63)**

Zarela. Boisterous yuppie hangout serving decently authentic Mexican food.... *Tel 212/644–6740. 953 Second Ave., 6 train to 51st St. $$–$$$* **(see p. 61)**

Zen Palate. Asian health food.... *Tel 212/582–1669. 663 Ninth Ave., N/R, 1/2/3/9, or 7 to Times Sq.; tel 212/614–9291. 34 Union Sq. E., N/R, 4/5/6, or L train to Union Sq. $–$$* **(see p. 65)**

Uptown Dining

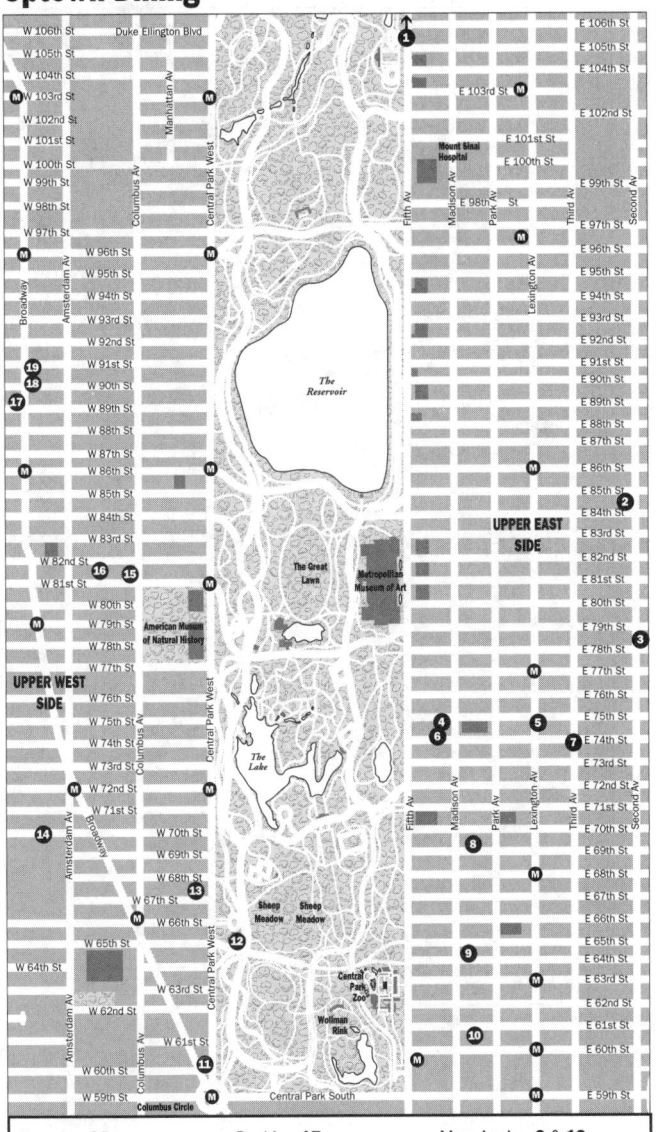

Aureole **10**	Dock's **17**	Mary Ann's **3** & **19**
Cafe des Artistes **13**	DT UT **2**	Mortimer's **5**
Cafe Luxembourg **14**	Ici **8**	Rain **16**
Carmine's **18**	Jean Georges **11**	Le Regence **9**
Coco Pazzo **6**	J.G. Melon **7**	Sylvia's **1**
Daniel **4**	Main Street **15**	Tavern on the Green **12**

Midtown Dining

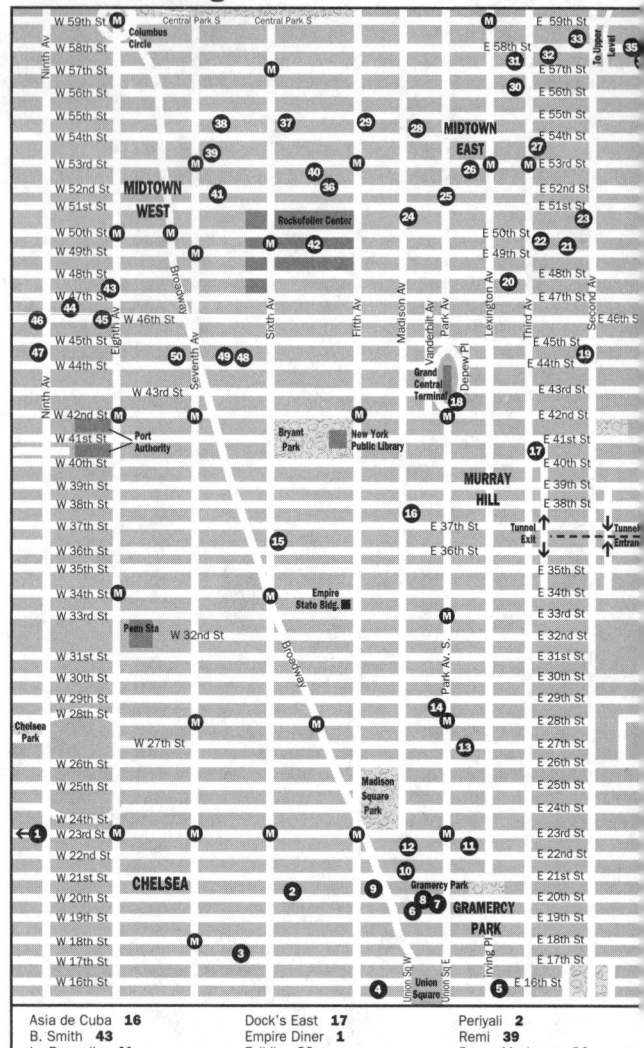

Asia de Cuba **16**
B. Smith **43**
Le Bernadin **41**
Bolo **12**
Brasserie **26**
Cafe Buelah **6**
Cafe Un Deux Trois **48**
Campagna **10**
Carmine's **50**
Chiam **20**
Chin Chin **21**
China Grill **40**
Le Cirque 2000 **24**
Le Colonial **31**
La Cote Basque **37**
Da Umberto **3**
Dawat **32**

Dock's East **17**
Empire Diner **1**
Felidia **33**
Firebird **44**
The Four Seasons **25**
Gramercy Tavern **7**
Jezebel **47**
Keens Steakhouse **15**
Lespinasse **29**
March **35**
Oceana **28**
Orso **45**
Osteria del Circo **38**
Oyster Bar **18**
Palm **19**
Park Bistro **14**
Patria **8**

Periyali **2**
Remi **39**
Rossa Mexicano **34**
Sea Grill **42**
Shun Lee Palace **30**
Smith & Wollensky **22**
T Salon & T Emporium **9**
I Trulli **13**
'21' Club **36**
Union Pacific **11**
Union Square Cafe **4**
Virgil's Real Barbecue **49**
Vong **27**
Yama **5**
Zarela **23**
Zen Palate **46**

Greenwich Village Dining

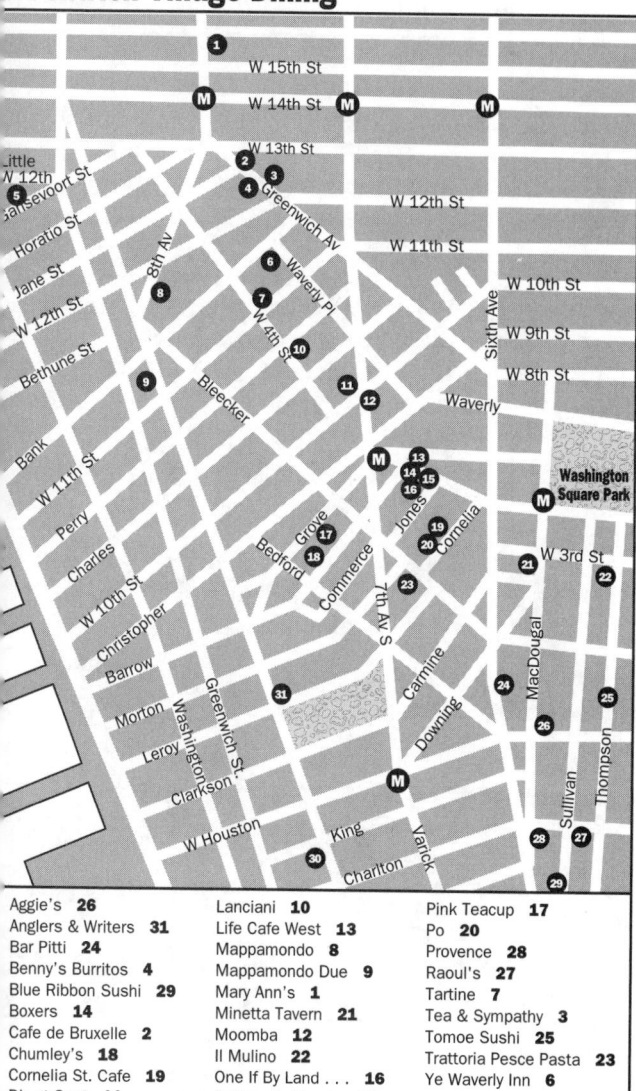

East Village Dining

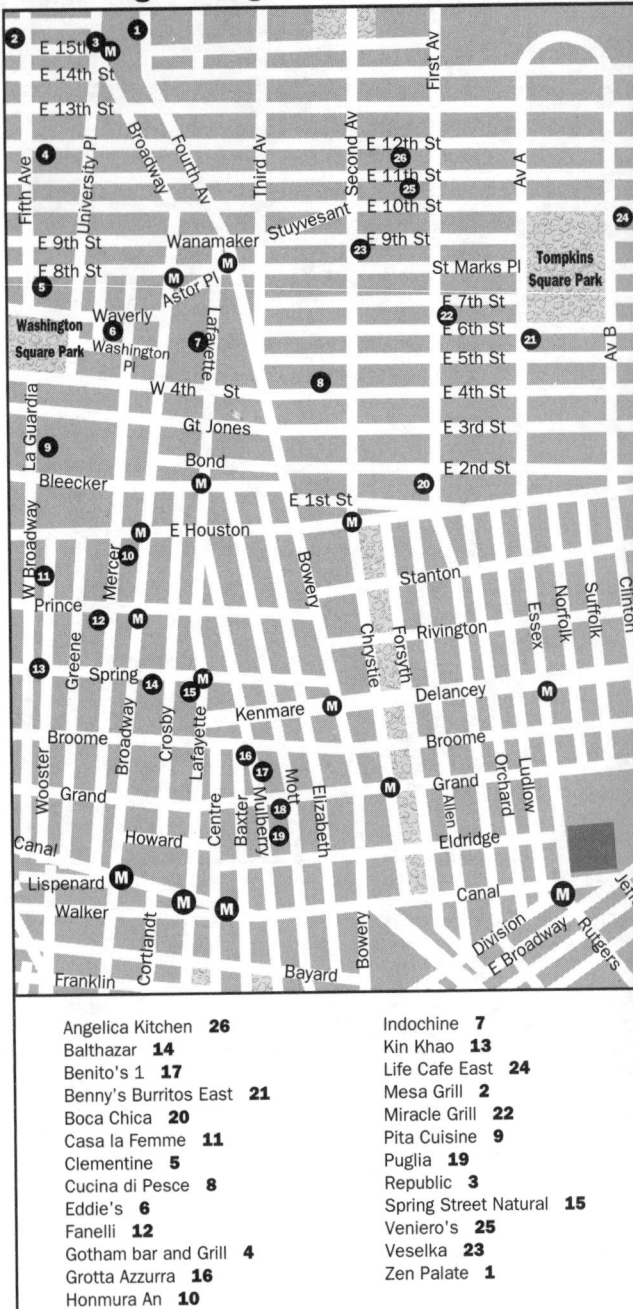

Angelica Kitchen **26**
Balthazar **14**
Benito's 1 **17**
Benny's Burritos East **21**
Boca Chica **20**
Casa la Femme **11**
Clementine **5**
Cucina di Pesce **8**
Eddie's **6**
Fanelli **12**
Gotham bar and Grill **4**
Grotta Azzurra **16**
Honmura An **10**

Indochine **7**
Kin Khao **13**
Life Cafe East **24**
Mesa Grill **2**
Miracle Grill **22**
Pita Cuisine **9**
Puglia **19**
Republic **3**
Spring Street Natural **15**
Veniero's **25**
Veselka **23**
Zen Palate **1**

Downtown Dining

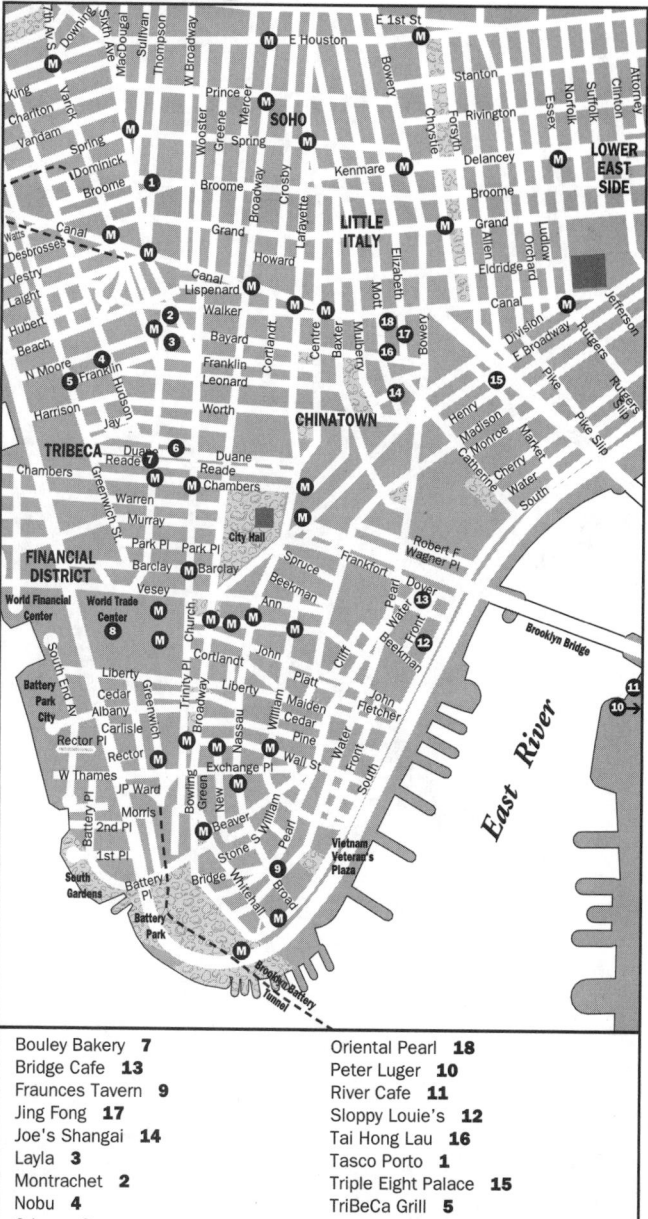

Bouley Bakery **7**	Oriental Pearl **18**
Bridge Cafe **13**	Peter Luger **10**
Fraunces Tavern **9**	River Cafe **11**
Jing Fong **17**	Sloppy Louie's **12**
Joe's Shangai **14**	Tai Hong Lau **16**
Layla **3**	Tasco Porto **1**
Montrachet **2**	Triple Eight Palace **15**
Nobu **4**	TriBeCa Grill **5**
Odeon **6**	Windows on the World **8**

3

sions

New York Harbor
and Miss Liberty,
Times Square, the
Empire State
Building, the
Brooklyn Bridge—
that's the short

list of New York City's must-sees. The unabridged list would take up volumes, not even counting city sights that are totally ephemeral—city squares mantled in snow and icicles, bike messengers flying like dervishes down the avenues, subway musicians playing at a certain stop one day and then gone the next. Taking in everything could drive a person to distraction. So make it easy on yourself by picking out one or two top attractions to visit each day. After you visit them, roam around the neighborhoods where they lie, taking the distinct pulse of the place by simply sitting on a park bench or in a cafe. Then wander on, preferably by foot. As novelist Elizabeth Bowen wrote of Rome, "to be anything but walking is estrangement." It's just as true of New York.

Getting Your Bearings

The kingdom of New York is composed of five boroughs: Staten Island (which is always agitating to secede from the union), the Bronx, Queens, Brooklyn, and the island of Manhattan, 13.5 miles long and 2.3 miles across at its widest point. The population is 7.3 million, with 1.5 million packed into Manhattan's high-rise apartment buildings, rowhouses, and fire-escape-filigreed tenements, lining 504 miles of streets. Access to the island is provided by three tunnels, some 12 bridges, the Staten Island and Hudson River ferries, and Roosevelt Island's aerial tram. From 14th Street all the way up to the northern tip of Manhattan, getting the lay of the land is a cinch because in 1811 urban planners laid the city out on a virtually unvarying grid. Numbered avenues run north and south. Sixth Avenue is also known as the Avenue of the Americas. Between Fifth and Third lie three named avenues—Madison, Park, and Lexington (Park turns into Fourth Avenue below 14th Street)—and east of First Avenue you'll find York and East End Avenue uptown, while the Upper West Side confuses everything by renaming its avenues: Central Park West, Columbus, Amsterdam, and West End. Numbered streets run east and west—though traffic moves alternately east or west, since most streets are one-way, except for the major cross-streets: 14th, 23rd, 34th, 42nd, 57th, 72nd, 79th, 86th, and 96th. Broadway cuts across the grid on one sweeping, 17-mile northwest diagonal. Fifth Avenue is the city's "Continental Divide" in terms of addresses; east and west of it, cross-street addresses start at zero, and are prefixed by an E. or W. (Hence 240 E. 37th Street or 315 W. 53rd Street). Avenue addresses baffle everybody—while 633 Third Avenue is at 40th Street, 633 Madison Avenue is at

59th. There's a way to find out that involves cancelling part of the address, dividing by two, and adding or subtracting a magic number, but who remembers? Your best bet is to call ahead and ask what the nearest cross street is.

Figuring out where you are is a lot harder downtown. Take a look at a map and you'll see why—the street grid looks like it's gone through a Cuisinart. I still get lost in parts of the Village and **Lower East Side**, and am always (delightedly) coming upon streets I never heard of before, like Weehawken, Attorney, and Lispenard. Back in the old days, streets were laid out along property lines, and useless marshlands covered large swatches of the littoral; the Village grew up as a jumbled tent encampment for refugees during the yellow fever epidemic of 1822, and strong, straight major arteries like Seventh Avenue weren't even extended south of 14th Street until 1911. This explains the loony, skewed, logic-defying layout of downtown.

You could just stay uptown—but wouldn't that be sad! So venture into the maze, remembering that the farther south you go, the closer together everything is (you can walk from the **West Village** to **SoHo** or from the **South Street Seaport** to the **World Trade Center** in a handy 10 minutes). Hang onto the lifeline of Broadway, and think of downtown in three parts, from north to south: The Village lies between 14th and Houston streets; SoHo is sandwiched between Houston and Canal streets (the name comes from "south of Houston," in fact); and everything below Canal Street is downtown, including the financial district, TriBeCa (the "triangle below Canal"), Chinatown, and the Lower East Side. **Heritage Trails of New York** has marked off four prime sightseeing routes in the lower

---

Talk City

You can sit in on a taping of one of the many talk shows shot in New York, including the "Late Show with David Letterman", "Conan O'Brien", "Regis and Kathie Lee", "Montel Williams", "Rosie O'Donnell", "Jesse Raphael".... you get the idea. Call for addresses, and write in advance. There are some age requirements, so check when you call. Late Night With Conan O'Brien. Tapings Mon–Fri 5:30pm.... Tel 212/664-3056. Late Show with David Letterman. Tapings Mon–Wed 5:30pm, Thur 5:30 and 9.... Tel 212/975-5190. Live with Regis and Kathie Lee. Tapings Mon–Fri 9am.... Tel 212/456-3054. The Montel Williams Show. Tapings Mon, Tues, Wed, 10am, 1 and 3pm.... Tel 212/989-8101. The Rosie O'Donnell Show. Tapings Mon–Fri 10am.... Tel 212/664-3056. Sally Jesse Raphael. Tapings Mon–Thur 11am and 1pm.... Tel 212/582-1722.

DIVERSIONS | INTRODUCTION

Manhattan area by painting more than 4 miles of dots on the sidewalks. The green route meanders between Wall Street and Battery Park; the blue starts at the Chase Manhattan Plaza; the red explores the City Hall area; and the orange winds from the American Stock Exchange to the World Financial Center. But if you see red footprints on the pavement, watch out, because there's a phantom painter on the loose downtown, whose markings lead you nowhere in particular and then mysteriously peter out.

The Lowdown

Partytime in Gotham... Back in New York's Dutch days, folks got crazy on the eve of Lent by playing an unsavory sort of game that, as far as I can make out, involved mutilating the greased carcass of a goose. I'd like to claim we've come a long way since then, but that wouldn't be just, considering the drunken brawling that goes on during the St. Patrick's Day Parade (March 17). The stomach is feted and then sated at the Ninth Avenue International Food Festival (mid-May), when Ninth Avenue from W. 57th to 42nd streets turns into one giant global-village smorgasbord; booths purvey everything from empanadas to Thai spring rolls. Gay Pride Week (in mid-June) culminates in another wild ride of a parade (generally on Sunday morning), with guys in such exquisite drag it would put RuPaul to shame. The Fourth of July just isn't the same (thank goodness!) since the city cracked down on illegal fireworks. Don't worry, though—you can still have a bang-up time around 9pm on the waterfront between Battery Park and South Street Seaport, with a fireworks show full of displays to remember, gorgeously mirrored in the water. Mid-August brings Harlem Week, with celebrations centering around 125th Street. Come September, Brooklyn is the scene of the West Indian American Day Carnival, when the air along Eastern Parkway is so thick with hot Afro-Latin music that you could cut it with a machete. Count on New York to put a few twists in the old recipe for fun, which it does in spades during the Greenwich Village Halloween Parade (October 31, after nightfall, of course), which winds up Sixth Avenue from Spring to 23rd streets. This is New York's version of Mardi Gras, with great attention paid to costumes. More wholesome by a mile is the

Macy's Thanksgiving Day Parade, when kids zipped up into warm winter coats line the curbs of Central Park West and Broadway from W. 77th Street to Herald Square, growing rosy-cheeked and enchanted at the sight of celebrity-laden floats and gigantic helium-filled balloon effigies of Mickey Mouse and all their favorite cartoon characters. If some of the grownups look bleary–eyed, they probably went to W. 77th Street and Columbus Avenue after midnight the night before to watch the giant balloons being inflated.Or you could just happen to strike it lucky and land in the city for a ticker-tape parade, which is how New York celebrates great civic and national events, on Broadway from Battery Park to City Hall.

The king of Museum Mile, and his minions...

Sticklers note that Museum Mile actually runs a mile and a half along Fifth Avenue from the **Frick Collection** at E. 65th Street to **El Museo del Barrio** at E. 105th Street. Over a score of museums line this stretch of wide pavement, making it something of a magic carpet for art lovers. But only one of them occupies a site on the western, Central Park side—the vast **Metropolitan Museum of Art**, which lies above E. 82nd Street. The Met's encyclopedic collection includes over three million works of art from all ages and corners of the globe, purchased or donated by Rockefellers, Sacklers, Lehmans, and other wealthy patrons and housed in myriad, mazelike wings. The Met can seem daunting. In a long half day you might be able to cruise past most of its hits, like the Assyrian Nimrud Ivories dating from the 13th to the 7th century BC, Botticelli's 1490 *Annunciation*, the Dogon sculptures from the western Sudan, the *Temple of Dendur*, Degas's gemlike *Dancing Class*, and Picasso's portrait of Gertrude Stein, not to mention some 40 sculptures by Rodin. I've done this once or twice, but it's really better to limit yourself to a handful of wings—maybe the half acre of 19th-century European Paintings, masterpieces from the Neo-Classicists to the Impressionists; or the Rockefeller Wing, featuring "primitive" art from Africa, Oceania, and South America; the tombs and reliquaries of pharoahs in the Egyptian Wing; or the Greek and Roman Galleries. For lovers of Asian art there's the Ming Dynasty-era Astor Chinese Garden Court; the stunning American Wing picks up long before the Whitney Museum starts, with Duncan Phyfe furniture, handsome portraits by John Singer Sargent, and a painstakingly recreated Frank Lloyd Wright room. Before leaving, climb up to the rooftop sculpture garden, if only to see the city skyline fringing Central Park. Many masterworks from the Met's medieval collection aren't in the Met at all, but way up on Manhattan's west side, in Fort Tryon Park: **The Cloisters** holds, among other treasures, the Unicorn Tapestries, an illuminated manuscript called *Les Belles Heures du Duc de Berry*, and the 12th-century Bury St. Edmunds Cross. But many will find the Cloisters most memorable for its dramatic Hudson River cliffside setting and bizarre composition, a Frankenstein-like amalgamation of medieval architecture from all over Europe: a Romanesque chapel, a 12th-century Spanish apse, and portions of cloisters from five different monasteries. Back on Museum Mile, above the Met, you'll find the **Museum of the City of New York**, with fine historical interiors; the **International Center of Photography**; and the **Cooper-Hewitt National Design Museum**, overseen by the Smithsonian Institution. Of the three, I'd choose the Cooper-Hewitt in a flash, partly because it occupies a mansion built by Andrew Carnegie in 1901, and because its rotating displays of decorative arts—from Japanese kimonos to Bauhaus chairs—never fail to beguile. But to my mind the **Frick Collection** is the apogee of Museum Mile, a lovely, intimate place for some of life's transcendent moments. Among all the famous paintings hanging on museum walls in New York, the one I care for most is at the Frick—Whistler's stunningly pink *Valerie, Lady Meux*, who eyes the viewer with the subtlest sort of come-on, while a signature Whistler butterfly floats in front of her.

I know what I like, and I like modern art... Go directly to the **Museum of Modern Art** (MoMA), which covers all of contemporary art beginning with the Post-Impressionists. MoMA opened in 1929 on Fifth Avenue, but then moved to new International-style digs on W. 53rd Street 10 years later, with its Philip Johnson-designed sculpture garden. The collection consists of 100,000 paintings and sculptures, 10,000 films, and 100,000 books—but numbers don't tell the MoMA story at all, because this museum has more masterworks by late 19th- and 20th-century artists than any other in the world. You will stop, all agog, by Vincent Van Gogh's *Starry Night*, Henri Rousseau's *Sleeping Gypsy*, Piet Mondrian's *Broadway Boogie-Woogie*, and Pablo Picasso's *Desmoiselles d'Avignon*. The **Whitney Museum** is a logical stop for contemporary art lovers, housing a collection of American painting, sculpture, and graphic arts in styles as various as Pop, Conceptual, Social, and Magical Realist. The permanent collection contains works by George Bellows, Edward Hopper, Andy Warhol, Jasper Johns, and Louise Nevelson; and Whitney Biennial shows are considered the last word in cutting-edge art. Way west in Chelsea, you can sit on the rooftop at the **Dia Center for the Arts**, and then wander into sculptor Dan Graham's glass and metal "reflective experience." SoHo has three important modern art forums: the **Alternative Museum**, dedicated to works with a social or political agenda; the **New Museum of Contemporary Art**, featuring such whimsical curios as Jimbo Blachly's *Unperturbed Abstraction*, a streetside window installation which the artists often enter for stints of performance art; and the **Guggenheim Museum SoHo**, with a rotating schedule of exhibits shown in a bare loft space with towering ceilings. But when I have a spare Sunday afternoon, the museum I visit is the **Solomon R. Guggenheim Museum**. The permanent collection contains Chagalls, Matisses, Van Goghs, Picassos, and Kandinskys till the cows come home, and there's always some intriguing special exhibit; the last time I was there huge piles of penny candy were on display—an exhibit I tried hard to contemplate before stashing some pieces in my purse (don't worry, this was allowed). But forget all that, it's the building that provides transcendent moments. Frank Lloyd Wright was the architect, and in the Guggenheim he sought to suggest a ziggurat. It's one immense concrete spiral, with a seven-story tower alongside, ascended via a half-rounded elevator. You zoom to the top, then cruise slowly on foot down a long spiral ramp, past the artworks.

Coming to America... Technically speaking, nearly all Americans are immigrants—no matter how long ago their ancestors made the trip. But the greatest wave lasted from about 1890 to 1950, when 12 million people arrived from places like Eastern Europe, Russia, Ireland, and Italy, with the crest coming in 1907. What they first saw upon entering New York Harbor was the **Statue of Liberty**, still perhaps the city's most stirring sight. Copper-coated Miss Liberty, standing 150 feet from base to torch, was designed by Frederic-Auguste Bartholdi, Alexandre Gustave Eiffel, and Richard Morris Hunt. Take a ferry to the statue from Battery Park; an elevator whisks you to the top of the pedestal, from which it's a 12-story climb to the crown. The ticket booth is, appropriately, at Battery Park's **Castle Clinton**, an old fort that served as the city's prime disembarkation point for immigrants until 1892, when the federal government opened new processing facilities on **Ellis Island** (also reached by ferry from Battery Park). The Great Hall has been carefully restored; displays of immigrant memorabilia can be toured and if you had ancestors pour through this island, you may be able to look up their entrance date on a public computer. The American Immigrant Wall of Honor outside, skirting the waterfront, is moving to behold, with the names of 420,000 immigrants inscribed. When newcomers finally reached Manhattan, most carried their baggage up Broadway, then veered right to the Lower East Side, a neighborhood of tenement buildings and sweatshops that spans 4 square miles from Broadway east to the river, between Houston and Canal streets. Italians, Irish, Chinese, and Jews lived in close, squalid quarters there, with Hispanics joining them more recently. **Sara Delano Roosevelt Park**, running along Chrystie Street between Houston and Canal streets, remains the district's center, the scene of a bustling open-air bazaar. Just east lies the Jewish commercial hub of Orchard Street and the **Lower East Side Tenement Museum**, housed in an 1868 tenement, with dioramas that reveal the rigors of life in a cramped railroad apartment, with a bathtub in the kitchen and a toilet down the hall. A different, infinitely more poignant side of Jewish life in our century is portrayed in the recently-inaugurated **Museum of Jewish Heritage: A Living Memorial to the Holocaust**, where artifacts, documents, photographs, and film clips shed a wrenching light on Jewish immediate life before, during, and after World War II.

New York stories... Great poets have left their marks all over New York, beginning with that dauntless American oracle, **Walt Whitman**, raised in a house on **Cranberry Street** across from Plymouth Church in Brooklyn Heights. As a reporter for the *Brooklyn Eagle* he roamed far and wide, drinking in New York and its people, result-ing in his poetic masterpiece *Leaves of Grass*, which he set at a printshop once located at **170 Fulton Street**. Master of the macabre, **Edgar Allen Poe**, had a hard time settling down in any one place for long, but we know he helped to run a boarding house at **113 1/2 Carmine Street**, was treated for a head cold in 1837 at the **Northern Dispen-sary** (Christopher Street and Waverly Place), and retreated with his invalid wife to a farmhouse on the Upper West Side (on the site of a tenement at **206 W. 84th Street**) where he finished *The Raven*. The modernist, **e.e. cummings**, grew old, crusty, and reclusive at **4 Patchin Place**, a secretive little mews off 10th Street west of Sixth Avenue; **Bob Dylan** haunted clubs around the intersec-tion of **Bleecker** and **MacDougal streets**. Welsh poet **Dylan Thomas** became a permanent fixture at the **White Horse Tavern**, at the southwest corner of Hudson and west 11th streets, where you can still down a beer and imagine his sonorous voice; he spent his last bleerily alco-holic days at Victorian Gothic **Chelsea Hotel** (222 W. 23rd Street), also inhabited at various times by **Tennessee Williams**, **Yevgeni Yevtushenko**, and **Arthur Miller**. In the East Village, kind-hearted **W.H. Auden** lived for many years above a bar at **77 St. Marks Place**, today marked by a plaque bearing this line of his verse: "If equal affection cannot be, let the more loving one be me." Beat poet **Allen Ginsberg** hung out at the **St. Mark's Church-in-the-Bowery**. It remains headquarters for other younger poets, who join in weekly readings at the long-running **Poetry Project**. A more recent addition to the East Village scene is the **Nuyorican Poets Cafe**, featuring poetry slams and rap. But if all you want to do is cuddle up with a book of verse, stop by the **Poets House**, started in 1985 by Stanley Kunitz and Elizabeth Kray, where there are deep easy-chairs and 30,000 volumes of poetry.

Beautiful buildings, Downtown... "Look up!" exclaims the estimable *American Institute of Architects Guide to New York City*. This is the only way to appreciate Manhattan's grand, gorgeous buildings, though with so much to absorb at street level, it's easy to pass them by. So make a special trip to the **Woolworth Building** at 233 Broadway just below City Hall, a 60-story skyscraper with enchanting Gothic embellishments and known as the "Cathedral of Commerce" when dimestore magnate F.W. Woolworth

DIVERSIONS | THE LOWDOWN

had it erected (paying $13.5 million in cash) in 1913, employing Cass Gilbert as architect. I know of no finer lobby in the city—go inside and gaze at the marvelous glass-mosaic vaulted ceiling, where you'll find a gargoyle-ish likeness of Mr. Woolworth counting coins at the top of a crossbeam on the south side. Step over to City Hall Park to view it from a distance, then turn to note the fine neo-classical Federal lines of **City Hall**, itself, and the hand-some twin towers of the **Park Row Building** across the traffic island to the south (15 Park Row between Ann and Beekman streets), Manhattan's tallest edifice from 1899 to 1908. The foyer of the **American Telephone and Telegraph Building** (195 Broadway), a fascinating forest of columns, nearly rivals the Woolworth lobby. There was little chance that **Jefferson Market Courthouse** (now a branch of the **New York Public Library**, at Sixth Avenue and 10th Street) would start an architectural trend when it went up in 1876, because the building is simply too bizarre—but delightfully so. With its red brick, myriad gables, slender arched windows, and towers, it is one part Bavarian castle, one part Venetian palazzo.

Beautiful buildings, Midtown... Everyone stops short when they come upon the **Flatiron Building**, which rises in an awesome wedge at the skinny triangular meet-ing of Broadway, Fifth Avenue, and 23rd Street. It went up in 1902, and boasts one of the city's earliest struc-tural steel frames. In 1930, the 1,048-foot-tall **Chrysler Building** (405 Lexington Avenue at 42nd Street) sur-passed the Woolworth Building in height. To get a good view of this Art Deco landmark, find a spot on Lexington Avenue in the high Forties and look down-town, marveling above all the building's outlandish crown, composed of six levels of brilliant stainless steel arches topped by a dramatically lit lancet spire. Closer up you'll find brickwork designs inspired by automobile hubcaps, and a Jazz Age fantasy in African marble in the lobby. The Chrysler Building only held onto the world's tallest title for a few months, until the **Empire State Building** (Fifth Avenue and 34th Street) opened its doors. Just down the street from the Chrysler Building you'll find another architectural wonder from 1930, the **Daily News Building** (220 E. 42nd St.), with a power-ful red-and-black-striped composition; check out the huge globe and weather instruments in the lobby, but don't look for the newspaper, because the *Daily News* moved to cheaper digs in 1995. Two stone lions greet visitors on the broad stone steps of the **New York Public Library** (Fifth Avenue and 42nd Street), where there are al fresco cafes and plenty of shady spots for brown-bag lunches. The main reading room is undergoing a massive renovation and so the lions are temporarily adorned with their very own hard hats. This 1911 building is New York Beaux Arts at its best, with a grand, airy lobby, Romanesque arches, and two sweeping side staircases. Those who favor modern architecture should stop by the **Seagram Building** (375 Park Avenue), designed in the International Style by Mies van der Rohe in 1958, with interiors (including the lobby-level **Four Seasons** restaurant—see Dining) by Philip Johnson. This simple, black-mirrored rectangle looms powerfully, fronted by a plaza—actually one of the first introduced in the high-rent district of Midtown. Equally impressive is **Lever House**, completed in 1952, which opened up the whole block of Park Avenue between East 53rd and 54th streets; one stainless-steel-and-glass slab sits on columns occupying the site horizontally, while another rises at the north end, creating one gigantic, backwards L. The **Citicorp Center** (Lexington Avenue between 53rd and 54th streets) shot up in 1978, cantilevered over St. Peter's Lutheran Church, with two lower-level shopping and eating arcades and a height of 900 feet; its top 130 feet have been sliced diagonally, yielding the building's signature angled crest. One final modernistic landmark lies at 909 Third Avenue: New Yorkers call it the "**Lipstick Building**," due to its tall, rounded shape. John Burgee and Philip Johnson were the architects, which must have been convenient for Johnson, since he lived virtually around the corner at 242 E. 52nd Street, in a shockingly contemporary townhouse he designed, now the **Museum of Modern Art Guesthouse**.

On the square... In the last ten years or so, many of New York's finest squares, containing parks, have undergone dramatic restoration. Once the domain of junkies, pushers, and the homeless, Midtown's **Bryant Park** (Sixth Avenue between 40th and 42nd streets) now seems a little patch of Versailles, with pebbled paths, very Continental green iron folding chairs, clean restrooms, a wide central lawn, and a stage hosting free midday con-

DIVERSIONS | THE LOWDOWN

certs and free Monday night movies in summer. Fashion designers set up runways there for showings of their newest collections. **Union Square** (Broadway and Park Avenue South, 14th to 16th streets) isn't bordered by buildings of great architectural distinction (indeed, the atmosphere is busy and rattling), but it has an interesting red-tinted past: In the thirties, orators held forth on soapboxes here, stirring up the city's Left Wing sensibilities. Now a splendid **greenmarket** takes over the concrete flats at the north end of the square, open for business on Monday, Wednesday, Friday, and Saturday, and a chic cafe called **Luna Park** (see Dining) has blossomed in the center of it all. Sedate **Gramercy Park** (20th to 21st streets, at the foot of Lexington Avenue) is surrounded by a distinguished residential neighborhood, where the townhouses are decorated with New Orleans-style wrought-iron porticoes and porches. Only residents have keys, but guests at the **Gramercy Hotel** get to use the key of house.

It takes a village... Tompkins Square Park is, in many ways, the heart of the **East Village**. At the turn of the century Eastern European immigrants settled in, leaving behind pleasing traces like **B & H Dairy** (see Dining) and the **Russian and Turkish Baths**, where you can sip borscht, sizzle in the Russian room, or sweat out your toxins in the Turkish Room. When the wild sixties rolled in, the East Village was transformed into New York's Haight-Ashbury, with avant-garde artists bunking in communal apartments, flower children wandering freely, and artistic meccas like the innovative theater **La Mama E.T.C.** (74 E. 4th Street) and the **St. Mark's Church-in-the-Bowery Poetry Project**. East of Tompkins Square Park, **Alphabet City** (so named because the avenues bear letters not numbers) sprawls toward the East River, a dodgy urban netherland with a large Hispanic population and fearless Gen-X homesteaders. In the **West Village**, where Seventh Avenue South crosses west 4th and Christopher streets, little **Sheridan Square** (historically, Christopher Park, founded in 1837) saw violence of a different kind in 1967, when homosexual protestors clashed with cops in the Stonewall Riot, sparking the beginning of the country's gay activism. The **General Philip H. Sheridan monument** strikes an odd note there, with white-wrapped lifelike statues of gay and lesbian couples taking up bench space below him. If you stop in only one square during your visit to New York, make it **Washington Square**, where Fifth Avenue dead-ends at 10th Street with a grand triumphal arch designed by Stanford White. A trout stream ran through this area in the 18th century, and one corner of what is now the square was used as a Potter's Field. In the early part of the 19th century, wealthy denizens from downtown moved up to its environs—including Henry James's grandmother, who owned a now-demolished rowhouse at 19 10th Street. James would be amazed to see it now, because Washington Square Park is a veritable circus. The wide fountain is the city's top stage for street performers; its fenced-in dogwalk yields canine shows; chess is the park's prime sport, played at stone tables at the southwest corner; and NYU students use the place for a quad (indeed, it's the scene of the university's commencement ceremonies every spring). Certainly, there are streetpeople, pickpockets, and pushers, too—but not in disproportionate numbers. The Village mixes here, generally with a very positive attitude.

Knockin' on heaven's door... With so much of New York's art lining the walls of museums, most tourists don't venture into the city's churches, unless maybe to go to a gospel service up in Harlem (see "Way Uptown," below). During the week, however, Manhattan churches remain deeply peaceful places, where one can sit, breathe, and think. **St. Patrick's Cathedral** (Fifth Avenue and 50th Street) is a cavernous edifice designed by James Renwick in the mid-19th century, skirted by wide stone steps and pinnacled by twin 330-foot Gothic spires. Also in Midtown, **St. Bartholomew's Episcopal Church** (Park Avenue at 51st Street), built in 1918, has grand Romanesque vaulting, Byzantine decorations, and, being a socially responsible sort of congregation, a homeless shelter in the foyer. A little farther east, tucked beneath the northwest corner of the **Citicorp Center** (Lexington Avenue and 54th Street), is **St. Peter's Lutheran Church**, often the showcase for Off-Off Broadway theatrical productions; the miniscule **Erol Beker Chapel** at the north side is what really makes it worth a stop—pure white, and designed by Louise Nevelson. Uptown, the **Cathedral of St. John the Divine** (Amsterdam Avenue at 112th Street) still struggles toward completion. It was started in 1892, and conceived on an incredibly grand scale—indeed, if the last gargoyle is ever finally sculpted and set, it will be the

DIVERSIONS | THE LOWDOWN

biggest Gothic cathedral in the world. The most recent building spurt, during the 1980s, faded out leaving one of the two planned towers at the front a lot taller than the other. Somehow the effect is to make what ought to be an imposing structure look like a gangly teen. Graceful, Gothic **Riverside Church**, over at 120th Street and Riverside Drive, was a hotbed for Vietnam War opposition, fueled by the wise, reasoned voice of the Reverend William Sloane Coffin. You can ascend its belfry for a peaceful refuge 392 feet high, with sweeping views of the Hudson River and New Jersey beyond; the carillon has 74 bells weighing 100 tons, and chimes daily at noon and on Sundays at 3pm. On lower Broadway, at the end of Wall Street, the first **Trinity Church** was built in 1696. But the original church was burned down by British General Howe in 1776; the lovely Gothic gem that stands here now was completed in 1846, with huge bronze doors designed by Richard Morris Hunt and a bucolic colonial-era cemetery wrapped around it. One of Trinity's chapels, **St. Paul's** (at Broadway and Vesey Street), survives as the city's only pre-Revolutionary War structure, built in 1766 with Scotsman Thomas McBean as architect. The heart of the building is a modest Georgian hall, topped 30 years later by a somewhat ostentatious spire. Inside you'll find the pew where George Washington worshipped from 1789 to 1790, when New York briefly served as the nation's capital.

Reel to reel... The movie industry started in the New York area (New Jersey, to be exact, where Thomas Edison had his lab), and so many films and televison shows have used the city for a backdrop that walking around here gives many folks a disconcerting sense of déjà vu. Christopher Reeve and Margot Kidder posed at the entrance to the **Daily News Building** (220 E. 42nd Street) in the 1978 film version of *Superman*; the **New York County Court-house** downtown (Centre and Pearl streets) served in 1957 as the opening setting for *Twelve Angry Men*, which starred Henry Fonda; a white townhouse at **171 E. 71st Street** was Audrey Hepburn's East Side digs when she wasn't window-shopping at 57th and Fifth in *Breakfast at Tiffany's*; the **New York Public Library** was de-spooked in 1984's *Ghostbusters* (the ghostbusters operated out of a firehouse in TriBeCa at 14 Moore Street). **Tom's Restaurant** at 112th and Broadway is the hangout for

Jerry and his pals on TV's "Seinfeld"; an apartment building at the **corner of Grove and Bedford streets** in the
West Village is supposed to be home base for the characters of "Friends". The **Ed Sullivan Theatre** (Broadway at
53rd Street) holds powerful memories of the days when
Sullivan's Sunday-evening variety show presented everyone from Elvis to the Beatles to an Italian mouse puppet
named Topo Gigio; today it's home to CBS's "The Late
Show with David Letterman", which has made celebrities
of every small-business proprietor on the block (Mujibar
and Sirajul work up the block at a store called Rock
America, Rupert Gee at the Hello Deli around the corner). The **Museum of Television and Radio** in Midtown,
founded by CBS titan William S. Paley, has 60,000 old
television programs and 7,000 vintage radio shows in its
stacks, which can be checked out for sampling at custom-
built consoles. (Most requested tape: The 1964 "Ed
Sullivan Show" introducing the Beatles to American audi-
ences.) The museum also mounts displays and organizes
special screenings, and has a fun gift shop on its first floor.
Out in Queens, near the old but still functioning Kaufman
Astoria Studios, is the **American Museum of the Moving
Image**, a classily put-together place for movie addicts to
indulge themselves. It has a theater, screening room,
changing exhibits, complete sets from famous films, and
60,000 pieces of movie memorabilia.

Crossroads of the world... Times Square, situated at the
giant X-shaped intersection of Broadway, Seventh
Avenue, and 42nd Street, is Gotham's theater district, as
well as the town's latest Cinderella story. Long the
stomping ground of peepshows, pimps, pickpockets, and
pushers, it is now being redeveloped into a tourist and
entertainment center. Ratso Rizzo, the hustler played by
Dustin Hoffman in the 1969 movie, *Midnight Cowboy*,
wouldn't know the place. The stately old theaters that had
sunk to showing XXX double features are being renovated
for live drama and splashy musicals. The Walt Disney
Company has poured money into reviving the old **New
Amsterdam Theater** on what used to be the most
wretched block of 42nd Street. A new **Warner Brothers
Store** and a branch of London's **Madame Tussaud's** are
on their way. And just up the street is the **Virgin
Megastore** that likes to call itself the world's largest music
store... and maybe it is!

DIVERSIONS | THE LOWDOWN

Park it here... **Riverside Park**, which runs alongside the Hudson River from W. 76th to 129th streets, and **Prospect Park** in Brooklyn, considered the masterwork of the the 19th-century landscape design team of Frederick Law Olmsted and Calvert Vaux, are two emeralds in the city's treasure trove. But **Central Park** is indisputably the diamond, if only because it's so...well, so *central.* Stretching from 59th to 110th streets, it occupies 840 acres of prime Manhattan real estate, but if the city ever tried to sell it off the populace would revolt. It's crowded as a circus on weekends, when it becomes everybody's backyard. Always in need of renovation or trash collection somewhere, and not very safe in the off-hours, all in all it's dearly beloved. The city bought the marshy, rock-strewn property for the park in 1851; at the time, one newspaper reporter called it "a pestilential spot where miasmic odors taint every breath of air." But then Olmsted and Vaux took over, filling the lowlands, extracting boulders, erecting rustic stone bridges and Beaux Arts lampposts, and running four major crosstown arteries (65th, 79th, 86th, and 96th streets) through it—though due to the clever way they've been engineered, the park's integrity remains unspoiled. The designers' goal was to create not a formal greenspace but a rich natural landscape, where urban denizens could briefly forget they lived in a city. The sweeping greenswards of the 22-acre **Sheep Meadow** (north of 65th Street) and the 36-acre **Great Lawn** (midpark between 79th and 86th streets) were seeded, 58 miles of pedestrian paths were laid, and wonderful architectural follies rose, like **Belvedere Castle** overlooking **Turtle Pond** (now housing a children's learning center and U.S. Weather Service Station, just above 79th Street). The Victorian Gothic **Dairy** (midpark at 65th Street) currently serves as the park's information center and rents queens, kings, and pawns for those who want to test their skill in the **Chess House** nearby. Woodland sections like the **Ramble** (lining the northern shores of the **Lake**) and the **Ravine in the North Woods** (midpark around 103rd Street—go here only on weekend days, and never alone), were left intact, and have since become rest stops for flocks of migrating birds. Of course, the park has changed since Olmsted and Vaux's time. In 1880 the **Metropolitan Museum of Art** moved into a site on the east side at 82nd Street. Around 1950 another urban planner put his own imprint on the park—Robert Moses, the city's tireless highway builder, who cut tennis courts, playgrounds, recreation centers, and baseball diamonds into the greenswards. And, more recently, the Sheep Meadow and Great Lawn have become great open-air stages for the Metropolitan Opera, singers like Paul Simon and Garth Brooks, the New York Philharmonic, and (on those rare occasions when he comes to visit) the Pope. Begin by entering at 59th Street and Fifth Avenue, where paths winding to your left take you along the placid **Pond**, **Wollman Skating Rink**, the **Dairy**, and a delightful 1903 **Carousel**. Or walk straight into the small though engaging **Central Park Zoo**, where snow monkeys, polar bears, and red pandas roam in natural settings. Just north of the zoo entrance, an archway leads under the fanciful **Delacorte Clock**; on the hour two monkeys strike a bell, an elephant plays the accordion, goats pipe, penguins drum, and hippos fiddle. Right on the other side of the clock tower is the entrance to the new **Tisch Children's Zoo** with more than 25 species of animals, an Enchanted Forest with interactive displays, and a variety of live performances. South of 72nd Street lies **the Mall**, lined with statues of great men like Robert Burns, Shakespeare, and Christopher Columbus; and great Rollerbladers, who've claimed this as their turf. **Bethesda Terrace**, one of the only formal settings in Central Park, graces the central sector above 72nd Street, with the *Angel of the Waters* fountain, sculpted by Emma Stebbins in 1870; rowboats from the **Loeb Boathouse** (which has a restaurant and snack bar) ply the waters of the lake below. **Strawberry Fields**, Yoko Ono's garden tribute to John Lennon, is at 72nd Street and Central Park West. On the north side of the Lake, midpark at 79th Street, the **Delacorte Theater** presents two Shakespeare plays every summer. Tickets are free, but in great demand—so you must line up at the box office as early as noon on the day of a performance. Runners follow the jogging path around the **Jacqueline Kennedy Onassis Reservoir**, midpark from 87th to 95th streets, with the **Tennis House** northwest of that. Contrary to popular fears, the northern reaches of the park can be navigated safely on weekend afternoons—they hold seldom-visited glories like the **Great Hill** (on the west side at 106th Street), a popular picnic spot; the recently renovated **Harlem Meer**, stocked with fish; and the **Conservatory Garden**, perhaps my favorite place in Central Park. Enter through the Vanderbilt Gate (taken from the Vanderbilt

DIVERSIONS | THE LOWDOWN

mansion downtown) at 105th Street and Fifth Avenue; stroll along the crabapple allées with overarching bows and shady benches; stop for a moment in the Japanese wisteria pergola, decked with blooms in the spring; gaze at the delightful *Three Maidens* statue in the French Garden; and then find your way to the **Secret Garden** on the south side, where heliotropes, snapdragons, hollyhocks, phlox, butterflies, and bumblebees run riot on hot summer days.

Way uptown... **Harlem** is the vast area north of Central Park, stretching from 125th to 168th Street, with **Spanish Harlem** occupying a lower eastern portion from 96th to 125th streets and Fifth Avenue to the East River. Dutch farms and roadside taverns were scattered across it in New York's early years, but in the 1890s it was developed as a semi-suburban getaway for affluent whites. By the 1920s black New Yorkers, driven out of Midtown by high rents, moved up (and all but a very small number of whites bailed out). Harlem blossomed thereafter, with jazz spiraling out of clubs like the **Apollo Theatre** (happily, still open), Small's, and the Cotton Club, where Josephine Baker danced and the floor shows were swank—though, ironically, only white patrons were allowed. Meanwhile, however, poverty spread in Harlem and housing projects rose up; the sixties brought racial protests, crystallized around the mesmerizing figure of Malcolm X. It is a sad fact that most white New Yorkers never venture into Harlem, and can't quite figure out why so many foreign visitors wish to do so. (Most make the trip with an organized tour. I'd suggest **Harlem Your Way Tours Unlimited, Inc.,** or **Harlem Spirituals, Inc.**) And in truth, most of Harlem is desperately rough. Change is coming, though, but slowly. Recently Robert DeNiro bought the old **Minton Playhouse**, with plans to refurbish and reopen it, and the Harlem Chamber of Commerce is at work renovating numerous blocks. From the subway stop at 125th Street and Lenox Avenue (also known as Malcolm X Boulevard), Harlem's main commercial drag, the skyline of downtown Manhattan looks like a mirage. The cultural heart of Harlem is the **Schomburg Center for Research in Black Culture** (a branch of the New York Public Library, at Lenox Avenue and 135th Street), where you can see the collection of Puerto Rican-born Arturo Alfonso Schomburg (1874–1938). Taught in school that blacks had no history, Schomburg spent his life amassing a library that proves the lessons false. Just down the block is the **Liberation Bookstore** (tel 212/281–4615, 421 Malcolm X Blvd.), a friendly, packed little place; west on 135th is the **Harlem YMCA**, where Harry Belafonte and James Baldwin studied. The **Abyssinian Baptist Church**, on 138th Street between Lenox Avenue and Adam Clayton Powell Jr. Boulevard, is where all the Sunday morning tour groups stop to hear gospel voices raised. **Londel's**, around the corner (tel 212/234–6114, 2620 Frederick Douglas Blvd. [Eighth Avenue]), is a good place to stop for soul food before heading on to **Strivers' Row**, actually two rows of fine houses on 138th and 139th streets between Adam Clayton Powell Jr. Boulevard and Eighth Avenue. These are known as the richest blocks in Harlem. In **Hamilton Terrace**, another high-rent Harlem neighborhood, you'll find **Hamilton Grange**, a yellow frame house that would look at home on Maryland's Eastern Shore. It was briefly the summer home of Alexander Hamilton, first Secretary of the Treasury (he's the guy on the $10 bill). Born in the West Indies, Hamilton is thought to have been part black, which makes it a fitting coincidence that this house should be one of Harlem's crown jewels.

On the waterfront (and on the water)... There's water, water everywhere around Manhattan, though getting to it can be tricky. A move is under way to encircle the island with a thin ribbon of parks, which will probably be a long time in coming, given the city's tight budget. Until then, folks in the know find ways to take in the waterfront, beginning way up north in **Washington Heights** at the new **Pier and Marina in Inwood**. Situated at the eastern foot of Dyckman Street, it has a snack bar selling fried calamari and shrimp, and at the moment just 12 private boats moored here. But there are fine views up toward **Fort Tryon Park** and the treacherous confluence of the Hudson and Harlem rivers, dubbed **Spuyten Duyvil** by the Dutch. Moving on down the west side, you'll find the salty little houseboat colony at the **79th Street Boat Basin in Riverside Park**. At **The Intrepid–Sea–Air–Space Museum**, occupying a World War II aircraft carrier permanently berthed at the end of W. 46th Street, you can climb a gun turret, board a submarine, and learn about great sea disasters of the past. The *Lusitania* once docked at the foot of W. 23rd Street, which is now home to the

Chelsea Piers Sports and Entertainment Complex; lining the Hudson River from piers 59 to 62 (see Getting Outside), it's now the embarkation point for **Spirit Cruises**. Down at Christopher Street, West Villagers encroach on rattletrap piers to sunbathe, or Rollerblade, bike, and jog on **Hudson River Park**'s concrete waterfront path (which after nightfall becomes the realm of transvestite hookers). Romantics favor a little pocket of shorefront turf known as **South Cove**, tucked into **Battery Park City**. But the **Circle Line** is uncontestably the best way to take to the water in New York, on three-hour daytime sightseeing cruises. You round the southern tip of the island, sampling nonpareil views of the harbor and Statue of Liberty, cruise past Brooklyn and right under the Brooklyn Bridge, then head up the East River to glimpse the United Nations, cutting to port at the Harlem River, and so back into the Hudson River's broad, deep channel. Amplified commentary is provided, along with plenty of snack food—and, on a bright summer day, possibly a sunburn. Down at **Battery Park**, on the island's southern tip, you'll feel as if you're perched at the prow of a gigantic ship headed out into New York Harbor. Seagulls cry, vendors sell hot dogs, soft drinks, and souvenirs, and benches line the waterfront. From the park's southeast corner, you can catch a ride on the *Petrel*, a 76-foot yacht with teakwood decks, formerly owned by John F. Kennedy, cruises last about 45 minutes. The **Staten Island Ferry Terminal** sits at the far end of the park (at the foot of Whitehall Street), and head over the waves to the little community of St. George on Staten Island, passing Governor's Island, Miss Liberty, and the Brooklyn container port. Farther out, you get a sterling view of the Verrazano Narrows Bridge, which connects Staten Island to Brooklyn, near Coney Island. The round-trip takes 50 minutes, and best of all it's free! **South Street Seaport** is a veritable shrine to matters nautical, situated at the foot of stone-paved Fulton Street, where the old Fulton Ferry landed from 1814 until 1883, when the Brooklyn Bridge opened. The riverside block of Fulton Street, lined with shops, restaurants, and pubs, turns into one giant Wall Street frat party after the financial markets close on Friday night. The visitors center for the **South Street Seaport Museum** lies halfway down a row of early 19th-century buildings on the south side of Fulton Street—note their handmade brick, stonework details, and imperfect old glass. The museum encompasses five historic seaport blocks of Fulton, Water, Front, and South streets, but above all, a handful of antique ships berthed at Pier 16: the *Peking*, the largest sailing ship ever built; a fishing schooner from 1891; and the *Ambrose*, a lightship built in 1907. **Liberty** and **Pioneer schooner cruises** can be booked here, as well. The Seaport's handsomely restored **Pier 17** has more shops and restaurants, concerts on summer nights, and, at the north end, a fine Brooklyn Bridge vantage point, from which you can just make out Brooklyn's **Fulton Ferry Landing**, illuminated by the white Christmas lights of the **River Cafe** (see Dining).

In bloom... At almost any time of year, a trip to the **Brooklyn Botanical Garden** is most highly recommended, but when spring comes, what a blooming wonderland this 50-acre park becomes! The Beaux Arts administration building is lined with lily ponds and beds of tulips. Nearby there's a sweet swelling of the earth called "Daffodil Hill." Down the path, a wooden teahouse sits beside a gemlike pond with a bright red *torii* gate near the far shore; this is the landmark Japanese Garden, a favored backdrop for wedding pictures. Then it's on to the cherry esplanade, which blossoms in late April; the Rose Garden hits its prime in June. Recently renovated greenhouses, a renowned collection of fabulously gnarled bonsai, and a nice little al fresco cafe complete the picture. Five times as large, the **New York Botanical Garden** in the Bronx is easy to reach; it's the first stop on Metro North's Harlem division. Enter via the Enid A. Haupt Conservatory, a series of graceful domed glass houses built in 1901 to recall the Great Palm House in England's Kew Gardens. A bit of a hike will take you through a hemlock forest, native plant garden, and rhododendron valley—with perhaps a final stop at the **Old Lorillard Snuff Mill**, built in 1840, where terraces overlook the Bronx River and there's a pleasant tea service. And if you have a bit of time on your hands, venture north to **Wave Hill**, a 28-acre 1840s estate in **Riverdale** (an hour by subway from Midtown), with a lawn sloping down toward the Hudson River and carefully planted gardens everywhere. Previous owners of the estate include Teddy Roosevelt, Arturo Toscanini, and Mark Twain; now it's managed by the city, which charges no admission on weekdays.

DIVERSIONS | THE LOWDOWN

Getting high... Make your way to the **Empire State Building** on Fifth Avenue at 34th Street, occupying the site of two old Astor family mansions. Call me old-fashioned, but I still prefer this 1,250-foot skyscraper to the much taller **World Trade Towers**. This is, after all, where a big gorilla held, in one gargantuan paw, a delightfully writhing Faye Wray in the 1933 flick *King Kong*. Get there early, because later on the lines wind all the way around the block. The **World Trade Towers** down in the financial district top the Empire State Building by 100 feet. These plain, white, rectangular twin giants were built between 1966 and 1976, with a wide, windy plaza skirting them. Tourists zip upward via elevator (in 58 ear-popping seconds) to the observation deck on the 107th floor of building number two.

Art where you least expect it... Not so long ago I took a shortcut through the lobby of the **Equitable Center** at 797 Seventh Avenue, never expecting to encounter two marvelous large-scale murals by Roy Lichtenstein and Thomas Hart Benton; I made myself late for an appointment admiring the latter, a sweeping paean to Jazz Age New York. The lobby is actually one of several outposts of the Whitney Museum (another one occupies the lower level of the **Philip Morris Building** at 120 Park Avenue), but the beauty part is that entrance is free. Stop into the **Church of the Ascension** on Fifth Avenue and 10th Street to take a gander at the elaborate marble altar by Augustus Saint-Gaudens and the vast altarpiece behind it, painted by John La Farge. Up the street lies another surprising free gem, the **Forbes Magazine Galleries**, housing a warren-like exhibition of eccentricities collected by the late publishing magnate Malcolm Forbes—golden panels from the ocean liner *Normandie*, 12,000 toy soldiers struggling against opponents in wonderfully detailed dioramas, delightful model yachts, antique Monopoly gameboards, and 12 glorious Fabergé eggs. And way downtown, beneath the stunning oval rotunda of the **United States Custom House** at One Bowling Green, you'll find Reginald Marsh's cheering rendering of the history of the city, commissioned by the WPA (the Depression-era Work Projects Administration).

Secret gardens... For a moment put aside any notions of picnicking in Central Park, and instead imagine yourself coming upon a green place full of flowers and bees where it ought not to be—for instance, at Houston Street and Second Avenue in the lower East Village. Houston Street is blighted there, and nearby the Bowery begins, known for its boozy bums (these days we call them streetpeople). But in the **Liz Christy Garden** you can sit on a wooden bench amid rose bushes and snapdragons and feel apart from the city, fantasizing yourself in Stratford, England, or York. It's the work of a marvelous group of urban pioneers called the **Green Guerillas**, who make little patches of earth bloom all over town; they also have delightful gardens on **W. 89th Street** between Columbus and Amsterdam avenues and on **W. 48th Street** between Ninth and Tenth avenues. **Hudson River Park**, just north of the World Financial Center, has the unbeatable benefit of fronting directly onto the Hudson River; on weekends people jog or blade down to this park along a concrete path that starts on the riverfront near Christopher Street, where they play volleyball, drink bottled water, then strip down to teeny-weeny bathing suits (at least the gay men do) to soak up a few rays. **City Hall Park** (lower Broadway, at Fulton Street and Park Row) is entirely more demure, frequented by lunching secretaries during the workweek, but almost no one on the weekends. **Clement Clark Moore Park** on W. 22nd Street brightens up Chelsea, and happens to lie just across the street from the **Empire Diner** (see Dining). Up on the West Side, you can take a moment to smell the natural perfume at the **W. 91st Street Flower Garden**, along the esplanade in **Riverside Park**. In springtime, I have often contemplated jumping the wrought-iron fence of the **Sheridan Square Viewing Garden** (on W. 4th Street at Barrow Street); instead I content myself by wending my way back behind the church of **St. Luke's in the Field** (Hudson and Grove streets) to its private garden (behave circumspectly and no one should mind your intrusion). Summertime brings a rich, peonied hush to this place. The **Vale of Cashmere** in Brooklyn's **Prospect Park** is where I go for rhododendrons, blooming in the late springtime in a deep valley much cherished and manicured by park volunteers. At nighttime it's a strut for gay hookers—don't they have taste!

The commute... Every day, millions commute in from the environs, and the experience is well worth sampling, though not at rush hour. Besides, you get to begin your

THE LOWDOWN | DIVERSIONS

excursion at **Grand Central Terminal** (E. 42nd Street and Park Avenue); of course, you could go to Long Island or New Jersey from the concrete barnlike **Pennsylvania Station**, but that place is just no fun. Grand Central, however, is an urban epiphany, with a vast main concourse 275 feet long, 120 feet wide, and 125 feet high; the clock in the center is the city's prime rendezvous point. The facade is part Art Nouveau, part Viennese Secessionist, and an even bigger part Beaux Arts, with the whole colossal hulk of the building lying over a cavernous train shed with 10 unique loop tunnels, sending inbound trains right back out again. (Technically it's not a station but a terminal, at the end of numerous lines.) The terminal, which opened in 1913 and has a "kissing gallery" at its western end for farewell embraces, was described in a 1937 radio broadcast as the "crossroads of a million private lives! Gigantic stage on which are played a thousand dramas daily."

Utter childishness... Kids must have a special kind of radar for **F.A.O. Schwarz** (see Shopping); whenever they pass near the renowned toy store (as seen in the movies *Big* and *Home Alone 2*), they've got to go in, entering via a veritable zoo of stuffed animals. There are real zoos in the metropolitan area too, or rather Wildlife Conservation Centers, as the correct term is these days: the **Central Park Wildlife Center** at the southeast corner of Central Park, and especially for kids, the nearby **Tisch Children's Zoo**, and Brooklyn's **Prospect Park Wildlife Center**, which used to be such a decrepit old place that once plotted a mystery novel that began with the finding of a corpse there. It has since been beautifully renovated with children in mind, and just southeast of it there's a vintage carousel that still works, with dashing horses from Coney Island. The **Bronx Zoo** is something of a schlep from Manhattan, though it can be reached via subway. Its 4,000 animals live in naturalistic environments spread over 265 acres—younger kids may find it's too much to walk. But they can ride camels, cruise over 38-acre Wild Asia on a monorail, spy on nocturnal animals in the World of Darkness display, and walk through Jungle World, a tropical rain forest environment. In Central Park, marionettes cavort at the **Swedish Cottage Theatre**, and the **Conservatory Garden** (Fifth Avenue and 105th Street) has a delightful statue of Mary and

Dickon (from *The Secret Garden* by Frances Hodgson Burnett) standing over a lily pond. But frankly, it's the long-extinct creatures at the **American Museum of Natural History** that thrill young ones most. This world-famous repository of fossils, minerals, and anthropological material just refurbished its two spectacular dinosaur halls, which hold wonders like a 65-million-year-old T-Rex skeleton. Mechanized skulls of Triceratops and Anatotitan demonstrate how the behemoths chewed, and at computerized video **Lifeline Stations** kids can time-travel to three ages when the dinosaurs lived, viewing what their home turf looked like. Downstairs in the Teddy Roosevelt Rotunda there's a five-story-high cast of Barosaurus. The **Naturemax** theater here shows films on a giant IMAX screen. But what I really love here are the extraordinarily detailed dioramas in which stuffed grizzlies and gorillas and gnus pose like flies trapped in amber, their entire ecosystems lovingly recreated. Sure beats studying this stuff in science class.

Must-sees for second-time visitors from Peoria... Sorry to be prescriptive, but there really are a few must-see sights in New York. Foremost of these is the **Brooklyn Bridge**, designed by John Roebling, whose toes were crushed by a ferryboat while he was surveying along the waterfront. He died of tetanus a few days later, and it was left to his son, George Washington Roebling, to oversee the building of the great bridge. The Brooklyn Bridge lies south of the Williamsburg and Manhattan bridges, closest to the East River's confluence with New York Harbor. A long ramp near City Hall in lower Manhattan provides access to the pedestrian walkway, perhaps the city's finest promenade of all. It will take you less than an hour to cross the bridge, stopping often to take in the exquisite views. When you reach the Brooklyn side, turn right on Cadman Plaza West, and right again on handsome Clark Street to reach the **Brooklyn Heights Promenade**, cantilevered over the Brooklyn-Queens Expressway. Here you can see the great bridge you just traversed, the spires of downtown, and the harbor in all their splendor. At the very heart of midtown Manhattan lies 21-acre **Rockefeller Center**, a virtual city-within-a-city, composed of 18 office buildings, two shopping concourses, Radio City Music Hall, the Channel Gardens, and the glorious Lower Plaza, where skaters glide beneath a brilliant golden statue of Prometheus, and the flags of U.N. member nations fly. The whole sweeping complex was the brainchild of John D. Rockefeller, who built the center during the Great Depression. The Art Deco, 70-story **GE Building**, formerly the home of RCA, fronts on Rockefeller Plaza, which runs between West 48th and 51st streets; this is where the the holiday season begins with the raising and lighting of the city's colossal Christmas tree. Down the block, on Sixth Avenue, marvelously sleek and neon-lit **Radio City Music Hall** celebrates the season on into January with its famous *Christmas Spectacular*, in which cartoon characters romp and the Rockettes kick high. (You can tour both Radio City and the NBC studios in the GE Building, or stop by the information booth at the east entrance of the GE Building to get Rockefeller Center walking tour brochures.) On Fifth Avenue at 82nd Street lies the magnificent **Metropolitan Museum of Art**, the largest museum in the U.S. and the fourth largest in the world: The little aluminum button that proclaims you paid to enter the Met is a true badge of Manhattan. If there's a snowstorm or a hurricane on the way, you might find this museum empty; otherwise there's always a crowd, even during Friday and Saturday evening hours. The **United Nations Center**, which presides over the East River between 42nd and 49th streets, remains a striking complex. Tours depart from the north entrance, where there's an excellent gift shop, and a lovely garden wraps around the U.N., with a half-mile esplanade overlooking the East River. Downtown's premier attraction is the **New York Stock Exchange** on Wall Street between New and Broad streets. George Post designed the building's colonnaded facade in 1903; to the left is a modern addition, where you can enter for an interesting trip to the visitor's gallery above the frenzied trading floor. **Lincoln Center** lies on on a 15-acre site on Columbus Avenue between West 62nd and 65th streets. Opened in 1962, it includes **Avery Fisher Hall**, where the New York Philharmonic performs, the **Metropolitan Opera House**, the **Vivian Beaumont and Mitzi E. Newhouse Theatres**, and the **New York State Theatre**, home to the New York City Ballet and School of American Ballet (see Entertainment). Catching a performance at one of these beauty spots is well-nigh mandatory; even when the major companies are on break, artistic activity never lulls. Even if you don't get a ticket for a performance, stroll through the wide plaza, where there's a cafe and a reflecting pool surrounding a statue by Henry Moore. At dusk, as well-dressed crowds swarm towards brightly lit lobbies, it's magical indeed.

The Index

Abyssinian Baptist Church. Everybody's favorite Sunday morning gospel service, up in Harlem.... *Tel 212/862–7474. 132 W. 138th St., 2/3 train to 135th St. Sun service at 11am. Donation suggested.* **(see p. 107)**

Alternative Museum. Avant-garde art in SoHo.... *Tel 212/966–4444. 594 Broadway, E/F train to Prince St., 6 train to Spring St. Open Tues–Sat 11–6. Donation suggested.* **(see p. 95)**

American Museum of Immigration (Statue of Liberty and Ellis Island). Reached by ferries that depart from Battery Park and Liberty Park in New Jersey.... *Tel 212/363–3200; ferry information 212/269–5755. Open daily 9:30–5 (until 7 in summer), first ferry departs 9:15. Admission charged.* **(see pp. 95, 96)**

American Museum of Natural History. The last word in rocks, fish, mammals, birds, and bones—plus knock-out dinos.... *Tel 212/769–5100. Central Park West at 79th St., B/C train to 81st St. Open Sun–Thur 10–5:45, Fri–Sat 10–8:45. Donation suggested.* **(see p. 113)**

American Museum of the Moving Image. An interesting museum all about the movies, located on the site of Paramount Pictures' original New York home.... *Tel 718/784–0077. 36—01 35th Ave., Astoria, Queens, R/G train* to *Steinway St. Open Tues–Fri 12–5, Sat–Sun 11–6. Admission charged.* **(see p. 103)**

Apollo Theatre. The Harlem Jazz Age landmark, reopened in 1978, with popular amateur nights on Wednesdays.... *Tel 212/749–5838. 253 W. 125th St., 2/3 train to 125th St. Call for schedule. Admission charged.* **(see p. 106)**

Bronx Zoo. Largest city zoo in the U.S.... *Tel 718/367–1010. 185th St. and Southern Blvd., 2 train to Pelham Parkway, Metro North to Fordham Rd. (then Bx9 bus), or BxM11 Liberty Line bus (tel 212/652–8400). Open daily 10–5. Admission charged (pay what you wish Wed).*
(see p. 112)

Brooklyn Botanical Garden. Fifty acres of flora in the heart of Brooklyn.... *Tel 718/622–4433. 100 Washington Ave., D train to Prospect Park. Open Tues–Fri 8–6, Sat–Sun 10–6 (closes at 4:30 Oct–Mar). Admission free.* **(see p. 109)**

Castle Clinton National Monument. A fort, then immigrant processing center, then music hall—but now an historical museum and ticket booth for Statue of Liberty and Ellis Island trips.... *Tel 212/344–7220. Battery Park at Broadway, 1/9 train to South Ferry, N/R to Whitehall St. Open daily 9–5, closed Jan–Feb. Admission free.* **(see p. 96)**

Central Park. 840 green acres in the heart of Manhattan; the visitors center is at the Dairy, midpark at 65th St.... *Tel 212/794–6564. For information on park events and walking tours call 800/201–PARK.* **(see p. 104)**

Central Park Wildlife Conservation Center. Beautiful though small zoo right in Central Park.... *Tel 212/861–6030. 5th Ave. at 64th St., N/R train to 5th Ave. Open Mon–Fri 10–5, Sat–Sun 10:30–5:30. Admission charged.*
(see p. 112)

Circle Line. Circumnavigations of the island of Manhattan, a city classic.... *Tel 212/563–3200. Pier 83 at W. 42nd St., 1/2/3/9/7/S to Times Square, or A/C/E to Port Authority. Call for schedule. Admission charged.* **(see p. 108)**

The Cloisters. The Metropolitan Museum of Art's Fort Tryon branch, given over to medieval art.... *Tel 212/923–3700.*

Fort Tryon Park, A train to 190th St. Open Tues–Sun 9:30–4:45 (until 5:15 Mar–Oct). Admission charged.

(see p. 94)

Cooper-Hewitt National Design Museum. The decorative arts in Andrew Carnegie's uptown mansion.... Tel 212/849–8420. 2 E. 91st St., 4/5/6 train to 86th or 96th St. Open Tues 10–9, Wed–Sat 10–5, Sun 12–5. Admission charged. **(see p. 94)**

Dia Center for the Arts. Contemporary art studio/museum in West Chelsea digs.... Tel 212/989–5912. 548 W. 22nd St., C/E train to 23rd St. Open Thur–Sun 12–6, closed July–Aug. Donation suggested. **(see p. 95)**

Ellis Island. See **American Museum of Immigration**, above.

Empire State Building. Glassed-in observation deck on the 102nd floor, open-air on the 86th.... Tel 212/736–3100. 5th Ave. and 34th St., 4/5/6 train to 33rd St. or B/D/F/N/R/Q to 34th St. Open daily 9:30–midnight. Admission charged.

(see pp. 98, 110)

Forbes Magazine Galleries. Toy soldiers, model yachts, Monopoly gameboards, and other collectibles.... Tel 212/206–5549. 62 5th Ave., 4/5/6/N/R train to Union Square. Open Tues–Sat 10–4. Admission free. **(see p. 110)**

Frick Collection. A turn-of-the-century palace on Fifth Avenue containing gems by the likes of Gainsborough, Turner, Titian, and Whistler.... Tel 212/288–0700. 1 E. 70th St., 6 train to 68th St. Open Tues–Sat 10–6, Sun 1–6. Admission charged.

(see pp. 93, 94)

Guggenheim Museum. Frank Lloyd Wright's ziggurat, marvelous special exhibits, and lots of contemporary old favorites.... Tel 212/423–3500. 1071 5th Ave., 4/5/6 train to 86th St. Open 10–6 (until 8 Fri and Sat), closed Thur. Admission charged (pay what you wish after 6pm on Fri). **(see p. 95)**

Guggenheim Museum SoHo. Downtown outpost of famed Museum Mile star, with a rotating exhibit schedule.... Tel 212/423–3500. 575 Broadway, N/R train to Prince St. Open 11–6 (until 8 on Sat), closed Mon–Tues. Admission charged. **(see p. 95)**

Hamilton Grange National Memorial. A fine yellow clapboard house once occupied by Alexander Hamilton, in the distinguished Hamilton Terrace neighborhood of Harlem.... *Tel 212/283–5154. 287 Convent Ave., A/C/D train to 145th St. Open Wed–Sun 9–5. Admission free.*

(see p. 107)

Harlem Spirituals, Inc. Gospel, jazz, soul food, and sightseeing tours up in Harlem....*Tel 212/391–0990. 690 8th Ave., 1/2/3/9/7/S to Times Square. Call for schedule. Admission charged.* **(see p. 106)**

Harlem Your Way! Tours Unlimited. Walking tours of Harlem, meeting at a turn-of-the-century rowhouse.... *Tel 212/ 690–1687. 129 W. 130th St., 2/3 train to 125th St. Call for schedule. Admission charged.* **(see p. 106)**

Heritage Trails of New York. Walking tour brochures of lower Manhattan, available at the visitors information center at Federal Hall National Memorial.... *Tel 888/487–2457. 26 Wall St., 2/3/4/5 train to Wall St. Open weekdays 9–5. Admission free.* **(see p. 91)**

International Center of Photography. Rotating photographic exhibits and an interesting permanent collection.... *Tel 212/860–1777. 1130 5th Ave., 4/5/6 train to 96th St. Midtown branch: Tel 212/768–4680. 1133 6th Ave., 1/2/3/7/9/N/R to Times Square. Open 11–6 (until 8 Tues), closed Mon. Admission charged.* **(see p. 94)**

Intrepid Sea–Air–Space Museum. A great World War II aircraft carrier displays its gun turrets, batteries, hangers, and fighter bombers.... *Tel 212/245–0072. Pier 86, W. 46th St. at 12th Ave., A/C/E train to 42nd St. Open Wed–Sun 10–5. Admission charged.* **(see p. 107)**

Lower East Side Tenement Museum. An immigrant walk-up displaying life as poor, ethnic New York lived it at the turn of the century.... *Tel 212/431–0233. 90 Orchard St., F train to Delancey St., J/M to Essex St. Open Tues–Fri 11–4, Sun 12–5. Donation suggested.* **(see p. 96)**

Metropolitan Museum of Art. The big house, in terms of NYC art.... *Tel 212/879–5500. 5th Ave. at 82nd St., 4/5/6 train* to 86th St. Open 9:30–5:15 (until 8:45 Fri–Sat), closed Mon. Admission charged.   **(see pp. 93, 104, 114)**

El Museo del Barrio. Hispanic art, with a Puerto Rican emphasis.... Tel 212/831–7272. 1230 5th Ave., 6 train to 103rd St. Open Wed–Sun 11–5. Donation suggested.
(see p. 93)

Museum of Jewish Heritage: A Living Memorial to the Holocaust. Manhattan's newest museum, and its most moving.... Tel 212/968–1800. 18 First Place, at West St. and Battery Place, 1/9 train to Cortlandt St. Open Sun–Wed 9–5, Thur 9–8, Fri 9–2. Admission charged.   **(see p. 96)**

Museum of Modern Art. The world gone abstract, in masterworks; nice Garden Cafe and lobby bookstore; exquisite Sculpture Garden.... Tel 212/708–9480. 11 W. 53rd St., E/F train to 5th Ave. Open Sat–Tues and Thurs 10:30–6, Fri 10:30–8:30. Admission charged.   **(see p. 94)**

Museum of Television and Radio. Displays and thousands of vintage shows on tape.... Tel 212/621–6600. 25 W. 52nd St., E/F train to 5th Ave. Open 12–6 (until 8 Thur), closed Mon. Admission charged.   **(see p. 103)**

Museum of the City of New York. Famed NYC interiors, vintage firefighting equipment, toys, theatrical memorabilia, and more.... Tel 212/534–1672. 5th Ave. at 103rd St., 6 train to 103rd St. Open Wed–Sat 10–5, Sun 1–5. Admission charged.   **(see p. 94)**

New Museum of Contemporary Art. Videos, installations, and exhibitions of artists at work now in the city.... Tel 212/219–1355. 583 Broadway., E/F train to Broadway–Lafayette, 6 to Spring St. Open 12–6 (until 8 Sat), closed Mon–Tues. Admission charged.   **(see p. 95)**

New York Botanical Garden. 250-acre botanical park and renowned horticultural research center.... Tel 718/817–8700. 100th St. and Southern Blvd, the Bronx, Metro North from Grand Central to Botanical Gardens station. Open 8–6 (until 7 Apr–Oct), closed Mon. Admission free. **(see p. 109)**

New York Public Library. The great research library on Fifth

THE INDEX | DIVERSIONS

Avenue, where you read "between the lions".... *Tel 212/340–0849. 5th Ave. at 41st St, B/D/F/7 train to 42nd St. Open Mon and Thur–Sat 10–6, Tues–Wed 11–7:30. Admission free.* **(see pp. 98, 99, 102)**

New York Stock Exchange Center. Down on Wall Street, of course, with displays explaining how the market works, how to read a stock table, etc. Plus an Exchange viewing gallery.... *Tel 212/656–5168. 20 Broad St., 2/3 train to Wall St. Open Mon–Fri 9:15–3:30. Admission free.*
(see p. 114)

Nuyorican Poets Cafe. East Village poetry haunt.... *Tel 212/505–8183. 236 E. 3rd St., F train to 2nd Ave. Call for changing schedule. Admission charged.* **(see p. 97)**

Petrel. A sleek 1938 racing yacht sailed by John F. Kennedy, offering daytime and sunset cruises.... *Tel 212/825–1976. Battery Park, R train to Battery Park, 4/5/6 to Bowling Green, 1 to South Ferry. Mid-May–mid-Oct. Admission charged.* **(see p. 108)**

Poets House. A poetry library in SoHo.... *Tel 212/431–7920. 72 Spring St., N/R train to Prince St., 6 to Spring St. Open Tues–Fri 11–7, Sat 11–4, closed Sun–Mon. Admission free.*
(see p. 97)

Prospect Park. Olmsted and Vaux's big Brooklyn park, and a real beauty.... *Tel 718/788–0055. Bounded by Eastern Parkway, Flatbush Ave., Parkside Ave., and Prospect Park West; 2/3/4 train to Grand Army Plaza, F to 15th St./Prospect Park, D/Q to Prospect Park.* **(see pp. 104, 111)**

Prospect Park Wildlife Center. A children's zoo grows in Brooklyn.... *Tel 718/399–7339. Prospect Park, Willink Entrance (off Flatbush Ave.), B/D/Q train to Prospect Park. Open Mon–Fri 10–5, Sat–Sun 10–5:30. Admission charged.* **(see p. 112)**

Radio City Music Hall. 6,000 seats, gorgeous Art Deco flourishes, and the Rockettes. Tours available.... *Tel 212/632–4041. 6th Ave. at 50th St., B/D/F train to Rockefeller Center. Call for schedule. Admission charged.* **(see p. 114)**

Russian and Turkish Baths. An old-fashioned hothouse, where you can drink borscht, take wet or dry heat, and chill in a Swedish shower. Swimming suits required, communal setting.... *Tel 212/674–9250. 268 E. 10th St., 6 train to Astor Pl. Open 9–10 (Mon, Tues, Fri, and Sat coed; Thur and Sun men only, Wed women only). Admission charged.*
(see p. 100)

Schomburg Center for Research in Black Culture. Programs, exhibitions, and library facilities for scholars—all on black history and culture.... *Tel 212/491–2265. 515 Malcolm X Blvd. (Lenox Ave.), 2/3 train to 135th St. Open Mon–Wed 12–8, Thur–Sat 10–6, Sun 1–5. Admission free.*
(see p. 106)

South Street Seaport. Historic ships to tour, antique buildings to stroll by, cobblestones beneath your feet.... *Tel 212/748–8600. 12 Fulton St., 2/3/4/5 train to Fulton St. Open 10–6 (Thur until 8). Admission charged.*
(see pp. 91, 108)

Spirit Cruises. Lunch, brunch, cocktail, dinner, and moonlight cruises around the island; somewhat more intimate than the Circle Line.... *Tel 212/727–7735. Pier 62 in Chelsea, A/C/E train to W. 23rd St. Call for schedule. Admission charged.*
(see p. 108)

St. Marks Church-in-the-Bowery. Historic East Village church with a long-running poetry program.... *Tel 212/674–0910. 131 E. 10th St., 6 train to Astor Pl. Admission charged to poetry readings.* **(see pp. 97, 100)**

Statue of Liberty. See **American Museum of Immigration**, above.

Swedish Cottage Theatre. Marionette theater in Central Park.... *Tel 212/988–9093. Mid-park at 81st St., B/C train to 81st St. Performances Tues–Fri 10:30 or noon, Sat noon or 3pm, reservations required. Admission charged.*
(see p. 112)

Tisch Children's Zoo in Central Park. It's child-friendly, it's environmentally correct, and it's great fun.... *Tel 212/861-6030. 5th Ave. at 64th St., N/R train to 5th Ave. Open*

DIVERSIONS | THE INDEX

Mon–Fri 10–5, Sat–Sun 10:30–5:30. Admission charged.
(see pp. 105, 112)

United Nations Center. Le Corbusier's Secretariat and General Assembly buildings, overlooking the East River. Tours available.... *Tel 212/963–7713. 1st Ave. between 42nd and 48th Sts., 4/5/6/7/S train to Grand Central. Open 9:15–4:45. Admission charged for tours.* **(see p. 114)**

Whitney Museum of American Art. Contemporary American specialist.... *Tel 212/570–3600. 945 Madison Ave., 6 train to 77th St. Open Wed, Fri–Sun 11–6, Thur 1–8. Admission charged.* **(see p. 95)**

World Trade Center. Observations of New York from the 107th floor deck of building number two.... *Tel 212/435–4170. W. Church, Vesey, and Liberty Sts.; 1/9 train to Cortlandt St. Open 9am–9:30pm. Admission charged.* **(see p. 91)**

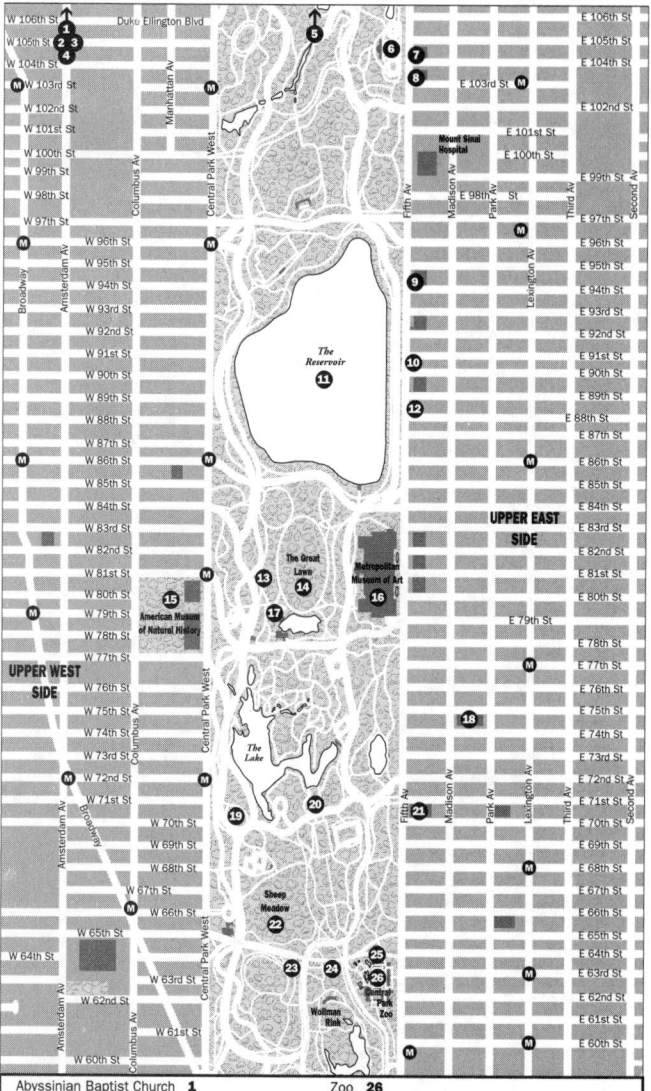

Uptown Diversions

Abyssinian Baptist Church **1**
American Museum of Natural History **15**
Apollo Theatre **3**
Central Park
  Bethesda Terrace **20**
  Carousel **23**
  Conservatory Gardens **6**
  Dairy **24**
  Delacorte Theatre **17**
  Great Lawn **14**
  Jackie O. Reservoir **11**
  Sheep Meadow **22**
  Strawberry Fields **19**
  Swedish Cottage **13**
  Tisch Children's Zoo **25**

Zoo **26**
The Cloisters **4**
Cooper/Hewitt National Design Museum **10**
El Museo del Barrio **7**
Frick Collection **21**
Guggenheim Museum **12**
Hamilton Grange National Monument **2**
International Center of Photography **9**
Metropolitan Museum of Art **16**
Museum of the City of New York **8**
Schomberg Center **5**
Whitney Museum of American Art **18**

Midtown Diversions

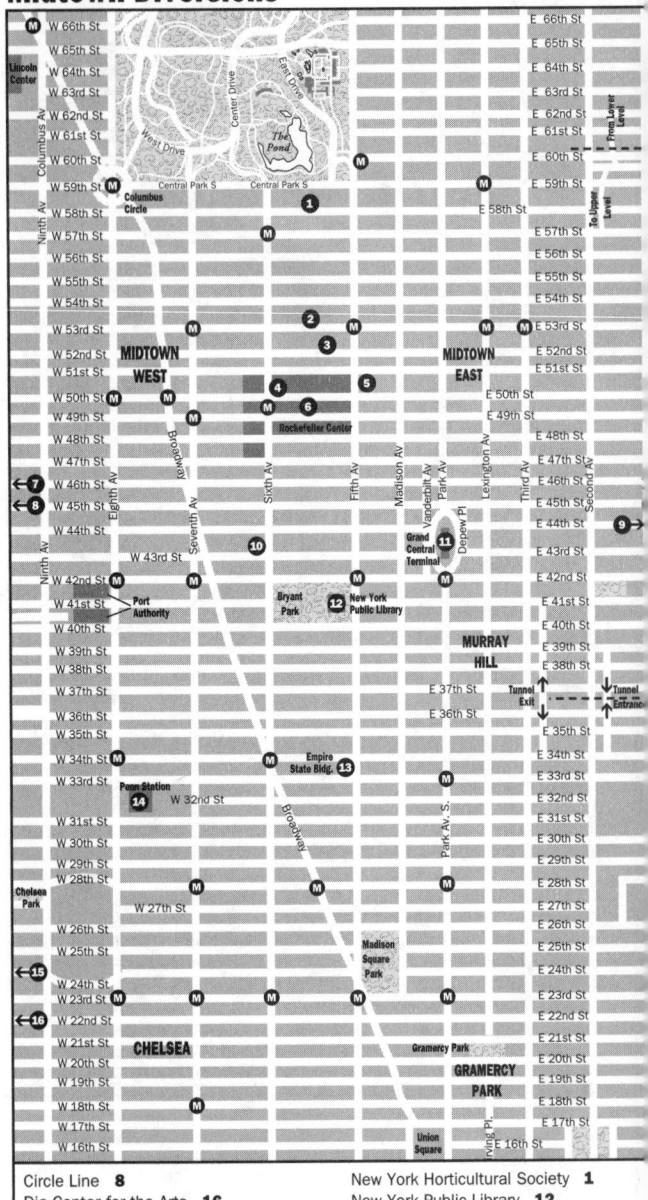

Circle Line **8**
Dia Center for the Arts **16**
Empire State Building **13**
Grand Central Station **11**
International Center of Photography **10**
Intrepid Sea-Air-Space Museum **7**
MoMA **2**
Museum of Television & Radio **3**

New York Horticultural Society **1**
New York Public Library **12**
Pennsylvania Station **14**
Radio City Music Hall **4**
Rockefeller Center **6**
St. Patrick's Cathedral **5**
Spirit Cruises **15**
United Nations **9**

Downtown Diversions

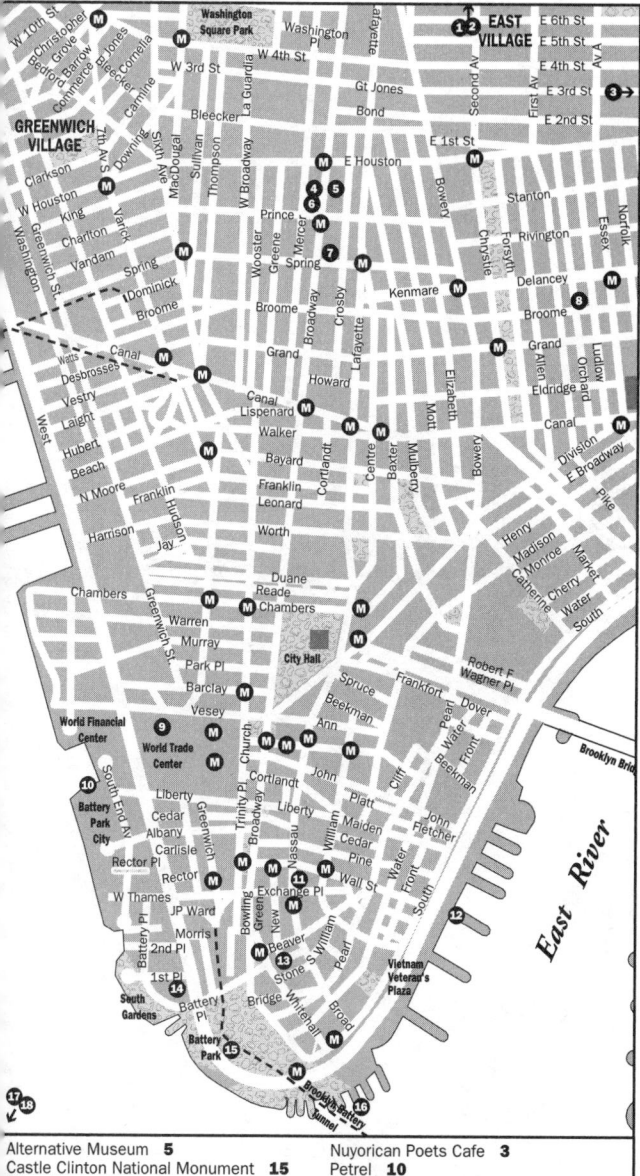

getting

4

outside

Despite rumors
that Americans
are returning to
their La-Z-Boy
recliners in legion
numbers, that's
one trend New

Yorkers aren't buying. Workaholics chained to their desks for 10-hour days strive to keep in shape whenever they can grab an hour to run on busy streets or ply the Stairmasters in sleek health clubs, watching MTV on monitors above. The exercise obsession is further fueled by the need to stay beautiful and young forever in this very vain city, not to mention the desperate hope of meeting a cute, trim mate at the Nautilus machine. The city boasts parks aplenty for pick-up softball games, running, cycling, and blading (all pursued with hyperintensity, of course). Chief among them is Central Park, of course, but long skinny Riverside Park on the West Side and Prospect Park in Brooklyn are also top sports spots.

The Lowdown

Born to run... The extraordinary popularity of the New York City Marathon every November is a testament to New Yorkers' penchant for running, which they pursue in heavy traffic, in fair or foul weather, on hard, uneven surfaces, and despite never-ending streetside diversions. Serious runners join the **New York Road Runner's Club** (tel 212/860–4455), which sponsors a Central Park Safety Patrol, a year-long schedule of races, and clinics in all five boroughs (including marathon prep and a New Year's Eve run), and more loosely organized Central Park runs at 6:30pm weekdays, and at 10am on weekends (meet at club headquarters, 9 E. 89th Street, a block from the 90th Street entrance to Central Park). You see runners puffing their way around just about every park in the city, from the Battery to Washington Square to Carl Schurz on the Upper East Side. But without a doubt, the best place to run in Manhattan is **Central Park**, where you can chalk up distances; the Outer Loop of the park's circular drive is 7.02 miles, the Middle Loop 4.04 miles (enter the park at 72nd Street and follow the drive around the south end of the park), and the soft-surface path around the Reservoir, 1.57 miles. Safety can be an issue here; unaccompanied women should run only at peak times and stay on the path. **Riverside Park** lines the Hudson River for 4 miles beginning at West 72nd Street, providing knock-out views for runners; there's also a quarter-mile, open-air track near the 72nd Street entrance. A jogging path along the **East River** can be caught near Sutton Place and followed all the way north to the mayor's digs at Gracie Mansion. Out in Brooklyn's **Prospect Park** (take the 2 or 3 subway train to Grand Army Plaza) is a gem of a landscape designed by the same 19th-century team who laid out Central Park. The big interior circuit passes shady woods and a colony of swans on the Lullwater, running approximately 3.5 miles in all. The New York dream of creating a narrow belt of parkland all around Manhattan is far from being realized, but a start has been made between **Hudson River Park** and the fenced-off piers at the foot of Christopher Street in the West Village; there's little green, but a 2-mile running/skating/biking path assumes the air of a carnival on sunny afternoons.

A bicycle built for one... Bikes can be rented for cruises through Central Park at the **Loeb Boathouse** (near W. 74th St., tel 212/861–4637), but you'll get equipment in better condition from **Metro Bicycles** (midtown shop at 360 W. 47th St., tel 212/581-4500, and six other locations around town). Wear a helmet, ride on the right with traffic, clearly claim space in a lane as opposed to riding on the side of the street where you can get hammered by opening car doors—and watch out for pedestrians. Most of the running paths mentioned above, with the exception of the reservoir in Central Park, are fine for reasonably carefree biking. But for some wild and woolly urban treks, try the **Lafayette Street bike lane**, which runs north only from Houston Street to 14th Street at Union Square; cross the East River on the **Brooklyn Bridge bike lane**, a steep but scenic 1-miler; catch the bike lane just north of South Street Seaport that leads through parking lots **under the FDR Drive** and some monster puddles; or take the aerial tramway at E. 60th Street to Roosevelt Island and then bike through **Lighthouse Park**, watching for speed bumps as you go. If you've got several hours, take a tour to the outer boroughs—or at least Brooklyn—cruising along the city's oldest dedicated bicycle path, which accompanies **Ocean Parkway** from Prospect Park's Church Avenue entrance all the way to Coney Island; study the shifting demographics of this once-grand boulevard as you pedal along. It's okay to take bicycles on the subway, but if you're headed farther afield you'll need to get a pass for trips on the Long Island, New Jersey

Transit, and Metro North railroads. The **New York City Cycle Club** (tel 212/886–4545) sponsors group rides and training clinics, while the **Century Road Club Association** (tel 212/222–8062) is particularly keen on racing. The **Central Park Bicycle Tour** (tel 212/541–8759) includes bike rental in the cost of a two–hour escorted cruise around the park.

Pounding the pavement... **Fifth Avenue** and **Broadway** are virtual yellow brick roads, fine especially on Sundays for hikes all the way from the south end of Central Park to downtown's Battery (I've done this walk in a little over two hours—the great thing about walking in New York is that there's so much to see en route, you forget how far you've tramped). **Upper Broadway** takes you right through the fascinating heart of the Upper West Side, and there's nothing prettier than a springtime ramble up the East Side's **Park Avenue**, when banks of flowers bloom in the neatly planted median strip and you can peer under canopies into the lobbies of luxury co-ops. **Riverside Park** has some wonderful riverview promenades, both in the park and along shady **Riverside Drive**. If you want to be led by the hand, not to mention edified by a trivia-nut tour guide (these folks could score big on "Jeopardy!"), check out the walking tours offered by the **92nd Street YMHA** (1395 Lexington Ave., tel 212/ 996–1100), which include such pleasures as Staten Island ferryboat rides, picnic hikes along the Old Croton Aqueduct Trailway, and brunch tours of Battery Park City. The **Urban Park Rangers** (tel 212/427–4040) know the city's parks like the backs of their hands, and take groups for jaunts absolutely free of charge.

For the birds... It's hard to believe that green wilderness exists anyplace near Manhattan, but it's there to rejuvenate walkers whenever the concrete canyons of the city threaten to close in. Bring a pair of binoculars so you can watch the birds while trailblazing in Central Park's prime patch of forest, the **Ramble**, where the Urban Park Rangers lead nature walks on Sundays at 9am, and the **New York Audubon Society** (tel 212/691–7483) organizes early-morning birdwatches in the spring and fall (believe it or not, Manhattan's located on a major North American migration flyway, and birders here make some spectacular sightings). If birding is your passion, take the upper promenade in **Riverside Park** between W. 114th and W. 120th streets for more bird sightings in the densely wooded sanctuary below. Nature and solitude await along the **Kazimiroff Nature Trail** at Pelham Bay Park (in the Bronx, accessible from the Hutchinson River Pkwy., tel 718/548–7070), or in the 14.5-square-mile birder's paradise of **Jamaica Bay Wildlife Preserve** in Queens (Exit 17, Belt Pkwy. or A train to Broad Channel, tel 718/474–0613).

Water, water everywhere... Watching the city glide by from the deck of a sightseeing tour boat (see Diversions) is a great way to feel the sun on your face and the breeze ripple through your hair. But for a more interactive experience, rent a rowboat from Central Park's **Loeb Boathouse** (near W. 74th St., tel 212/517–2233, spring through fall). Liliputian-style boating takes over the **Conservatory Water** in Central Park (also called the Boat Pond, east side of the park

Tour Time

"New Jersey is on the other side of the Hudson River." If this information is new to you, you might benefit from a stint aboard the bright red double-decker buses run by New York Apple Tour (tel 800/876–9868). They stop at major sights every fifteen minutes, letting visitors disembark, look around, and then climb back on the next Apple bus that comes along. New York Apple tours offer three itineraries: uptown and Harlem, downtown, or full–city, all conducted in Spanish, Japanese, German, English, Italian, and French. Gray Line (tel 212/397–2600) runs similar double–decker city tours; these two are the La-Z-Boy Recliners among NYC tours. You'll see and learn a lot more if you're willing to get off your duff and walk. Citywalks (tel 212/989–2456) offers weekend walking tours of historic districts like Greenwich Village, Chinatown, Soho, and Little Italy; call for a schedule. The Municipal Art Society (tel 212/439–1049) leads some fascinating tours, too, including one of Grand Central Station every Wednesday at 12:30, meeting at the east end of the main concourse (admission is free, but a hat is passed afterwards).

MANHATTAN | GETTING OUTSIDE

near West 74th street) on weekends, when enthusiasts with transistor-operated model boats (some so fancy that they cost an upwards of $3,000) hold their own regattas. You can launch a paper boat if you want, but remember:

If you're racing, international yachting rules are staunchly upheld. The 20-boat **Sheepshead Bay fishing fleet** in Brooklyn takes old salts out sightseeing or fishing for flounder, fluke, snapper, and night-time blue fishing in New York Harbor; half-day trips start at the Sheepshead Bay piers (D train to Sheepshead Bay) beginning at 8am, 10am, and 1pm; full-day trips leave at 6 and 7am, and nighttime excursions at 7pm; just show up at the dock. You can rent or bring your own bait and rods. The crowd this fleet attracts is inclined to embibe heavily, and resembles the cast of *Con Air*. City Island, which hugs the east coast of the Bronx, is the fishing and sailing capital of New York; it's just a mile and a half long, but about as close to Nantucket as you can get without leaving the five boroughs. If you have a car, you can reach it via the City Island drawbridge from Pelham Bay Park. Once there, you can watch a regatta, fish for porgies and flounder on the *Apache* (591 City Island Ave., tel 718/885–0843), rent a motorboat at The Boat Livery (663 City Island Ave., tel 718/885–1843), or become a certified scuba diver at **Capt. Mike's Diving Services** (634 City Island Ave., tel 718/885–1588).

Buoys and gulls... If you want to see eye–to–eye with Miss Liberty, try gliding a couple of hundred feet above New York harbor with **Parasail New York** (North Cove Yacht Harbor at Battery Park City, tel 212/691–0055). Find out how it feels to be a human kite. If you get dunked, the owner promises you a new outfit.

The pick-up game... Central Park's 55-acre Great Lawn (mid-park from 81st to 85th streets), after a two–year renovation, is once more the place to find yourself a pick-up game of softball or frisbee. And the big park's carefully maintained **Heckscher Ballfields** (near W. 64th St.) are often given over to established amateur leagues, who generally don't welcome drop-ins, but can be fun to watch. (Between the Broadway show leagues, ad agency leagues, and publishing leagues, you may catch some semi-celebrities at play.) You should be able to find a game of softball at **Riverside Park**'s play area, which runs from West 101st to 111th streets, or in **Central Park**, mid-park at 98th Street. Basketball pros like Julius Erving and Chris Mullen started out in the wild, fast games played at the

W. 4th Street cages (West 4th St. and Sixth Ave.). The **North Meadow Recreation Center** in Central Park (just above W. 97th St.) sees plenty of basketball action. And down at Piers 59-62, **The Chelsea Piers Sports and Entertainment Complex** (tel 212/336–6000, one-day pass $31) has basketball and volleyball courts (the latter with sand flooring). For further information on where to find softball, basketball, hockey, soccer, and volleyball pick-up games, keep your eyes open for a copy of the freebie newspaper *Sports City*, distributed in health clubs and sports equipment stores around town.

Skating—straight up or on the rocks... Skating at the diamond-like rink at **Rockefeller Center** (E. 50th St. at Fifth Ave., lower plaza, tel 212/332–7654, open in winter) or Central Park's **Wollman Memorial Rink** (near W. 64th St., tel 212/396–1010, open winter) is like stepping into a picture postcard of New York, especially when the snow flies; there are always a few hot-doggers slicing patterns in the ice, but even if you forgot your fur muff and little pink skirt, you can stash your bags in a locker, rent skates, and give it a whirl. At the extreme uptown end of Central Park there's a more neighborhoody place to hit the ice, **Lasker Rink** (near W. 110th St. and the Harlem Meer, tel 212/396–0388, winter). **Sky Rink**, another element of the Chelsea Piers scene (tel 212/336–6100), is roomier and less show-offy, not to mention indoors and open year-round; lockers, equipment rental, and skating instruction. Open ice-hockey frays are offered, too. But enough about ice skating; let's talk about in-line skating, the sport of the moment in New York—you see Rollerbladers with briefcases stroking their way to Wall Street, sparks flying from grind plates everywhere. During the warm months, Central Park's **Wollman Rink** (see above) goes in-line, but the hot places to Rollerblade are the **Dead Road** in Central Park (mid-park from 66th to 69th streets, no boom boxes please), Central Park's **slalom course** (weekends, on the circular drive across from Tavern on the Green), alongside the dilapidated piers in the **West Village**, the 2.5-acre in-line center at **Chelsea Piers**, and the big loop in Brooklyn's **Prospect Park**, for racers. Make sure to wear safety gear; it's a cool look, anyway. In-lines can be rented at **Blades East** (160 E. 86th St., tel 212/996–1644), **Blades West** (120 W. 72nd St., tel 212/787–3911), **Alex Sports** (128 Chambers St., tel 212/964–1944), and **Third Street Skate** (207 Seventh Ave. in Brooklyn, tel 718/768–9500). For skating instruction and two indoor rinks, try the **Chelsea Piers Roller Rinks** (at Pier 61, tel 212/336–6200); for roller hockey, head up to **Stanley M. Isaacs Park** (FDR Drive from 95th to 97th streets), where there's a brand-new roller rink.

Seesaws and sandboxes... Taking your children to a playground is a way to survey the more settled aspects of the New York City scene; go with a cup of java and the paper, then install yourself on a bench. Eavesdrop on discussions of whether Heather should go to the Dalton School or Brearley, and scope out the different nannying styles of the various Jamaican, Guyanese, and Irish babysitters. The playgrounds at **Union Square Park** (E. 16th St. and Broadway), **Bleecker and Hudson streets**, **Washington Square Park** (W. 4th and MacDougal streets), **Pierrepont Park** in Brooklyn Heights (Furman St. and Columbia Heights), **Riverside Park** (at W. 91st St.—the "hippo park," nicknamed after its statues that kids clamber over—or the "dino park" at W. 97th St.), **Sutton Place** (E. 53rd St. and the FDR Drive), and at East 67th, West 85th, and East 96th streets in **Central Park** are top-of-the-line.

Courting... To swing a tennis racquet with the city skyline on the horizon, head to the **Central Park Tennis House** (mid-park, near W. 93rd St., tel 212/280–0201) where 26 courts are sprucely maintained thanks to a recent $1 million endowment from a private citizen. You must have a season permit to reserve a court, but if you stop by the tennis house in person, for $5 per person you can get a single-play ticket for an hour on any unreserved court. Weathered-faced tennis junkies of a certain age hang out there waiting for a free court, sometimes bringing a folding table to play bridge or pinochle while sitting on the park benches courtside—it's a scene. **Riverside Park** also has a set of clay courts near West 96th Street, which neighborhood volunteers maintain now that park budgets have been slashed; play is on a first-come-first-served basis. Tennis players can use the courts at a few indoor private clubs like **Crosstown Tennis** (114 W. 31st St., tel 212/947–5780), **The Tennis Club** (15 Vanderbilt Ave., over Grand Central Station, tel 212/687–3841), **Sutton**

East (488 E. 60th St., tel 212/751–3452), and **Club La Racquette** (119 W. 56th St., tel 212/245–1144); call for fees and times. But this is New York, after all—do you think New Yorkers would be content with just a white-bread sport like tennis? No way. There are 12 handball courts in **Riverside Park** (at the W. 111th St. play area), and many more in **St. Vartan's Park** (35th St. between 1st and 2nd Aves.); bocce courts at **DeWitt Clinton Park** (52nd St. between 11th and 12th Aves.) and **Robert Moses Playground** (1st Ave. between 41st and 42nd Sts.); regulation croquet/lawn bowling facilities in **Central Park** (west side near 69th St., tel 212/360–8133); and horseshoe pitching at **Battery Park** (State and South sts.) and **J.J. Murphy Park** (E. 17th St. and Avenue C).

Swimming holes in the concrete jungle... Among city pools, probably the best are the **Carmine Street Pool** (tel 212/242–5228, 7th Ave. S. and Clarkson St.) and the pool in **John Jay Park** (tel 212/794–6566, E. 77th St. and Cherokee Place), though they're crowded all summer long. A few hotels have swimming pools: the **Days Inn Hotel** (Eighth Ave. and W. 48th St., tel 212/581–7000), **Le Parker Meridien** (118 W. 57th St., tel 212/245–5000), **The Peninsula** (700 Fifth Ave., tel 212/247–2200), **Vista International** (3 World Trade Center, tel 212/938–9100), and the **U.N. Plaza** (1 United Nations Plaza, tel 212/355–3400). The centrally located **Vanderbilt YMCA** (224 E. 47th St., tel 212/756–9600) allows walk-ins as well as Vanderbilt YMCA Hotel guests (see Accommodations) to use the clean and highly chlorinated pool for $20 a day. A big indoor pool with a sundecks is part of **The Sports Center** at Chelsea Piers (at Pier 60, tel 212/336–6000), which allows day-use guests. What is more, a number of health clubs in the city have indoor and outdoor pools, like **Manhattan Plaza** (482 W. 43rd St., tel 212/563–7001), **Printing House** (421 Hudson St., tel 212/243–7600), four branches of the **Vertical Club** (tel 212/355–5100), six branches of **New York Health and Racquet Club** (tel 800/HRC–BEST), and two branches of the **New York Sports** clubs (tel 800/796–NYSC). These are particularly worth noting if you're a member of a health club back home that offers reciprocal club rights elsewhere, and I must confess, I occasionally pose as a prospective club member, take a tour of the facilities, and then talk my way into a free trial use of the pool.

Indoor fitness... You may be a pro at getting into places you're not supposed to go, but the truth is you've got to be a member to use the facilities in most New York health clubs. At some independent clubs, taking a tour with a guide from the membership department can win you a free fitness class (plus a sauna and/or steambath, if such amenities are available); if you have friends in the city, convince them to get you a guest pass (which usually costs $10 to $20) at their club; or check with your club at home to see if it has reciprocal privileges someplace in New York. The hot health clubs these days are the high tech **Reebok Sports Club/NY** (160 Columbus Ave., tel 212/362–6800) that has everything from a pool to a swimsuit spin dryer; **David Barton Gym** (552 Sixth Ave., tel 212/727–0004, 623 Broadway, tel 212/420–0507 and 30 E. 85th St., tel 212/517–7577), where the best male bodies are made; **Equinox** (five branches, tel 212/780–9100), just a good all-around club; and the westside **Printing House** (421 Hudson St., tel 212/243–7600), with its largely gay clientele, postage stamp-sized rooftop pool, and sweat sundeck. As for hotels, fitness freaks should book the **Doral Park Avenue** (70 Park Ave., tel 212/687–7050), which has a complete health facility in its Saturnalia Fitness Center (guests at the Doral Court, Doral Tuscany, and Doral Inn are welcome, as well). **The Sports Center** at Chelsea Piers (Pier 60, tel 212/336–6000) includes everything a workout requires, including cardiovascular weight training, aerobics, two tracks, and an indoor pool; day-use passes are available to out-of-towners for $31. And, joy of joys, **Crunch Fitness** (54 E. 13th St, tel 212/475–2018; 66 Greenwich St., tel 212/366–3725; 162 W. 82nd St., tel 212/875–1902; and 404 Lafayette St., tel 212/614–0120) admits one-time users for $20 a day. Exercise machines are available, but what sets Crunch apart is its fitness classes, with names like "Washboard Abs," "Brand New Butt," and "Uninhibited Funk." Crunch teachers are so top-notch that most of them develop loyal followers; but watch out, because the classes are hard. Walk-in yoga classes are available at the **Yoga Zone** (146 E. 56th St., tel 212/935–YOGA, and 138 Fifth Ave., tel 212/647–YOGA). Realign your body-mind relationship at **Integral Yoga** (227 W. 13th St., tel 212/929–0585).For Chinese martial arts, try the **Northeastern Tai Chi**

Chuan Association (163 W. 23rd St., tel 212/741–1922) or the **New York Martial Arts Center** (598 Broadway, tel 212/431–1100).

Par for the course... Call me negative, but I don't think it makes a lot of sense to come to the city to play golf. Still, if you've just gotta get in 18 holes, no matter what, top courses in the tri-state area are: **Bethpage State Park** (in Bethpage, Long Island, tel 516/249–0701) with five 18-hole courses, including the impossibly difficult Black Course; **Tamarack Golf Course** (East Brunswick, NJ, tel 908/821–8881), ranked fourth-best in the state by *Golf Digest*; and **Split Rock** (Pelham Bay Park, the Bronx, tel 718/885–1258), one of the best public courses around, even if the cops have harvested 13 bodies from the woods adjacent to the fairways in the last 10 years. The golf cages at the **Chelsea Piers Golf Club** (tel 212/336–6400, at W. 23rd St. and the Hudson River) take up an entire pier, feature a 200-yard long driving range with sheltered, heated tee-off area. The nets are suspended from computerized 155-foot-tall towers that automatically lower them when the wind kicks up.

Back in the saddle... You can go horseback riding at the **Claremont Riding Academy** (175 W. 89th St., tel 212/724–5100); experienced riders get to go out on the bridle paths in Central Park from here, cantering under arched trees and 19th-century bridges and along the reservoir.

You bowl me over... I have a friend who celebrates his birthday every year with a party at **Bowlmor Lanes** (110 University Place, tel 212/255–8188); maybe next year I can get him to try **Leisure Time** (625 Eighth Ave., tel 212/268–6909), an improbable, modern bowlatorium above the Port Authority Bus Station.

shop

5

ping

A friend told me
about a New York
City woman who
arrived for her
first therapy
session deeply
distressed. "I need

help—*I can't shop*," the woman said. "I've tried everything—Bloomingdale's, Charivari, the Lower East Side—nothing seems to work." An extreme case, of course, and possibly an apocryphal tale. But you get the idea: New Yorkers shop—over the phone, on their lunch breaks, after work, and especially on weekends, when street fairs, flea markets, and peddlers transform the city into one giant, never-ending, seductive bazaar. Visitors to the city can't help but catch the bug. Even when the dollar is strong, deals on perennial New York draws like designer clothes, jewelry and watches, art and antiques, perfume, and toys can simply seem too good to pass up. The city has 10,000 shops and boutiques, including huge, new, value-driven superstores like **Barnes & Noble Bookstores**, **Bed, Bath & Beyond**, and **Filene's Basement**. So if you're wondering what to buy here, the answer is anything you want.

Target zones

Fifth Avenue from 32nd to 57th streets is perhaps the world's most famous shopper's stroll—10,000 pass this way every day between the peak hours of 11am and 3pm. It has wide sidewalks assiduously cleaned in the morning, antique cast-iron clocks, a thrilling view up towards Central Park, and vendors selling nuts, pretzels, hot dogs, and hot watches. It also has some of the city's finest turn-of-the-century architecture, along with Rockefeller Center, the 68-story Trump Tower, and St. Patrick's Cathedral—where it might be wise to light a candle for your bank account before you start to shop. You can binge at **Fendi**, **Gianni Versace**, **Cartier**, **Christian Dior**, **Bergdorf Goodman**, or **Henri Bendel**; if not, head one long block west to Sixth Avenue, where the same 32nd-to-57th street stretch offers plenty of bargain glad rags. Fifth Avenue has been changing, due to the advent of many mass-market, mall-type retailers who target shoppers under the age of 20: the **Coca-Cola** gift shop, the **Warner Brothers Studio Store**, **Tower Records**, the **Virgin Megastore**, the **Original Levi's Store**, **Niketown** and a **Disney Studio Store**. The intersection at 57th Street has come to be known as the "Four Carats" because its corners are occupied by high-end (if not boring) jewelers **Tiffany**, **Bulgari**, **Van Cleef & Arpels**—and carrot-chomping Bugs Bunny, who appears on T-shirts and mugs at the ever-packed Warner Brothers store.

Traditionalists rue the avenue's transmogrification, but young shoppers and foreign aficionados of American kitsch don't kvetch. The task of maintaining New York's high-class shopping standards has fallen to the **Upper East Side**, especially along Madison and Lexington avenues south of 76th Street. Classy **Bloomingdale's**, at 59th Street between Lexington and Third avenues, was for many years the last word in New York department stores until the ultra-chic **Barneys** came to Madison Avenue at 61st Street, making this intersection the city's top showplace for upscale stores, with **Ann Taylor** and **Armani** in residence. Small, posh specialty shops parade on up Madison, featuring clothing introduced on fashion show runways in Paris and Milan, elegant lingerie, and shoes that could turn any Cinderella into a princess. Farther downtown near Grand Central Station, **Madison Avenue** devotes itself to buttoned-up sorts of male attire, notably classic **Brooks Brothers** and **Paul Stuart**. The Upper West Side's **Columbus Avenue**, between 80th Street and Lincoln Center, came into the fore as a hip place to shop in the eighties, when trendy retailers like **Betsey Johnson** and **Putumayo** moved in. The neighborhood has calmed down somewhat now, remaining a pleasant, not too pretentious place to shop.

    Herald Square at the intersection of Broadway and Sixth Avenue was one of the city's busiest shopping districts in the thirties and forties, starring (along with a heart-stoppingly young Natalie Wood) in the Christmastime classic *Miracle on 34th Street*. It remains at the nerve center of the city's bustling garment district, but alas, the only department store left is immense middle-class **Macy's**, where you will find a lot of the same upscale designer labels as at the posher stores (and at pretty much the same upscale prices). A rash of upscale national chain stores has lately colonized 34th Street, replacing the junky variety stores and cut-rate electronics emporiums that had clogged the arteries for the past couple of decades.

    Shopping in the bohemian **East Village** (roughly everything east of Broadway between 14th and Houston streets) is almost always a wild ride. At **Astor Place**, street vendors hawk used jeans, tapes and records, books, and lamps that look utterly beyond reconditioning. From there, head east on St. Marks Place where the shops' wares spill out onto the sidewalk—punk regalia, sacrilegious jewelry, and cocktail dresses with more peek-a-boo holes than fabric. Broadway bisects the Village, becoming the artery of the trendy **NoHo** (North of Houston) neighborhood; join the New York University students browsing among the jammed shelves at just-about-always-open **Tower Records** on 4th Street. Staid in comparison to the East, the

SHOPPING | INTRODUCTION

West Village still has rewards for shoppers, like reasonably priced shoes and hipster clothes on 8th Street between Fifth and Sixth avenues, vintage comic books arrayed on sidewalk tables along Sixth Avenue, Italian comestibles on Bleecker Street, and in the region around Sheridan Square, erotic leather goods, sex gear, condoms in all tastes and textures, and clothing stores catering to the gay male. Stroll across Houston Street to reach **SoHo**, with its turn-of-the-century cast-iron warehouses. Rediscovered by artists 20-odd years ago, SoHo has since become the display case for contemporary New York style. SoHo's art galleries (like **G.W. Einstein** for original photographs), hip designer showrooms (like **Comme des Garçons** and **J. Morgan Puett**), and remarkable furniture stores (like **Poltrona Frau**) are too good to miss. In many of the best SoHo stores the merchandise bears the stamp of the creator, not of an assembly line, so of course prices are astronomical. Or wind your way down Broadway below Spring Street, where you'll find discounters like **Canal Jeans** and the **Soho Mill Outlet**. **Downtown**, upscale Wall Streeters gravitate to the high-end shops inside the World Financial Center, and rank-and-file office workers shop the subway concourse mall below the World Trade Center or the discount stores around Nassau and Fulton streets; **Century 21** on Cortlandt Street is one of the city's best discount department stores. For exotic groceries, gaudy souvenirs, and a thick ethnic atmosphere, wander through **Little Italy** and **Chinatown**. Intrepid bargain hunters brave **Orchard Street** on the **Historic Lower East Side**, where there are some incredible buys to be found (note that shops are closed for the Saturday sabbath, but open again on Sunday).

Bargain Hunting

Thrift stores and flea markets offer good buys in the open air, and, of course, there are the devoted discounters like **Century 21**, **Daffy's**, **Loehmann's**, and **S&W**. Most clothing retailers and department stores hold big sales in August (sundresses and bathing suits), December (linens), and January (coats), and around major holidays like the Fourth of July, Columbus Day, and Presidents' Weekend (look for humongous newspaper ads with banner headlines touting "Blowout," "Midnight Madness," and "Spectacular Clearance"). The "Sales and Bargains" column in *New York* magazine offers excellent insider advice on sales at specialty stores and galleries.

Hours of business

As a rule, New York shops open at 10am and close at 5 or 6pm
Monday to Saturday. Downtown is shut tight as a tomb on
weekends, and the Lower East Side observes the Jewish sabbath on Friday afternoons and Saturdays. Saturdays are great
for shopping during the day on the Upper East and West
sides, but many stores take Sunday off. In the East and West
Village and SoHo merchants are apparently nocturnal; some
don't open up until noon, and take Monday rather than
Sunday off. Remember, though, that New York is the city that
never sleeps—in an emergency, you can almost always find
what you need 24 hours a day by checking the Yellow Pages.

Sales Tax

The sales tax is 8.25% in New York City, unless the store ships
your purchases out of state for you. It is non-refundable—
foreign visitors will not be reimbursed at the airport. Recently,
the mayor implemented a tax-free shopping week in January.

The Lowdown

For aspiring Martha Stewarts... For serviceable, stylish,
reasonably-priced interiors and entertaining storefront
window displays, check out **Crate & Barrel** at the
Madison and 59th crossroads. Or let yourself fantasize in
SoHo at **Portico Bed & Bath** and **Portico Home**, where
romantically-styled beds have names like "Soleil" and
"Nathalie"; **Barton-Sharpe, Ltd.,** which specializes in
handmade 18th-century American recreations; **Modern
Age**, where the styles bespeak the fifties; and **Scott
Jordan Furniture** for handsome Mission-style beds,
shelves, and tables. The **Manhattan Art & Antiques
Center** and the **Chelsea Antiques Building** are excellent
antiquers' target zones. New furniture with a chic edge is
a speciality at **Wyeth**. For gargoyles and walnut panelling
salvaged from old New York buildings, try **Urban
Archaeology**. But for something different, try **Old
Japan, Inc.,** the art-deco **Wooster Gallery**, or **Jacques
Carcanagues, Inc.** where that Korean step tansu you've
been looking for can finally be found.

Incredible edibles... Among the city's gourmet grocery
stores, **Zabar's** rules the Upper West Side, **Dean &**

Deluca reigns in SoHo, and **Balducci's** is king of the West Village; but don't forget the neighborhoody **Jefferson Market** (in the West Village) and **Gourmet Garage** (in SoHo). **Florence Meat Market** makes no bones about selling the best veal in town. Up on the East Side, **Sherry Lehmann** is a virtual wine museum (fancy a jeroboam of Château Lafite-Rothschild 1966 for $1,100?), with a staff of connoisseurs posing as clerks. The Village's **Astor Wines & Spirits** takes more of a bargain-basement approach to alcohol, but the selection alone could make you drunk. Coffee beans are available everywhere, but I make a steady diet of Peter's blend from my Village local, **Porto Rico Importing Company.** **Ferrara Foods and Confections** has been baking mini-sfogliatella and chocolate-dipped biscotti in Little Italy since 1892, and wrapping them up for carry-out in the loveliest little parcels. Fresh pasta comes in almost all the colors of the rainbow and tastes of the garden at **Raffetto's** in SoHo, nicely topped by gorgonzola or fontina from **Murray's Cheese Shop** in the West Village. And just to prove that the sun never sets on the British Empire, there's **Myer's of Keswick**, a Village village grocer late of the Lake District, where lovers of fresh kidney pie and Milo Chocolate Food Drink will find happiness at last.

Everything under one roof... There was a time, in the late 19th century, when almost all the city's department stores lined up in handsome, multi-storied buildings with exquisite cast-iron facades along the so-called Ladies Mile (Sixth Avenue from 8th Street to 23rd Street); B. Altman & Company was there, complete with a 500-horse stable for deliveries. In the early 1900s, most stores moved to what's now Midtown, and it's been downhill all the way since then. (Alas, poor Altman's closed its dowager store at 34th and Fifth in the late eighties.) **Bloomingdale's** and **Barneys** both have personal shopping departments for those who need help deciding what to buy, and both offer the very latest in clothing and furnishing styles; Barneys is postmodern-spare, Bloomie's so Upper-East-Side that it's become a cliché. **Macy's** has clunky wooden escalators that shuttle shoppers from merchandise-packed floor to floor, and **Saks Fifth Avenue** is quite simply a New York institution, especially for Christmas shopping and post-Christmas fancy dress sales. Beguilingly chic **Felissimo**, is a fine old Midtown mansion with a grand curving staircase and tea room on the top floor.

Finding the New You... If you're looking for scents, soaps, and unguents you won't find in malls all over the world, try the East Side's **Floris of London**. Americans since George Washington have been splashing on scents from **Caswell-Massey**, you can join them by visiting the flagship store on the East Side. Or seek out **Kiehl's**, an ever-crowded little pharmacy that's been making its own natural beauty products since 1851. The **Elizabeth Arden Red Door Salon** on Fifth Avenue has mainstream posh attractions (like Oribe, famed colorist from Vogue). **Bergdorf Goodman** has its beauty-world mecca, the **Frederic Fekkai Beauty Center**, and the Waldorf-Astoria Hotel has the **Kenneth Salon**. But if all you want are pots of paint try **MAC** (Makeup and Cosmetics Limited), based in the West Village but with outposts at Saks and Henri Bendel. Get a haircut at SoHo's **Girls And Boys** or **Mud Honey**, where the prices are surprisingly reasonable and your locks get clipped in an art gallery atmosphere; or Midtown's industrial-chic **Bumble & Bumble**, where you and Broadway stars get revamped.

The vintage vantage point... New York's favorite flea market—where you might catch Barbra Streisand rummaging—is the **Annex Antiques Fair and Flea Market**, which takes over empty parking lots along Sixth Avenue between 24th and 27th streets on Saturdays and Sundays. About 425 vendors offer up costume jewelry, old bicycles, wigs, hats, bibelots—in short, oddities and treasures (you just have to be able to tell the difference). Two fine street markets seem to have settled in permanently, one just south of Tower Records on Broadway (in the Village) and the other at Wooster and Spring streets (in SoHo), where the goods tend toward thigh-high socks, strappy sundresses, tapes, and cast-off lots from The Gap; a newer one has turned up on Fifth Avenue at 42nd Street. The thrift shop at the **Church of St. Luke in the Fields** in the West Village sometimes has startlingly wonderful women's clothes, and special Saturday sales. Prices are higher at the East Village's **Screaming Mimi**, but the buyers are hip and the clothes are so well reconditioned that they seem new. On the Upper East Side, **Encore** has been reselling "gently used" European and American designer fashions for 40 years, and anything you buy at **Repeat Performance**, near Gramercy Park, benefits the New York City Opera (watch for freshly donated batches of brand new clothes). And then—dare I mention it?—there's the **Ritz Thrift Shop**, where the lynx, sable, and fox coats are secondhand but a far cry from ratty.

Kid stuff... If you didn't bring the kids to New York, take it back to them. You could brave the 57th Street crowds for a Daffy Duck cap from **The Warner Brothers Studio Store** or a Mickey Mouse backpack from **The Disney Studio Store**, but why not astonish them with a one-of-a-kind toy from SoHo's **The Enchanted Forest?** Funky kids' clothes like a tutu that plays *It's a Small World After All* can be found in the West Village at **Peanut Butter and Jane**; for a pretty satin dress-up frock or perfect sailor suit, go to the Upper East Side's **Jacardi** or **Wicker Garden's Children**—then pick up a Japanese kite or toy plane from **Big City Kites**, or Italian building blocks and German jigsaw puzzles from **Penny Whistle Toys**. If the kids are along, **FAO Schwarz** is unavoidable—two stories of toys, including a whole department for Barbie dolls, the very latest in action figures, and a whole zoo of immense stuffed animals.

Gadgets and gizmos... You've got to stay sharp when shopping for electronics in New York. Midtown west of Fifth Avenue is loaded with electronics stores, but you're better off downtown. Near City Hall is **J&R**, with computer, TV/VCR, video game, home and car stereo, small appliance, and tape and CD departments (in several buildings), and a whole army of helpful salespeople.

Exotica... Two East Village shops, **Enchantments** and **Lady in the Moon** cater to the witches among us, selling candles and personalized incense mixtures that come complete with a spell; stop in around Halloween or when there's a full moon. In Soho **Kate's Paperie** is a showplace for fine stationery, handmade cards, beautifully bound blank books, and marbleized wrapping paper too pretty to throw away. Up near the American Museum of Natural History is a fitting location for **Maxilla and Mandible**, which stocks bones and fossils (weird but actually cool). At **Gotta Have It! Collectibles Inc.** on chic 57th Street, you'll find one-of-a-kind specialty items, like a signed Bob Dylan guitar.

For L.L. Bean types... Centrally located **Paragon Sporting Goods** is a great place to gear up for athletic endeavors from step aerobics to lacrosse, on three levels of a cavernous warehouse near Union Square; it offers reasonable prices and frequent sales. **Eastern Mountain Sports** can help you with sleeping bag pads, skis, rock-climbing equipment, and ice picks, though these days "gear heads" are making a beeline down to **Patagonia**, a link in the environmentally-conscious California sportsretailing chain. Nearby **Smith & Hawken** supplies stylish gardeners with seeds, bulbs, trowels, and mud boots.

Diamonds are a girl's best friend... If you can't find **Tiffany & Co.**, you're not trying hard enough. It's a shame that Tiffany's is actually more mass-market than it used to be, but it's still a Fifth Avenue lodestar, intimately bound up with the mythology of glamorous New York. Make a pilgrimage to the Tiffany Diamond, 287.42 carats cut in 1877, and then, if you're still a starry-eyed shopper with a money-burning hole in your pocket, you can bag something slightly less pricey like a paper-thin Peretti brandy snifter for about $30. At the other end of the jewelry spectrum, there's the **Diamond District**, one discount jewelry store after another lined up along 47th Street between Fifth and Sixth avenues, where more than a few young grooms have purchased starter rings for their intendeds. A **La Vieille Russie** and **Ares Rare Jewelry** are pricy East Side purveyors of museum-quality antique glitter—Fabergé eggs, enameled snuff boxes, Egyptian scarabs, and the like. Gaudy costume gems can be found in the Village at **Out of Our Drawers, Inc.**, where ear piercing is painless and free for the cost of a pair of posts. All the major jewelry shops and department stores sell timepieces, but to get a Tourneau at the source, stop in at Midtown's **Tourneau**, where you'll also find the latest tony watch styles from Tag Heuer, Omega, Rolex, and Longines.

SHOPPING | THE LOWDOWN

100-percent leather... Well-heeled men get that way at **To Boot** (West Side) and **McCreedy & Schreiber** (East Side), both of which feature big American name brands like Bass, Rockport, and Timberland, plus too-cool Italian loafers and English ankle boots. **T.O. Dey** makes boots and shoes for hard-to-fit feet (male or female) in an unprepossessing Garment District warehouse; John Travolta's ostrich-skin boots and Liza Minelli's sequined pumps were custom made here. On the Madison Avenue boutique strip, **Cole Haan** shoes traditionalist male and female feet, and the first American location of **Patrick Cox**, otherwise of London, rivets high-end shoe fetishists of both sexes with such eye-poppers as fuchsia-toned jelly shoes; unaccountably, the shop also sells antiques from the 1950s. Madison Avenue is also home to **Arche**, the source for hip, pricey French shoes in a luscious range of colors. Down in SoHo there's a cluster of chic little shoe boîtes like **Freelance**, **Varda**, **Jenny B.**, **Peter Fox**, and **Sacco**. Walking into any of the small leather stores in the West Village always makes me want to eat a good steak—the jackets, gloves, and handbags are that genuine. Try the **Village Tannery** or the **New York Leather Company**. Or head east to **Jutta Neumann Leather** for handmade designer bags, belts, and sandals.

The printed page... **Gotham Book Mart** is an anomalous island in workaholic Midtown, perilously crammed with used, new, and rare finds under a little emblem that says "Wise men fish here"; **Three Lives** is a living-room-sized West Villager devoted to fiction, with a staff full of real readers; and **Coliseum Books** is a richly-stocked independent on the West Side. In the Village, the **Strand** has 2.5 million used volumes ("eight miles of books"), including half-price review copies. Then there are the wonderful little specialists—**The Drama Book Shop**, in the theater district, naturally, featuring play scripts and practical volumes for actors and directors; the Village's **Biography Book Shop**; **The Ballet Co.** near Lincoln Center; and **Murder Ink** on the Upper West Side, to name only a few. Of course, these days in New York, smaller bookstores are closing in droves. The superstore chains are absolutely dominating the market.

The gallery scene... Every decade or so the New York art scene reassembles itself from the ground up; galleries open and close, artists come and go. But the **Leo Castelli Gallery**, one of the early champions of the works of Jasper Johns, has endured, as has **Mary Boone**, Julian Schnabel's champion. **Pace Wildenstein**, on E. 57th Street's gallery strip, and the **Gagosian Gallery**'s two branches are other extremely reliable showplaces for the latest trends in contemporary art.

To the highest bidder... The art and antiques auction game is played nowhere with more white-gloved aplomb than on Manhattan's Upper East Side at **Sotheby's** and **Christie's**, home of the multi-million-dollar collectible (a pair of Rudolph Nureyev's ballet slippers once fetched $9,000 at a Christie's auction). If you're serious about joining the oh-so-glamorous fray (night auctions are the real glitterati draws), attend the preview and study the catalogue before raising your hand. Both auction houses have somewhat less high-profile branches, **Sotheby's Arcade** and **Christie's East**, where one can swing excellent deals on porcelains, furniture, lamps, silver, and jewelry from family estates. As of late, bereaved clingers-on of Jackie and Diana have taken a crack at their discarded elegance. The clothing auctions at **William Doyle Galleries** bring out the genteel blue-haired ladies of the Upper East Side; a more rambunctious gang finds furniture treasures at surprisingly low prices (which don't include often woefully needed reconditioning) at the **Tepper Galleries**.

Right out of GQ... Perhaps clothes don't make the man, but when they're from **Bergdorf Goodman for Men** (just across the street from the elegant main Fifth Avenue store) gentlemen can count on cutting fine figures. Stylish foreign and American sweaters, sportswear, and accessories are on hand, not to mention scads of perfectly tailored suits. Drop-dead ties are the sole pursuit at the East Side's **Robert Talbott**. **Paul Stuart** is the current top contender among the traditional male outfitters clustered on Madison Avenue near Grand Central Station. Hip but tasteful downtown looks for men, with little retro touches, can be found at SoHo boutiques like **Agnès B.**, **New Republic Clothier**, and **Yohji Yamamoto**.

Women in Vogue... You know about the department stores, right? And that all the fancy designers (your **Valentinos**, **Yves Saint Laurents**, **Norma Kamalis**, **Chanels**, and **Nicole Millers**) hang out on Madison Avenue and E. 57th Street? And that you can put together a fetching city look by shopping the hipper chains like **Express Ltd.**, **Putumayo**, and **Urban Outfitters**? You've found the knock-off bargains at **Daffy's**? So now graduate to some of the special kinds of threads Manhattan weaves, all to be found below 14th Street in SoHo and the Village. Start an affair with **Harriet Love**, a little closet of a shop with sweet, chic suits hinting at the 1940s, and little black dresses to die for. **Ibiza** makes an art of the gypsy look, Parisian **Stephane Kelian** has simple, subtly sexy styles for girls with tall-drink bodies, **J. Morgan Puett** could blow you away with its fantastical cottons and gauzes, **Kanae and Onyx** has bargains on urban teeny-bopper attire, and **Cynthia Rowley** does the sixties with all the vinyl and polka dots you could dream of, plus a little bit of whimsy. **Mark Montano** has cool but classic silks and chiffons; **Todd Oldham** does high-style women's shoes, accessories, and gowns; and **Calypso St. Barth** does cutting-edge retro.

The Index

Agnès B. Handsome, wearable styles for men, women, and kids.... *Tel 212/925–4649. 116 Prince St., N/R train to Prince St.; tel 212/570–9330. 1063 Madison Ave., 4/5/6 to 86th St.;* and other locations. **(see p. 149)**

À La Vieille Russie. Art, antiques, and little bits of czarist Russia.... *Tel 212/752–1727. 781 5th Ave., N/R train to 5th Ave. Closed Sun, and Sat in summer.* **(see p. 147)**

Ann Taylor. Updated classic clothes for women.... *Tel 212/832–2010. 645 Madison Ave., 4/5/6 to 59th St.; and other locations.* **(see p. 141)**

Arche. French suede shoes in wonderful colors.... *Tel 212/439–0700. 995 Madison Ave., 6 train to 68th St.; and other locations.* **(see p. 148)**

Ares Rare Jewelry. Exquisite antique jewels.... *Tel 212/758–5340. 608 5th Ave., E/F train to 5th Ave. Closed Sun, and Sat in summer.* **(see p. 147)**

Armani. Grand boutique that displays the couture line.... *Tel 212/988–9191. 760 Madison Ave., 6 train to 68th St. Closed Sun.* **(see p. 141)**

Astor Wines & Spirits. The booze warehouse in the Village.... *Tel 212/674–7500. 12 Astor Place, 6 train to Astor Place or N/R to 8th St. Closed Sun.* **(see p. 144)**

Balducci's. Gourmet comestibles, very fresh fish, and meat in the pink.... *Tel 212/673–2600. 424 6th Ave., F or L train to 14th St.* **(see p. 144)**

The Ballet Co. Books on la danse.... *Tel 212/246–6893. 1887 Broadway. 1/9, B/D, or A/C train to 59th St./Columbus Circle.* **(see p. 148)**

Barneys. After a move uptown, the place for wretched excess.... *Tel 212/826–8900, 660 Madison Ave., N/R to 5th Ave.* **(see pp. 141, 144)**

Barton-Sharpe, Ltd. For handsome 18th-century hand-crafted furniture recreations.... *Tel 212/925–9562. 66 Crosb, 6 train to Spring St.* **(see p. 143)**

Bed, Bath & Beyond. A huge array of reasonably priced home furnishings.... *Tel 212/255–3550. 620 6th Ave., F train to 23rd St.* **(see p. 140)**

Bergdorf Goodman. High fashion for traditionalists mostly, in a landmark building.... *Tel 212/753–7300. 754 5th Ave., N/R train to 5th Ave.* **(see pp. 140, 145)**

Bergdorf Goodman for Men. Mecca for male styles.... *Tel 212/753–7300. 745 5th Ave., N/R train to 5th Ave.*
(see p. 149)

Betsey Johnson. Glitter, glad rags, too-short tubes and minis—all for girls who just wanna have fun.... *Tel 212/362–3364. 248 Columbus Ave., 1/2/3/9 or B/C train to 72nd St.; and other locations.* **(see p. 141)**

Big City Kites. Japanese and Chinese wind-worthy lovelies, plus toys.... *Tel 212/472–2623. 1210 Lexington Ave., 4/5/6 train to 86th St.* **(see p. 146)**

Biography Book Shop. Small, very West Village, for the lives of the greats.... *Tel 212/807–8655. 400 Bleecker St., 1/9 train to Christopher St.* **(see p. 148)**

Bloomingdale's. The Upper East Side shops in this classy older department store.... *Tel 212/705–2000. 1000 3rd Ave., 4/5/6 train to 59th St. or N/R to Lexington Ave.*
(see pp. 141, 144)

Brooks Brothers. Ivy League clothes.... *Tel 212/682–8800. 346 Madison Ave., 4/5/6/7 train to Grand Central.*
(see p. 141)

Bulgari. Jewels and watches, in two words.... *Tel 212/315–9000. 730 5th Ave., B/Q train to 57th St. or N/R to 5th Ave. Closed Sat–Sun.* **(see p. 140)**

Bumble & Bumble. Star-quality haircuts and color.... *Tel 212/521–6500. 146 E. 56th St., 4/5/6 to 59th St. or N/R to Lexington Ave.* **(see p. 145)**

Calypso St. Barth. New/old designs with a whiff of the Caribbean.... *Tel 212/965–0990. 280 Mott St., B train to Broadway/Lafayette; Tel 212/334–5555. 240 Centre St., N/R train to Prince St.* **(see p. 150)**

Canal Jean Co. Sportswear and some vintage, discount prices.... *Tel 212/226–1130. 504 Broadway, B/D/Q/F train to Broadway/Lafayette or N/R to Prince St.* **(see p. 142)**

Cartier. Another Fifth Avenue jewelry legend.... *Tel 212/*

753–0111. 2 E. 52nd St., E/F to 53rd St. Closed Sat–Sun in summer. **(see p. 140)**

Caswell-Massey. America's oldest perfumers.... *Tel 212/ 755–2254. 518 Lexington Ave., 6 train to 50th St.; and other locations.* **(see p. 145)**

Century 21. Department store bargains.... *Tel 212/ 227–9092. 22 Cortlandt St., 1/9 or N/R train to Cortlandt St., 2/3 to Park Place, or C/E to World Trade Center. Closed Sun.* **(see p. 142)**

Chanel. Classic French women's styles, especially suits and evening gowns.... *Tel 212/355–5050. 15 E. 57th St., N/R train to 5th Ave. Closed Sun.* **(see p. 150)**

Chelsea Antiques Building. Antiques emporium in a Chelsea warehouse.... *Tel 212/929–0909. 110 W. 25th St., 1/9 train to 23rd St.* **(see p. 143)**

Christian Dior. Women's clothing, fresh from Paris.... *Tel 212/ 223–4646. 703 5th Ave., N/R train to 5th Ave. Closed Sun.* **(see p. 140)**

Christie's. Art and antiques auctions, beloved of the blue-bloods.... *Tel 212/546–1000. 502 Park Ave; 4/5/6 train to 59th St. or N/R to Lexington Ave. Closed Sun in summer.* **(see p. 149)**

Christie's East. Christie's less pricey spin-off, good for furni-ture.... *Tel 212/606–0400. 219 E. 67th St., 6 train to 68th St.* **(see p. 149)**

Church of St. Luke in the Fields Thrift Shop. West Village cast-offs.... *Tel 212/924–9364. 487 Hudson St., 1/9 train to Christopher St. Closed Sun.* **(see p. 145)**

Coca-Cola Fifth Avenue. Kitschy Coke collectibles.... *Tel 212/ 355–5475. 711 5th Ave., N/R train to 5th Ave.*
(see p. 140)

CHC: Cole Haan. Classy shoes and accessories for women and men.... *Tel 212/421–8440. 667 Madison Ave., N/R train to 5th Ave.* **(see p. 148)**

SHOPPING | THE INDEX

Coliseum Books. Two floors of books, and an excellent magazine rack.... *Tel 212/757–8381. 1771 Broadway, 1/9/A/B/C/D train to Columbus Circle.* **(see p. 148)**

Comme des Garçons. Japanese unisex cutting-edge styles.... *Tel 212/219–0660. 116 Wooster St., N/R train to Prince St.* **(see p. 142)**

Crate & Barrel. Stylish baskets, glassware, lamps, rugs, and other accessories for the upwardly mobile home.... *Tel 212/308–0011. 650 Madison Ave., N/R train to 5th Ave.* **(see p. 143)**

Cynthia Rowley. Women's styles from the high sixties, only slightly updated.... *Tel 212/334–1144. 108 Wooster St., N/R train to Prince St.* **(see p. 150)**

Daffy's. Bargain threads for men, women, and children. Lotsa labels.... *Tel 212/529–4477, 111 5th Ave., 4/5/6 or N/R train to Union Square; and other locations.* **(see pp. 142, 150)**

Dean & Deluca. Specialty foods.... *Tel 212/226–6800. 560 Broadway, N/R train to Prince St.* **(see p. 143)**

The Disney Studio Store. The expected memorabilia.... *Tel 212/702–0702. 711 5th Ave., E/F train to 5th Ave.* **(see pp. 140, 146)**

The Drama Book Shop. Essential for plays and theater books.... *Tel 212/944–0595. 723 7th Ave., 1/9 train to 50th St.* **(see p. 148)**

Eastern Mountain Sports. Outfits backpackers, hikers, and other outdoor enthusiasts.... *Tel 212/397–4860, 20 W. 61st St., 1/9/A/B/C/D train to Columbus Circle; tel 212/505–9860, 611 Broadway, B/D/Q/F to Broadway/Lafayette.* **(see p. 147)**

Elizabeth Arden Red Door Salon. Facials, manicure, make-up advice, and massages on two luxurious floors.... *Tel 212/546–0200. 691 5th Ave., E/F train to 5th Ave.* **(see p. 145)**

Enchanted Forest. Handcrafted toys with a SoHo feel.... *Tel*

212/925–6677. 85 Mercer St., N/R train to Prince St.
(see p. 146)

Enchantments. Incense, spells, and candles for witches.... *Tel 212/228–4394. 341 E. 9th St., F train to 2nd Ave.*
(see p. 146)

Encore. The Upper East Side's most reliable clothing resale shop.... *Tel 212/879–2850. 1132 Madison Ave., 4/5/6 train to 86th St.* **(see p. 146)**

Express Ltd. French clothing units for women.... *Tel 212/421–7246. 133 E. 58th St., N/R train to 5th Ave.; and other locations.* **(see p. 150)**

FAO Schwarz. The first and last word in toys.... *Tel 212/644–9400. 767 5th Ave., N/R train to 5th Ave.* **(see p. 146)**

Felissimo. A small department store with handsome women's clothes and home furnishings.... *Tel 212/247–5656. 10 W. 56th St., N/R train to 5th Ave. or B/Q to 57th St.*
(see p. 145)

Fendi. Designer clothing and accessories.... *Tel 212/767–0100. 720 5th Ave., N/R train to 5th Ave.* **(see p. 140)**

Ferrara Foods and Confections. Italian cookies, pastries, and ices, to take out or eat in.... *Tel 212/226–6150. 195 Grand St., B/D/Q train to Grand St.* **(see p. 144)**

Filene's Basement. A branch of the discount clothing store from Boston.... *Tel 212/873–8000. 2220–2226 Broadway, 1/9 train to 79th St.; and other locations* **(see p. 140)**

Florence Meat Market. The city's top restaurants get their meats here.... *Tel 212/242–6531. 5 Jones St., A/C or B/D/Q/F train to W. 4th St. Closed Sun.* **(see p. 144)**

Floris of London. The British perfumery.... *Tel 212/935–9100. 703 Madison Ave., N/R train to 5th Ave. Closed Sun.* **(see p. 145)**

Frederic Fekkai Beauty Center. For shampoos, scalp massages, and haircuts among the stars.... *Tel 212/753–9500. 15 E. 57th St., N/R train to 5th Ave.* **(see p. 145)**

SHOPPING | THE INDEX

Freelance. New Wave Japanese and Italian footgear.... *Tel 212/925–6641. 124 Prince St., N/R train to Prince St.*
(see p. 148)

Gagosian Gallery. Perhaps the hottest contemporary art gallery on the scene.... *Tel 212/744–2313, 980 Madison Ave., 6 train to 77th St.; tel 212/228–2828, 136 Wooster St., N/R to Prince St. Open Tue–Sat, 10 to 6; summer hours, Mon–Fri, 10 to 6.* **(see p. 149)**

Gianni Versace. Sexy, loud, fun styles from Italy.... *Tel 212/ 744–5572. 817 Madison Ave., 6 train to 68th St.; tel 212/317–0224. 647 5th Ave., E/F train to 5th Ave.*
(see p. 140)

Girls And Boys. A SoHo hair salon.... *Tel 212/226–2084. 529 Broome St., N/R train to Prince St.* **(see p. 145)**

Gotham Book Mart. Used and new volumes in a bibliophile's midtown oasis.... *Tel 212/719–4448. 41 W. 47th St., B/D/ Q/F train to Rockefeller Center. Closed Sun.* **(see p. 148)**

Gotta Have It! Collectibles Inc. For one-of-a-kind signed collectibles.... *Tel 212/750–7900. 153 E. 57th St., 4/5/6 train to 59th St. or N/R to Lexington Ave. Closed Sun.*
(see p. 147)

Gourmet Garage. Specialty foods, especially fruits and vegetables, at lower-than-Balducci's prices.... *Tel 212/941– 5850. 47 Wooster St., N/R train to Prince St.; tel 212/663–0656. 2567 Broadway, 1/2/3/9 train to 96th St.*
(see p. 144)

G.W. Einstein. A SoHo photography showplace.... *Tel 212/226–1414. 591 Broadway, N/R train to Prince St.*
(see p. 142)

Harriet Love. Women's clothes with a 1940s cast.... *Tel 212/966–2280. 126 Prince St., N/R train to Prince St.*
(see p. 150)

Henri Bendel. Distinguished fashions.... *Tel 212/247–1100. 712 5th Ave., N/R train to 5th Ave.* **(see p. 140)**

Historic Lower East Side. Free guided tours; learn where the bargains are.... *Tel 212/226–9010. 261 Broome St., 4/5/6 train to Spring St.* **(see p. 141)**

Ibiza. Flowy, costumey women's clothing and dramatic accessories.... *Tel 212/533–4614. 42 University Place, 4/5/6 or N/R train to Union Square.* **(see p. 150)**

Jacardi. Parisian chic for the small set.... *Tel 212/535–3200. 787 Madison Ave., 6 train to 68th St.; tel 212/369–1616. 1281 Madison Ave., 6 train to 96th St.* **(see p. 146)**

Jacques Carcanagues. Antiques from all over the world.... *Tel 212/925–8110. 106 Spring St., 6 train to Spring St.* **(see p. 143)**

Jefferson Market. Fine foods, virtually next door to Balducci's—but a lot less crowded.... *Tel 212/533–3377. 450 6th Ave., F train to 14th St.* **(see p. 144)**

Jenny B. Dashing, strappy shoes.... *Tel 212/343–9575. 118 Spring St., C/E train to Spring St.* **(see p. 148)**

J. Morgan Puett. Fairy-tale styles for women, all gossamer and gauze.... *Tel 212/267–8004. 159 Duane St., N/R train to Prince St.* **(see pp. 142, 150)**

J&R. The downtown electronics hub.... *Tel 212/238–9000. 15, 23, 27, and 31 Park Row, N/R or 4/5/6 to Brooklyn Bridge/City Hall or J/M/Z to Chambers St.* **(see p. 146)**

Jutta Neumann Leather. Handmade bags and sandals with moxie.... *Tel 212/982–7048. 317 E. 9th St., 6 train to Astor Pl.* **(see p. 148)**

Kanae and Onyx. East Village hip youth.... *Tel 212/254–7703. 75 E. 7th St., 6 train to Astor Place or N/R to 8th St.* **(see p. 150)**

Kate's Paperie. Pretty stationery, desk accessories, and wrappings.... *Tel 212/633–0570. 8 W. 13th St., 1/2/3/9 train to 14th St.; tel 212/941–9816. 561 Broadway, N/R to Prince St.* **(see p. 146)**

SHOPPING | THE INDEX

Kenneth Salon. Spa treatments at the Waldorf.... *Tel 212/ 752–1800. 301 Park Ave., 6 train to 51st St. Closed Sun.*
(see p. 145)

Kiehl's. Natural beauty aids, since 1851.... *Tel 212/677– 3171. 109 Third Ave., L/N/R/4/5/6 train to Union Square. Closed Sun.*
(see p. 145)

Lady in the Moon. Equipment for witchery.... *Tel 212/ 473–8486. 115 St. Mark's Place, 6 train to Astor Place.*
(see p. 146)

Leo Castelli Gallery. Long-time leader in contemporary painting.... *Tel 212/431–6729. 578 W. Broadway, N/R train to Prince St.*
(see p. 149)

Loehmann's. The Bronx-basd bargain-hunter's dream comes to Manhattan.... *Tel 212/352–0856. 101 7th Ave., 1/9 train to 18th St.*
(see p. 142)

Macy's. The Herald Square department store standard.... *Tel 212/695–4400. 151 W. 34th St., 1/2/3/9 train to Penn Station or B/D/Q/F/N/R to 34th St.*
(see pp. 141, 144)

MAC Cosmetics. Expensive and model-worthy cosmetics.... *Tel 212/243–4150. 14 Christopher St., 1/9 train to Christopher St.; tel 212/334–4641. 113 Spring St., N/R train to Prince St. Also at Henri Bendel and Saks Fifth Avenue.*
(see p. 145)

Madison Avenue. A free guided exploration of the world's greatest concentration of designer fashion boutiques.... *Tel 888/462–3476. 59 E. 79th St., 6 train to 77th St.*
(see pp. 141, 148, 150)

Manhattan Art & Antiques Center. One hundred dealers on three floors, less pricey than Madison Avenue.... *Tel 212/355–4400. 1050 2nd Ave., 4/5/6 train to 59th St. or N/R to Lexington Ave.*
(see p. 143)

Mark Montano. Whimsical women's wear.... *Tel 212/505– 0325. 434 E. 9th St., 6 train to Astor Place.*
(see p. 150)

Mary Boone Gallery. Major contemporary art gallery.... *Tel 212/725–2929. 745 5th Ave., N/R train to 5th Ave. By appointment in summer.* **(see p. 149)**

Maxilla and Mandible. Collectible bones, fossils, and all the skeletons in your closet.... *Tel 212/724–6173. 451 Columbus Ave., B/C train to 81st St.* **(see p. 147)**

McCreedy & Schreiber. Men's shoes, especially boots.... *Tel 212/719–1552. 37 W. 46th St., D/E/F train to 47th-50th St.; tel 212/759–9241. 213 E. 59th St., 4/5/6 train to 59th St. or N/R to Lexington Ave.* **(see p. 148)**

Modern Age. Trend-setting interior design.... *Tel 212/966–0669. 102 Wooster St., 6 train to Spring St. Closed Sun.* **(see p. 143)**

Mud Honey. Haircuts in a SoHo gallery.... *Tel 212/533–1160. 148 Sullivan St., N/R train to Prince St.* **(see p. 145)**

Murder Ink. The original mystery bookstore.... *Tel 212/362–8905. 2486 Broadway, 1/2/3/9 train to 96th St.* **(see p. 148)**

Murray's Cheese Shop. A small crowded shop where they're happy to give samples.... *Tel 212/243–3289. 257 Bleecker St., 1/9 train to Christopher St.* **(see p. 144)**

Myer's of Keswick. For those craving British food staples, like PG Tips and Cornish pasties.... *Tel 212/691–4194. 634 Hudson St., A/C/E/L to 14th St.* **(see p. 144)**

New Republic Clothier. Handsome men's clothes.... *Tel 212/219–3005. 93 Spring St., N/R train to Prince St.* **(see p. 149)**

New York Leather Company. Jackets, bags, etc.... *Tel 212/243–2710. 33 Christopher St., 1/9 train to Christopher St.* **(see p. 148)**

Nicole Miller. Tastefully cool women's apparel.... *Tel 212/288–9779. 780 Madison Ave., 4/5/6 train to 59th St. or N/R to Lexington Ave.; tel 212/343–1362, 130 Prince St., N/R to Prince St.* **(see p. 150)**

SHOPPING | THE INDEX

Penny Whistle Toys. Small but smartly-stocked toy store.... *Tel 212/873–9090. 483 Columbus Ave., B/C train to 81st St.; tel 212/369–3868. 1283 Madison Ave., 6 to 96th St.*

(see p. 146)

Peter Fox. Attractive women's shoes.... *Tel 212/431–6359. 105 Thompson St., N/R train to Prince St.*

(see p. 148)

Poltrona Frau. For leather-upholstered furniture in knock-out contemporary styles.... *Tel 212/777–7592. 141 Wooster St., N/R train to Prince St. Closed Sun.* **(see p. 142)**

Portico Bed & Bath. Lovely bedroom and bathroom furnishings.... *Tel 212/941–7722. 139 Spring St., 6 train to Spring St.; and other locations.* **(see p. 143)**

Portico Home. Eclectic furnishings.... *Tel 212/941–7800. 379 West Broadway, 1/9 train to Canal St.* **(see p. 143)**

Porto Rico Importing Company. Great coffee, amazingly low prices, long lines.... *Tel 212/477–5421. 201 Bleecker St., 6 train to Bleecker St.; tel 212/533–1982. 40 1/2 St. Mark's Place, 6 to Astor Place or N/R to 8th St.*

(see p. 144)

Putumayo. Women's styles inspired by the Third World.... *Tel 212/595–3441. 341 Columbus Ave., 1/2/3/9 or B/C train to 72nd St.; tel 212/966–4458. 147 Spring St., N/R train to Prince St.* **(see pp. 141, 150)**

Raffetto's. Homemade pastry cut to size or shape right before your eyes.... *Tel 212/777–1261. 144 W. Houston St., N/R train to Prince St.* **(see p. 144)**

Repeat Performance. A thrift that supports the New York City Opera.... *Tel 212/684–5344. 220 E. 23rd St., 6 train to 23rd St. Closed Sat–Sun in summer.* **(see p. 146)**

Ritz Thrift Shop. Recycled furs.... *Tel 212/265–4559. 107 W. 57th St., B/Q to 57th St. Closed Sat–Sun in summer.*

(see p. 146)

Robert Talbott. Wide selection of exquisite ties.... *Tel 212/*

751–1200. 680 Madison Ave., 4/5/6 train to 59th St. or N/R to Lexington Ave. **(see p. 149)**

Sacco. SoHo shoes.... Tel 212/925–8010. 111 Thompson St., N/R train to Prince St.; and other locations. **(see p. 148)**

Saks Fifth Avenue. Sleek, traditional department store goods.... Tel 212/753–4000. 611 5th Ave., E/F train to 5th Ave. **(see p. 144)**

Scott Jordan. Mission-style furniture.... Tel 212/620–4682. 137 Varick St., 1/9 train to Canal St. **(see p. 143)**

Screaming Mimi. Wild old styles, recycled largely from the sixties.... Tel 212/677–6464. 382 Lafayette St., 6 train to Astor Place or N/R to 8th St. **(see p. 146)**

Sherry Lehmann. An extraordinary selection of wine.... Tel 212/838–7500. 679 Madison Ave., 4/5/6 train to 59th St. or N/R to Lexington Ave. Closed Sun. **(see p. 144)**

Smith & Hawken. Gardening goods, for stylish green thumbs.... Tel 212/925–0687. 394 W. Broadway, C/E train to Spring St. **(see p. 147)**

Soho Mill Outlet. Discount linens.... Tel 212/226–0656. 490 Broadway, 1/9 train to Houston St. **(see p. 142)**

Sotheby's/Sotheby's Arcade. Auctioneers of note.... Tel 212/606–7000. 1334 York Ave., 6 train to 72nd St.
(see p. 149)

Stephane Kelian. Cover-girl-quality frocks.... Tel 212/980–1919, 717 Madison Ave., 4/5/6 train to 59th St. or N/R to Lexington Ave.; tel 212/925–3077, 120 Wooster St., N/R to Prince St. or B/D/Q/F to Broadway/Lafayette. **(see p. 150)**

Strand Book Store. A browser's paradise for used books.... Tel 212/473–1452. 828 Broadway, L/N/R/4/5/6 to Union Square. **(see p. 148)**

S&W. Bargain women's clothes and accessories.... Tel 212/924–6656. 165 W. 26th St., 1/9 train to 28th St. Closed Sat. **(see p. 142)**

Tepper Galleries. Better bargains in auctions.... *Tel 212/677–5300. 110 E. 25th St., 6 train to 28th St.* **(see p. 149)**

Three Lives. West Village fiction specialists.... *Tel 212/741–2069. 154 W. 10th St., F train to 14th St.* **(see p. 148)**

Tiffany & Co. Gold, silver, gems, and crystal.... *Tel 212/755–8000. 757 5th Ave., N/R train to 5th Ave. Closed Sun.*
(see pp. 140, 147)

To Boot. Shoes and boots.... *Tel 212/724–8249. 256 Columbus Ave., 1/2/3/9 train to 72nd St.* **(see p. 148)**

Todd Oldham Store. Well-cut gowns and goofy pop designs.... *Tel 212/219–3531. 123 Wooster St., N/R train to Prince St.* **(see p. 150)**

T.O. Dey. Custom-made shoes.... *Tel 212/683–6300. 9 E. 38th St., B/D/Q/F train to 42nd St. or 7 to 5th Ave. Closed Sun.*
(see p. 148)

Tourneau. For high-end watches.... *Tel 212/758–6098. 500 Madison Ave., E/F train to 5th Ave.; and other locations.*
(see p. 147)

Tower Records/Tower Books/Tower Video. Grist for the CD player and VCR.... *Tel 212/505–1500. 692 Broadway, 6 train to Astor Place or N/R to 8th St.; tel 212/799–2500. 1961 Broadway, 1/9 train to 66th St.; tel 212/838–8110. 725 5th Ave., E/F to 5th Ave.* **(see pp. 140, 141)**

Urban Archaeology. Fascinating bits and pieces from demolished Manhattan.... *Tel 212/431–4646, 143 Franklin St., 1/9 train to Franklin St.; tel 212/431–6969, 285 Lafayette St., N/R train to Prince St.* **(see p. 143)**

Urban Outfitters. Mass-market hip, Timberland boots, for youths.... *Tel 212/475–0009. 628 Broadway, 1/9 train to Houston St.; tel 212/677–9350. 360 6th Ave., A/C/E/F train to W. 4th St.; tel 212/658–1200. 127 E. 59th St., 4/5/6 train to 59th St. or N/R to Lexington Ave.*
(see p. 150)

Valentino. The stylish designer showroom, sophisticated prêt à

SHOPPING | THE INDEX

porter.... *Tel 212/355–0051. 600 Madison Ave., N/R train to 5th Ave.* **(see p. 150)**

Van Cleef & Arpels. Fifth Avenue jewels.... *Tel 212/644–9500. 744 5th Ave., N/R train to 5th Ave. Closed Sat–Sun.* **(see p. 140)**

Varda. The latest word in Italian footgear.... *Tel 212/941–4990. 149 Spring St., N/R train to Prince St.; tel 212/472–7552. 786 Madison Ave., 6 train to 68th St.* **(see p. 148)**

Village Tannery. West Village leather goods.... *Tel 212/673–5444. 173 Bleecker St., A/C/E or B/D/Q/F to W. 4th St.; and other locations.* **(see p. 148)**

Virgin Megastore. If you can't find the CD you're looking for here, maybe it doesn't even exsist.... *Tel 212/921–1020. 1540 Broadway, 1/2/3/9/7/N/R/S train to Times Square; new location will be opening at Union Square on the NE corner of Broadway and E. 14th St.* **(see p. 140)**

Warner Brothers Studio Store. Cartoon and movie memorabilia.... *Tel 212/754–0300. 1 E. 57th St., N/R train to 5th Ave.* **(see pp. 140, 146)**

Wicker Garden's Children. Infant wear and clothing for well-clad kids.... *Tel 212/410–7001. 1327 Madison Ave., 6 train to 96th St. Closed Sat–Sun.* **(see p. 146)**

William Doyle Galleries. Classic furniture auction house, very East Side.... *Tel 212/427–2730. 175 E. 87th St., 4/5/6 train to 86th St.* **(see p. 149)**

Wooster Gallery. Art-deco furniture and fixtures, in SoHo.... *Tel 212/219–2190. 86 Wooster St., 6 train to Spring St.* **(see p. 143)**

Wyeth. Furniture with a smashing-loft-in-TriBeCa mood.... *Tel 212/925–5278. 151 Franklin St., 1/9 train to Franklin St.* **(see p. 143)**

Yohji Yamamoto. Hip, slightly Edwardian men's and women's clothes.... *Tel 212/966–9066. 103 Grand St., N/R train to Prince St.* **(see p. 149)**

Yves Saint Laurent. The classic French designer's Manhattan branch.... *Tel 212/988–3821. 855 Madison Ave., 6 train to 68th St.* **(see p. 150)**

Zabar's. All the food that's fit to eat, plus great housewares upstairs.... *Tel 212/787–2000. 2245 Broadway, 1/9 train to 79th St.* **(see p. 143)**

nigh

6

tlife

If Paris was
Hemingway's
"moveable feast,"
then Manhattan
is the moveable
club. Nightspots
dance in and out

of vogue (and *W* and *Elle* and *Paper*). One spot features dashing couples in evening dress twirling about an Art Deco ballroom; another stars painfully gaunt college kids in haute grunge (baggy skateboard apparel, tattoos, buzzcuts) straight out of *Trainspotting*. And there are places where the twain meet, and even go home together.

New York has always set the trends, but they're no longer set in stone. Some hardcore clubbies (and clubs) have become dated or, even worse, become parodies of themselves. There are increasingly fewer places where you are expected to enjoy the privilege of groveling: Democracy is in (of course, it never hurts if you drive up in a Rolls). If anything, the late 1990s have signaled a return to the freewheeling 1970s, when downtown types such as Andy Warhol, Robert Mapplethorpe, and Lou Reed would mingle with uptown stars like Liza Minelli and Halston, and society doyennes like Nan Kempner. No one's really trying to conjure up the old Studio 54 days, but the trend lately has been toward theme glamour–first lounges and tapas bars; more recently, champagne and caviar boites and recreations of cafe society a la El Morocco. Of course, gay is where it's at, darling: Follow the trannies on parade. Scattered in their wake you'll find a bunch of trust-fund pretties who, after swigging a few Cosmopolitans, adore flirting with bisexuality...as concept.

In the 1990s, clubs in New York have taken a much more thematic approach to their weekly schedules, too: What was clearly a straight scene on Monday night can be transformed into a queer extravaganza for Tuesday, from a relatively sedate evening of jazz-meets-rap on Thursday to a hard-core house-mix frenzy on Friday. Some clubs even shift locations from night to night, with the site a privileged secret among a select few hipsters—at least until the word spreads, which it inevitably does. Make a couple of new friends on the dance floor and your chances of being swept along for the ride increase. If the club gets too intense, there's Manhattan's burgeoning lounge scene to explore, where clubland intrigues can be pursued in vastly more subdued digs. Wind down the night at one of Manhattan's several notable after-hours eateries (see Dining); omelettes and coffee at 4am are as much a part of a quality clubbing experience as any dance hall pyrotechnics.

Black is always in (especially if it clings properly), but New York is far less fashion fascist than before. From Neo-Nazi skinheads with multiple piercings and combat fatigues to well-heeled loafers of the reptilian rep tie set, everyone fits in somewhere.

While certain neighborhoods are perennial bar-hopping classics, like the East Village and Greenwich Village, remember that New York is a scene on the move. The hot drags to cruise as the millennium approaches are lower West Broadway, Ludlow Street, and Park Avenue South: The watering holes on those three slices of real estate alone could provide fodder for their own nightlife chapter. Also bear in mind a stratum of New York restaurants that are no more than glorified watering holes (their food is mediocre at best); though we've relegated many of them to this chapter, check out the Dining chapter as well.

New York *is* an expensive place to party—unless, of course, you've perfected the art of looking pretty and sullen, in which case you might find someone to pick up the tab. Covers can be outrageous at some of the clubs (depending on the boite and the act, if any, $5–$45 cover alone), and the drinks ridiculously priced (here's a tip: as a rule, gay bars pour the strongest drinks). But who cares? This is New York, where almost anyone can be a member of the club somewhere, and some people-watching scenes are well worth the price of a drink, even at these prices.

The Naked City

Girls! Girls! Girls!... Live Nude Acts... *They used to call 42nd Street between Seventh and Ninth Avenues "The Deuce"; Eighth Avenue from 40th Street to Central Park West was "Minnesota Strip," because many of the hookers who patrolled here even in the dead of winter had toughened up back on Midwestern farms, where they grew up. The hinterlands of Times Square remain the domain of pimps, prostitutes, peep shows, and adult entertainment video stores. 42nd Street, though, is in the midst of a massive redevelopment project, spearheaded by the Disney Corporation's spectacular renovation of the New Amsterdam Theater, including glorious friezes, frescoes, and frolicking cherubs. (Jaded New Yorkers joke that Times Square as theme park will require its own peculiar authentic accents: audioanimatronic pimps, whores, pushers, and fire-and-brimstone preachers.) For now, the sleaze has simply crept south to the environs of the Port Authority Bus Terminal and Javits Convention Center, west of Eleventh Avenue between 34th and 38th streets.*

NIGHTLIFE | INTRODUCTION

Sources

Paper magazine, while not the clubgoers' bible it once was, is still the definitive guidebook to what's hot for many, not in the least because of its voracious appetite for ferreting out the newest, gaudiest scenes. If your tastes run to drag queens and teenage urchins done up like extras in "Speed Racer: The

Musical," then the pages of *Paper* are where you'll want to turn for tips. The ever-reliable *Village Voice* does a better job of chronicling the music scene than the club world, but the weekly alternative tabloid still devotes a sizable chunk of its back pages to nightlife advertising, and scenester-diva Michael Musto's dishy gossip column "La Dolce Musto" often catches the club-trotting fabulous with their pants down. *Time Out* magazine, which comes out weekly, provides exhaustive weekly listings of nightlife options. Depending on one's predilections, it's usually a good idea to stick to the first three, which are more professional and established, but for the anything-goes set, the personals in *H/X* (Homo-Extra) and *Next* are always a treat. Those slim, usually free (though you might be charged $2.50 in NYC, $1.50 out of town) gay weeklies cover the queer club scene (which has become increasingly indistinguishable from the club scene at large) in roughly the same manner that *Playbill* reports on theater: succinctly and in a easy-to-carry size. *Sound Views*, a free-in-New-York, $2-elsewhere fanzine has been reporting on the extremes of the subterranean music scene for more than 30 issues. If your interests run to bands with names like "Kurt Cobain Haiku," this is the rag for you. *aRUDE*, a new quarterly, follows the adventures of the neo-Warholian crowd, combining beefy interviews with cultural figures like Bill T. Jones alongside dishy and opinionated ruminations on downtown's endlessly percolating cafe society. On occasion, The "Style" section of the Sunday *New York Times* glosses over a club event in the course of chasing another trend or tracking a mainstream celebrity. If you have any interest at all in where Madonna was last seen, this would be a good place to start. *New York Press* includes a Dance Clubs listing in its weekly summary of events—clipped and generally reliable, but not exactly fabulous. It's good for a very quick take on a place you've never been.

Liquor Laws

Despite rumors that the legal drinking age in New York City is 10, one can get busted for proffering fake ID. Of course, if the clubs locked out all the underagers, their business would quickly evaporate, as would their cachet of youth chic. If you're not yet 21, New York State's legal drinking age, don't expect to get served once you get in. If you can't get in, go someplace else; chances are at least one benevolent doorman or bouncer somewhere will take a shine to the way you've worked your look. Some clubs offer special drinks, called "smart drinks," for patrons who've depleted themselves on the dance floor: these nutrient-addled beverages offer a quick fix for dehydration and decreased electrolytes, all without alcohol.

Drugs

"Just say no" is not the New York club tramp's motto. Cocaine is no longer the narcotic of choice, and crackheads are usually too busy getting toasted to think about dancing, but speed, special K (ketamine) and ecstasy help many a clubgoer keep up with a hammering techno beat. It's part of the scene, so look the other way.

The Lowdown

Scenes to see... Manhattan features model-wannabe waitstaff, clientele with movie-star looks, and its share of celebrity sightings, but **Bowery Bar** (a.k.a. B-Bar) is so snotty it demands reservations for *drinks*. It's the kind of place where you can't tell the heteros from the homos: everyone's hair is fashionably buzzed, the black clings perfectly to the bodies. The place is so crass, it actually throws an annual "Nude Year's Eve" party. **Spy** already seems about as dated as the KGB. Though a whiff of attitude (and a haze of unfiltered Camels) remains, they've relaxed their standards before midnight, making it perfect entry-level New York snobbishness. Lush multi-level **Pravda** is like Gorky Park meets Park Avenue—lounging in the intimate leather booths is an art form. The Concorde horde here sports a hard, glossy, metallic sheen. At **Sapphire**, everyone seems squeezed like sausages into their vinyl and leather. **bOb**, a laid-back scene on weeknights, is so crowded weekends that body armor is in order. **Flowers**, a French cafe, gives models another casual environment in which to drink mineral water, smoke cigarettes, and gaze longingly at the menu. **Fez** packs 'em in for its wildly varied theme nights and funky yet fab down-at-heels Tangiers decor, but the smart but smirky patrons may put you off. At the cigar bar **Club Macanudo**, you can expect to see lots of Brit lits and New York society types discreetly pointing their stogies at one another. **Waterloo** is a new, charming Belgian brasserie where Madonna sightings are frequent and you can spot the *W* and *Paper* crowds. The trendier-than-thou eatery **Lemon** sucks in the cosmetically-repaired set (you know, the ones who look like they're sucking on lemons), as well as literary brats and brokers on the rise. Buppies bop at **Cheetah** and **Shark Bar**, where there's enough gold jewelry to rival Fort Knox. On the gay side, even the ethnic types stand and pose as if they were neo-Nazi poster boys at **G**.

Lounge acts... There are those who claim the lounge trend is already passe. Au contraire: What chic Manhattanite doesn't want a plush banquette, kindly dim lighting, and an air of imminent conspiracy? Draw aside the chain-mail curtain, and enter time warp **Flamingo East**, one of the East Village's first—and hardiest—neo-lounges. It's dark, it's fashionable, it resembles a diner mutated into a nightclub, it's full of skinny boys with unwashed hair. On the even trashier (and comfier) side is **Art Bar**. The front room resembles an Edward Hopper diner on acid with half the lights blown out. **Bar d'O**, in a charming nook of the West Village, has picked up an unlikely neighborhood with its version of lounge meets drag. On Tuesdays and Saturdays, Joey Arias and several other high-heeled, high-camp divas put on a torchy, intimate show. Each new version of **Merchants N.Y.** has literally outgrown lounge status, but they all have cozy Edwardian nooks with overstuffed armchairs and over-heated fireplaces, decent wine lists, and palate-pleasing plates of baked chicken, sushi roll, or Thai dumplings. **Hell** is red red red and offers fun, sexy entertainment most evenings.

Cigars, cigarettes...? Yes, we all know what both Freud ("sometimes a cigar is just a cigar") and Churchill ("a woman is a woman but a good cigar is a smoke") said about cigars, but all genders seem determined to prove them both wrong as they mix a potent sex/power cock-tail in Manhattan's cigar bars. **Cafe Aubette** is a post-apocalyptic, Bauhaus-y vision of brick and glass where the staff light your cigars with a flame thrower. Nibbles are surprisingly tasty and there's a fine selection in the back room (the actual cigar bar). **Club Macunudo** is the true place for one-upmanship when it comes to cigars—the customers circle like barracudas if you don't know your Dominican from your Jamaican. The various branches of **Bar and Books** are for the literary, *Paris Review*-reading set. **Grand Havana Room** is for the power and glamour stogie (owned by actor Joe Pantoliano, this bar is also used for location shoots) and features swoony skyline views. It's a paean to conspicuous consumption. Wines on display seem as fiercely protected as the vault at Fort Knox. The three outposts of **Merchants N.Y.** all play up the neo-Victorian ambience, but the newest Upper East Side incarnation has its own glitzy cigar room.

Beer here.... There are several micro-breweries in Manhattan, but **Heartland Brewery** has proved to be the most enduring, even endearing. The decor is so nostalgically faux-Americana, you feel like saluting the numerous flags. **McSorley's** is a tiny, venerable East Village ale house that has retained its frat party air for decades. **Tribeca Tavern** serves over 100 hundred varieties of beers from around the world, as well as single malt scotches to die for, in a rather schizo space with chaise longues and chandeliers competing with the garish green light bulbs at the bar. **Waterloo** specializes in esoteric Belgian beers, which any aficionado will tell you are considered the world's finest.

Gotta dance... The newest thing to hit town, after rampant success in London, is jungle vibe, which has found a Monday-night home at **Wetlands**, Manhattan's most prominent neo-hippie joint. The scene is vibrantly multicult and the vibe deeply positive when an assortment of DJs and spoken-word poets brings Koncrete Jungle into the house. **Nell's** can no longer claim the central status it once held in New York's clubland zeitgeist of the 1980s, but its plush Victorian decor now plays host on Monday nights to Funky Buddha, a classy scene that attracts a lower-key clientele than the city's trendier boogie shacks. And forget not **The Roxy**, whose venerable dance-hall walls in Chelsea shelter Rollerballs on Monday nights, a carnival of classic-disco-meets-in-line-skating-tricksterism—just don't call it a rink! On Tuesday nights, **Mother**, far west on 14th Street, belongs to Jackie 60, ribald brainchild of DJ Johnny Dynell and MC Chi Chi Valenti, who preside over a decadent fall-of-Rome scenario where drag queens rub elbows with trashy club strumpets outfitted in T-shirts so tiny and tight that you'll never be in doubt over their body temperature. The scene at newly relocated, mostly gay **Sound**

Factory Bar is supremely down and has been for years: On Wednesday nights, Underground Network holds sway with Manhattan's hottest, most popular house mix. A must stop if high-impact aerobic clubbing is why you came to town. Veterans of 1980s clubbing remember the Tunnel as a splendid goth cavern where everyone looked scrumptiously pallid in the calculated gloom; well, Tunnel is back, featuring a Sunday night hip-hop fest called Mecca. If you want real fun, pretend to be a camera hound at China Club; an impressive phalanx of bodyguards protect the likes of Mike Tyson, Christy Turlington, Derek Jeter, and plain folks like Art Garfunkel and Donald Trump. It's plush, with lots of velvet and brass and mirrors, and so much door tude you'd swear they could tell if your Armani tux was rented. Life/The Ki Club offers a collection of rave-ing lunatics at its series of imaginative theme nights, including Get A Life, with some of the best spinners (in the booths and on the floor) in Manhattan. The Bank is the spot for industrial, techno, hiphop, and house—all at volumes designed to induce deafness, not that the collegiate crowd worries. The throwback Roseland offers everything from ballroom to salsa to diva disco. Cheetah is as sleek as its celebrity clientele; nominally it's an upscale Italian eatery, but the jungle decor and circular waterfall give it away. If you're over 30 and turned away at Nell's, head Uptown to the upscale, relatively urbane Decade (it doesn't say which), which plays good old rock and roll and disco and serves halfway decent food to a sea of suits, from Boss to Chanel.

Live and loud... No survey of the Downtown club scene is complete without a visit to CBGB/OMFUG, a dingy Bowery rathole with a sound system known throughout the tri-state area for its Homeric volume. Drop a few bucks on a bottle of Rolling Rock and settle in for an evening of eardrum torture—there might be a name act, might be just some Jersey kids who've just learned how to play in tune, sort of. For a more acoustic, folksy vibe, slip next door to CB's 313 Gallery, virtually a clean, well-lighted place in comparison to its older brother. Webster Hall, a huge space near an NYU dorm diversifies its offerings; some evenings, the scene is rhythm nation, on others it's a rising band of rude boys last glimpsed on MTV's "Buzz Cuts." Bill Clinton once stopped by here to blow a little sax, which ought to give an idea how mainstream this place really is. A welcome beacon in a scary neighborhood (the Lower East Side, for all its newfound boho credentials), **Ludlow Bar** has been home for countless Monday nights to Beat Rodeo, a butt-kicking, no-BS area band. **Mercury Lounge** opens its doors to the disaffected detritus that slinks nightly out of nearby pick-up palaces a beer-can's throw away. **Arlene Grocery** offers even hipper, less established acts than Mercury Lounge and their similar neighbors. It's also the local Irish kid's hangout, since the East Village's illustrious Siné closed down. There's no cover charge, so expect hats to be passed around. **Luna Lounge** specializes in bands hoping to attract record labels, so the crowd is a bizarre mix of T-shirts and suits. Mondays feature Eating It, one of New York's oddest, most delightful alternative comedy evenings; a wild grabbag that is a defining moment in Manhattan nightlife. **The Bank**, which was indeed a turn-of-the-century bank, now is a vast duplex that buzzes with metal so heavy it's off the periodic table. **Sidewalk Cafe** offers a mixed bag of free live bands to everyone from Hells Angels and skinhead performance artists to NYU students. Top country rockers like the Jayhawks and Wilco round up at the **Rodeo Bar**, a classic honkytonk right down to the peanut shells on the floor and the stuffed buffalo glowering over the bar.

Live and not as loud... The booking habits of **Wetlands**, that free-spirited West Village club, have exhibited a more adventurous edge in the past few years: Hear bands like Rise Robots Rise, a curious collective of rappers drunk on Frank Zappa. If fierce ole thumpin' base riffs and growling vocals are what you seek, **Tramps** might have your blues (or zydeco) medicine. Mighty loud on some nights, but almost always good as gold. **SOB**'s (Sounds of Brazil) is bossa nova's and world beat's residence this side of the equator; if Tito Puente or Astrud Gilberto is what you crave, this is where you should turn. The smoky souk **Fez** hosts eclectic entertainment (wicked satiric comedy, story-telling, as well as folk or acoustic acts) in the adjoining 200-seat theater, where the Mingus Big Band (yup, they jammed with Charlie) holds court every Thursday. **Zinc Bar** is a preeminent jazz/Latin/Brazilian spot, quite intimate and dimly lit, where the likes of Max Roach or Astrud Gilberto might drop by. **No Moore** offers one of the most diverse musical menus in town, with various ethnic sounds, as well as jazz and blues. Two outer-borough joints set the cadence for the cutting edge: **Maxwell's** in Hoboken, NJ, and **Lauterbach's** in Brooklyn. Maxwell's may make it into *The New Yorker* more often, but it's hard to argue with Lauterbach's ambience: it's like a double-wide trailer home crossed with the basement set of *Wayne's World*.

For chic poseurs... **Tenth Street Lounge** is where the East-Village-chic set convenes nightly for stylish posing, though lately the joint has been colonized by some bold out-of-towners toting Macy's bags. The desperately fashionable staff, however, continues to snub on an equal-opportunity basis. For the fearless, there's the frequently odious but always sexy **Bowery Bar**. If supermodel Veronica Webb, art dealer Larry Gagosian, or *Rolling Stone* publisher Jann Wenner are on your list of celebs to spot, the search begins here. A much more accessible, and sometimes even literary, crowd gathers around the corner at **Marion's**, a kitschy hole-in-the-wall bar drenched in 1950s lounge karma. The martini is what everyone eventually orders here, just because the decor demands it. (Reasonably good food, too.) The beautifully designed **M&R**, just off Houston Street, is transporting: Its imagined destination is Europe in the 1950s. Tenderly catered to by its conscientious staff, M&R also features a bar that sports some of the largest ashtrays in town.

Painting the town pink... Some of New York's gay and lesbian hangouts have become as widely known as Stonewall itself, the climactic event that set the whole homo-liberation movement in motion. The scenes vary, however, so know your tastes before stepping out. A great neighborhood to get started in (for men) is Chelsea—between the leather-boys and gym-bunnies, this is fag heaven (lesbians will have better luck in the West Village). **Splash** is a genial happytime cruising facility—the name suggests a pool party, and water metaphors abound, but the scene is so friendly you'll forget about all the queer-cruising cliches. Way over on the West Side is **The Spike**, a serious leather scene that, with the recent surge in S/M interest, now draws a more eclectic crowd. Monday is movie night, Tuesday club night, Wednesday bikers and blue jeans. It's advisable to wear something waterproof. Everyone eventually swings through **The Bar**, an East Village institution with a bohemian roadhouse/pool-hall persona. It's an excellent choice for beer and cruising. The cruising is both splendid and silly at **Wonder Bar**, a very friendly East Villager crammed with goofy erotica and colorful fixtures. **The Monster** screams West Village—shimmery, slightly garish, and full of attractive gay men—fulfilling every cruiser's dream while remaining devoted to cabaret and dancing. Though some have knocked it for appealing mainly to lesbian professional types, **Julie's**, a romantic piano lounge in Midtown, is really one of the most sophisticated rooms around, regardless of one's sexuality. For the most part, however, men are not particularly welcome, unless they come with company. **Crazy Nanny's** (just "Nanny's" to most regulars) and **Henrietta Hudson** are two of the most popular dyke bars in town, providing all the basics (pool table, jukebox, cheap drinks) plus dancing and (occasionally) comedy; men are made to feel at home (or at least ignored without huffy glares). On Friday nights the straighforwardly named Clit Club claims **Mother**. **G** is hardly gee whiz, given the posing of gay trophy boys who've seen (and done) it all. **The Townhouse** disproves the theory that there are no gays on the Upper East Side; everyone here is a "suit," probably works in retail (can you say Bloomie's?), and doesn't look a day over 47. **King** is king of sleaze, with homo homeboys hanging out on one of the many levels.

Getting lucky... When it opened in 1994, everyone thought it was going to be SoHo's contribution to the city's exploding lounge scene. But contrary to expectations, **The Cub Room** became a Wall Street–singles outpost, constantly shrouded in a testosterone and estrogen fog, where straight white girls in pumps ogle and get ogled by straight white boys in pinstripes and loosened ties. **America**, a vast space in the Flatiron district, owns not only the longest menu in Manhattan, but also a thriving pick-up scene. After business hours it's usually packed with predatory ad execs and wolfen market-jocks, so ladies should keep their legs crossed. **The Old Town Bar**, one of Manhattan's oldest and best-loved watering holes, shouldn't have a singles scene, but it does. After five, the place fills up remarkably fast with Flatiron-district office drones on the prowl. It's every man and woman for him- or herself at **Live Bait**, a sometimes terrifying Flatiron joint decorated like a beachcomber bar, where fashion and photographers' models get endlessly hit on by jobless guys who tool around on Harleys. On SoHo's main drag, the place to get cruised is **I Tre Merli**, an enormous bar and restaurant that can open its entire front facade to the parade of hunks and lovelies that stalk West Broadway after dark. **Lucky Strike**, a little farther south, reminds everyone of that bar they used to go to in college; with Gallic accent and Gautoise haze the aesthetic is barnyard bric-a-brac, but the crowd is hip and youthful. For a fabulous pastiche of different types, from multi-pierced men to women tottering on platform Adidas, **Stingy Lulu's** in the East Village is where the tattooed set goes.

Where to get your kinks... For those whose pleasures lean toward far left field, **The Vault** offers a heavily gothic S/M dungeon scene right out of Anne Rice: manslaves locked in cages, strapped to bondage crosses, or trussed from harnesses moan eagerly in response to insults from their mistresses. Women can play, too, or just watch, which is what a fair portion of the crowd does. Frankly, though, The Vault can be quite a turn-off if the sight of a dozen men engaged in group masturbation makes you uncomfortable. For more conventional kinkiness, there's **Billy's Topless**, one of Manhattan's most beloved strip joints, where you can blow 50 bucks on lap dances. **Scores** is about as high-tech and upscale as a strip club gets: this is where Demi Moore researched her role in *Striptease*, and the likes of Liam Neeson have been sighted in the V.I.P. Champagne Room (ostensibly doing research themselves).

The Index

America. Vast. Simply furnished. Scads of tables and a bar that's an event in itself.... *Tel 212/505–2110. 9 E. 18th St., N/R, 4/5/6, or L train to Union Square.* **(see p. 177)**

Arlene Grocery. The latest place for alternative sounds on the newly fashionable Lower East Side.... *Tel 212/358–1633. 95 Stanton St., F train to Second Ave., J/M/Z to Essex St.* **(see p. 175)**

Art Bar. Smoke, bad paintings, and cool sounds played at just the right volume.... *Tel 212/727–0244. 52 Eighth Ave., 1/9/2/3 or L train to W. 14th St.* **(see p. 172)**

The Bank. Loud, loud, loud music fills this high-ceilinged space, which also features a light-system borrowed from an arena-rock act.... *Tel 212/505–5033; hotline 212/414–8001. 225 E. Houston St., B/D/Q/F train to Broadway/Lafayette. Cover charge.* **(see pp. 174, 175)**

The Bar. Laid-back queer scene for leather, Levis, boho shaggi-ness, and khakis (everybody's welcome!). Truly happy hour Mon–Fri.... *Tel 212/674–9714. 68 Second Ave. (at 4th St.), F train to Second Ave.* **(see p. 177)**

Bar and Books. These cozy elegant hangouts play to nostalgia for the English country estate.... *Tel 212/717–3902, 1020 Lexington Ave., 6 train to 68th St. 212/980–9314. 889 First Ave., 6 train to 51st St. 212/229–2642. 636 Hudson St., 1/9 train to Christopher St.* **(see p. 172)**

Bar d'O. A comfortable lounge tucked away in the almost loun-geless West Village.... *Tel 212/627–1580. 34 Downing St., A/C/E/ or B/D/Q/F train to W. 4th St.* **(see p. 172)**

Billy's Topless. Yes, the ladies take their blouses off, but they take a back (or lap) seat to the kooky clientele.... *Tel 212/989–3373. 729 Sixth Ave., F Train to 23rd St.*
(see p. 178)

bOb. The lounge as weekend shimmy shack. Not a half-bad place on the Lower East Side for subdued drinks during the weeks, but on Friday and Saturday, the breathing room disappears.... *Tel unlisted. 245 Eldridge St., F train to Broadway/Lafayette.* **(see p. 171)**

Bowery Bar. An enormous walled garden encloses New York's tired wannabes as they steal drags from each other.... *Tel 212/475–2220. 358 Bowery, B/D/Q/F train to Broadway/Lafayette. Reservations required.* **(see pp. 171, 176)**

Cafe Aubette. Manhattan's first truly sexy cigar bar.... *Tel 212/686–5500. 119 E. 27th St., 6 train to E. 28th St.*
(see p. 172)

CBGB/OMFUG and CB's 313 Gallery. The aesthetic: untrammeled filth. The decor: layers of wheat-pasted posters and decades of graffiti. Suggested attire: something torn. Next door's 313 Gallery showcases quieter acts.... *Tel 212/982–4052. 315–313 Bowery, B/D/Q/F train to Broadway/Lafayette.* **(see p. 174)**

Cheetah. How hip-hopping and happening is it? Puff Daddy throws parties at this tropically-themed, soulful new club.... *Tel 212/206–7770. 12 W. 21st St., F/N/R trains to 23rd St.* **(see pp. 172, 174)**

China Club. Formerly a hip Upper West Side dive for jocks and the models who date them, reopened in 1997—appropriately in the Theater district.... *Tel 212/398–3800. 268 West 47th St., 1/2/3/ R/N trains to Times Square.* **(see p. 174)**

Club Macanudo. The swank room reeks of sophistication and cigar smoke.... *Tel 212/752–8200. 26 East 63rd St., N/R train to Fifth Ave.* **(see pp. 171, 172)**

Crazy Nanny's. One of the Village's lesbian standbys, a friendly room where girls will be girls.... *Tel 212/366–6312. 21 Seventh Ave. S., A/C/E or B/D/Q/F train to W. 4th St.*
(see p. 177)

The Cub Room. A scalding singles scene for both the sleazy and the button-down sets with comfy sofas and tables large enough to hold more than a gimlet.... *Tel 212/677–4100. 131 Sullivan St., C/E train to Spring St.* **(see p. 177)**

Decade. Sixties and seventies music plays for a baby boomer clientele. No piecings or torn clothes here.... *Tel 212/ 835–5979. 1117 First Ave., 4/5/6 to 50th St., N/R to Lexington Ave.* **(see p. 174)**

Fez. Cheap but chic sheik decor and some of the coolest acts around (both the performers and the clientele).... *Tel 212/533–3000. 380 Lafayette St., 6 train to Astor Place.* **(see p. 171, 175)**

Flamingo East. Neo-pioneer lounge for the downtown boho brood.... *Tel 212/533–2860. 219 Second Ave., 4/5/6, N/R, or L train to Union Square.* **(see p. 172)**

Flowers. This perfectly lovely bistro is one of the photo district's main venues for scoping out the starved and the leggy.... *Tel 212/691–8888. 21 W. 17th St., F train to 14th St.* **(see p. 171)**

G. A perfect example of the hell urban gay men create for themselves—and therefore immensely popular. The boys are so healthy, there's a juice bar.... *Tel 212/929–1085. 223 W. 19th St., 1/9 trains to W. 18th St.* **(see pp. 172, 177)**

Grand Havana Room. Swoony mahogany-paneled decor at this cigar bar where heavy hitters indulge in heavy petting. If the smoke doesn't get you, the views will take your breath away.... *Tel 212/245–1600. 666 Fifth Avenue, 6 train to 51st St.* **(see p. 172)**

Heartland Brewery. A rotating selection of stoutly made micro-brews helps wash down the juicy Kentucky whiskey burgers, cheese steak hoagies, and cheesy come-ons.... *Tel 212/645–3400. 35 Union Sq. W., 4/5/6 or N/R or L trains to Union Sq.* **(see p. 173)**

Hell. Janis Joplin or Astrud Gilberto on the juke, fine martini selection, red velvet and crystal chandeliers: a lounge classic in the meatpacking district.... *Tel 212/727–1666. 55 Gansevoort St., A/C/E/ trains to 14th St.* **(see p. 172)**

NIGHTLIFE | THE INDEX

Henrietta Hudson. Another of the Village's delightful dyke bars, where k.d. lang's singles have been retired from the jukebox.... Tel 212/924–3347. 438 Hudson St., 1/9 train to Christopher St. **(see p. 177)**

Julie's. Not just the mellowest and most dignified lesbian hangout in Midtown, but a jewel in the crown of the city's whole queer piano-bar scene.... Tel 212/688–1294. 204 E. 58th St., 4/5/6 train to 59th St. or N/R to Lexington Ave. **(see p. 177)**

King. Gay bar catering to banjee boys and the whitebread, well-bred types who worship them.... Tel 212/344–5464. 579 Sixth Ave., L train to Sixth Ave., F to 14th St. **(see p. 177)**

Lauterbach's. A rec room with a pool table in front and a stage in the back. Brooklyn's beautiful losers as well as legit talent blow in to shake the house.... Tel 718/788–9140. 335 Prospect Ave., Brooklyn; F train to 15th St./Prospect Park. **(see p. 176)**

Lemon. Hot Park Avenue South restaurant/bar hosts all sorts of bashes--lots of literary spottings.... Tel 212/614–1200. 230 Park Ave. South, 6 train to 23rd St. **(see p. 171)**

Life/The Ki Club. Possibly the hippest dance club of the moment, with international DJs and the jetset clamoring to get in. A model model hangout.... Tel 212/420–1999. 158 Bleecker St., 6 train to Bleecker St. **(see p. 174)**

Live Bait. If you leave this Flatiron dive lacking company, you just haven't been working hard enough on your mojo.... Tel 212/353–2400. 14 E. 23rd St., N/R train to 23rd St. **(see p. 178)**

Lucky Strike. You're liable to get pushed out the door and onto the street if you don't snag a table early at this SoHo bar for the young and groovy-looking.... Tel 212/941–0479. 59 Grand St., B/D/Q/F to Grand St. **(see p. 178)**

Ludlow Bar. Anchor of the Lower East Side's neo-bohemia. Somebody plays here almost every night of the week.... Tel 212/353–0536. 165 Ludlow St., B/D/Q/F train to Broadway/Lafayette. **(see p. 175)**

Luna Lounge. Short for Lunacy, probably, judging from Monday's hilarious theme-oriented comedy nights. An alternative must.... *Tel 212/260–2323. 171 Ludlow St., F train to Second Ave.* **(see p. 175)**

M&R. An admirably stocked bar gives way to an inviting dining room decorated with nudes that border on kitsch. Don't miss the Lower East Side's largest collection of truly gigantic liquor bottles.... *Tel 212/226–0559. 264 Elizabeth St., B/D/Q/F train to Broadway/Lafayette.* **(see p. 176)**

Marion's. Hep, man. One of the only bars in town to find even 22-year-olds huddled over silky, arid martinis.... *Tel 212/ 475–7621. 354 Bowery, B/D/Q/F train to Broadway/ Lafayette.* **(see p. 176)**

Maxwell's. New Jersey's main claim to the alternative music scene.... *Tel 201/798–4064. Washington and 11th St., Hoboken, NJ; NJ Transit or PATH train to Hoboken.* **(see p. 176)**

McSorley's Ale House. A tribal gathering-spot for NYU students, Manhattan's oldest beer space can get clogged with drunken louts who've had one stout too many.... *Tel 212/473–9148. 15 E. 7th St., 6 train to Astor Place.* **(see p. 173)**

Merchants N.Y. There are now three locations of this definitive lounge-cum-yuppieteria.... *Tel 212/366–7267. 112 Seventh Ave., 1/9 train to W. 18th St. Tel 212/721–3689, 521 Columbus Ave., 1/9 to W. 86th St. Tel 212/832–1551, 1125 First Ave., 4/5/6 train to 59th St., N/R to Lexington Ave.* **(see pp. 172, 173)**

Mercury Lounge. On it's way to becoming an East Village legend, with an eclectic schedule of bands offering something for every alternative taste.... *Tel 212/260–4700. 217 E. Houston St., F train to Second Ave.* **(see p. 175)**

The Monster. Sheridan Square's best-known fag bar.... *Tel 212/924–3558. 80 Grove St., 1/9 train to Christopher St.* **(see p. 177)**

Mother. Truly divine multi-sexual dance club with memorably wicked theme evenings like Trannie Trekkies (yes, just what the universe needed, Star Trek fans who cross-dress!!!!)... *Tel 212/366–5680. 432 W. 14th St., 1,2,3 train to West 14th St.* **(see pp. 173, 177)**

Nell's. No longer cutting edge, but still crazy after all these years, continuing to appeal to the shifting appetites of the '90s style tribes.... *Tel 212/675–1567. 246 W. 14th St., A/C/E train to 14th St.* **(see pp. 173, 174)**

No Moore. Cool, laid-back hangout with live music featuring everything from boleros to blues.... *Tel 212/925–2595. 234 W. Broadway, 1/9 to Franklin St.* **(see p. 176)**

The Old Town Bar. Nobody messes with The Old Town, and the slightly yupped-out but still polite crowd make sure no one wants to.... *Tel 212/529–6732. 45 E. 18th St., 4/5/6, N/R, or L train to Union Square.* **(see p. 177)**

Pravda. Everyone dresses in monochrome in this dazzlingly trendy (and full of itself) basement spot, bingeing on beluga and downing Stoli martinis as if they were water.... *Tel 212/226–4696. 281 Lafayette St, 6 train to Bleecker St.* **(see p. 171)**

Rodeo Bar. Rockabilly hangout for urban cowboys.... *Tel 212/683–6500. 375 Third Ave., 6 train to 28th St.* **(see p. 175)**

Roseland. Dowdy but endearing old New York ballroom offers everything from rock to salsa and merengue to old-fashioned Big Band touch dancing.... *Tel 212/249–8870. 239 W. 52nd St., 1/9, A/C, or B/D train to 59th St./Columbus Circle.* **(see p. 174)**

The Roxy. Strap on those skates and takes a turn around the immense dance floor at this longtime favorite among locals and tourists alike.... *Tel 212/645–5156. 515 W. 18th St., A/C/E train to 14th St.* **(see p. 173)**

Sapphire Lounge. A nightly hotspot for the fashionably bohemian Lower East Side set.... *Tel 212/777–5153. 249 Eldridge St., F train to Broadway/Lafayette.* **(see p. 171)**

Scores. This swank strip club is the spot for lap dances of luxury.... *Tel 212/421–3600. 333 E. 60th St., 4/5/6 to 59th St., N/R to Lexington Ave.* **(see p. 178)**

The Shark Bar. Tall, dark, and handsome soul food/music joint with matching clientele.... *Tel 212/874–8500. 307 Amsterdam Ave., 1/2/3/9 train to 72nd St.* **(see p. 172)**

Sidewalk Cafe. Slacker paradise, from cheap booze to the substantial portions of food. Live music several nights a week. No cover, but the tip jar usually goes around.... *Tel 212/ 473–7373. 94 Avenue A, F train to Second Ave.* **(see p. 175)**

SOB's (Sounds of Brazil). Got a taste for salsa? SOB's serves up a rich mixture.... *Tel 212/243–4940. 204 Varick St., 1/9 train to Houston St.* **(see p. 175)**

Sound Factory Bar. The definitive home to customized house mix, with some of the city's most sought-after DJs. Hyperyouthful.... *Tel 212/206–7770. 12 W. 21st St., F train to 23rd St.* **(see p. 173)**

The Spike. Lots of big moustaches and crotch-contorting Levis at this recently democratized S/M and leather paradise.... *Tel 212/243–9688. 120 Eleventh Ave., A/C/E train to 14th St.* **(see p. 176)**

Splash. A friendly gay bar scene; tasty musical offerings, too. If Chelsea pretty boys and professional types are objects of your desire, come on down.... *Tel 212/691–0073. 50 W. 17th St., F train to 14th St.* **(see p. 176)**

Spy. Persian carpets, crystal chandeliers, and caviar animate this sultry supper club where the C-list makes a beeline after hours.... *Tel 212/343–9000. 101 Greene St., 6 train to Spring St.* **(see p. 171)**

Stingy Lulu's. In summer the sidewalk tables here host a lively mix. Order the cheapest screwdriver in town and gawk at the freaks spilling out of Tompkins Square Park across the way.... *Tel 212/674–3545. 129 St. Mark's Place, 6 train to Astor Place or F to Second Ave.* **(see p. 178)**

NIGHTLIFE | THE INDEX

Tenth Street Lounge. So cool you might not be able to stand yourself after three or four $7 cognacs. Very comfortable if you can evade the attitude.... *Tel 212/473–5252. 212 E. 10th St., 4/5/6, N/R, or L train to Union Square.*

(see p. 176)

The Townhouse. Three rooms filled with aging gay preppies, including a piano bar.... *Tel 212/754–4649. 236 E. 58th St., 4/5/6 to 50th St., N/R to Lexington Ave.* (see p. 177)

Tramps. This blues club stands as one of Manhattan's true musical treasures.... *Tel 212/727–7788. 54 W. 21st St., F train to 23rd St.* (see p. 175)

I Tre Merli. A cavernous SoHo emporium for cruising the very beautiful.... *Tel 212/254-8699. 463 W. Broadway, C/E train to Spring St. or N/R to Prince St.* (see p. 178)

Tribeca Tavern. A perfect place to drink and talk, with soft jazz, brick walls, bronze sconces, and comfort food like Yankee Pot Roast.... *Tel 212/965–0141. 247 W. Broadway, 1/9 to Franklin St.* (see p. 173)

Tunnel. A subterranean club—literally and figuratively what its name says. Not the cheapest option around.... *Tel 212/695–7292. 220 Twelfth Ave., A/C/E train to 14th St.*

(see p. 174)

The Vault. Harsh, harsh, harsh, but always chock-full of consenting adults and the men who love to watch them (women, too, sometimes).... *Tel 212/255–6758. 565 W. 23rd St.., 1/9 train to 23rd St.* (see p. 178)

Waterloo. This casual but classy Belgian brasserie is one of the flavors of the moment for drinks and food.... *Tel 212/ 352–1119. 145 Charles St., A/C/E/ to 14th St.*

(see pp. 171, 173)

Webster Hall. Five spacious floors, each offering a different style of music to mostly college-aged crowds.... *Tel 212/ 353–1600. 125 E. 11th St., 4/5/6 train to Union Square.*

(see p. 174)

Wetlands. New York's hippie trippy love shack, where earnest young'uns gather for live music and poetry readings.... *Tel 212/966–4225. 161 Hudson St., 1/9 train to Christopher St.* (see pp. 173, 175)

Wonder Bar. A festival of silliness for gay men on the make, lipstick lesbians, and the straight students who are drawn to them. Not for older cruisers.... *Tel 212/777–9105. 505 E. 6th St., 6 train to Astor Place or F to Second Ave.*
(see p. 177)

Zinc Bar. Sexy, cozy jazz bar where the music, mood, and making out are all slinky.... *Tel 212/477–8337. 90 Houston St., A/C/E/B/D/F/Q trains to W. 4th St./Washington Square.*
(see p. 175)

enterta

7

nment

It's a big country,
but no one guzzles
culture quite like
New Yorkers. And
there are so many
entertainment
options

here, sometimes you can feel it's hopeless even to try to keep up. Frankly, it *is* hopeless. On a given day, a dozen must-see acts will pass through town, twice as many during the height of the spring and fall seasons, when all the opera companies and orchestras are in residence and every dance troupe in town is premiering new work. And these aren't just performances; they are world-class performances, in everything from acid jazz to chamber music to grand opera to cabaret to basketball.

In Manhattan, any old church can (and many do) host comic improv troupes, performance art pieces so cutting-edge they draw blood, and esoteric concerts such as Zimbabwean Mbira music (normally used to call spirits or change weather). Even museums such as the Guggenheim and the Met serve as venues for concerts and recitals, often accompanied by droning lectures. Best of all, there are umpteen freebie events that run the gamut from dungeon drag acts to chamber music recitals, to help New Yorkers remember how civilized—and forget how uncivil—city life can be. Central Park is the venue for major FREE performances by such luminaries as the New York Philharmonic, Metropolitan Opera (at least one of the Three Tenors may show up), Paul Simon, Garth Brooks, and (in)famously, Diana Ross. Hang out at Lincoln Center's plazas, where mimes, flutists, jugglers, stand-up comics, fire eaters, tap dancers congregate—a fun, free taste of all New York has to offer. Hell, even street musicians in the subways may be Juilliard-trained professionals.

Simple advice: Spend some time planning your entertainment itinerary before the plane lands. There are a lot of people in New York, and if an event is hot, that just means a lot of other people will have heard about it too. But for every failed plan in Gotham, an unexplored opportunity lurks in the wings. It's simply a matter of digging a little deeper.

Sources

The New York Times Sunday "Arts and Leisure" section contains a thorough list of the upcoming week's entertainment options, delivered in an even tone that makes few discernible attempts to help readers figure out what's worth their trouble. A helpful source, but not much fun. The unflaggingly comprehensive *Time Out*, a weekly newcomer to the New York scene, lists anything and everything you could want, spiced with a soupçon of catiness.

The New Yorker's "Goings On About Town" section provides a swift, disputatious rundown of the upcoming week's events, delivered in the magazine's arch, vaguely bemused style.

The film reviews are particularly useful, although not always extensive or exhaustive. Priceless bon mots from retired film critic Pauline Kael (the grande dame of American film criticism, actually) often adorn the revival-house listings, and witty hatchet jobs are frequently tucked away in the section's columns of tiny print. The magazine hits the stands each Monday.

The *Village Voice*, available for free bright and early every Wednesday morning, performs for the Downtown scene the service that *The New Yorker* supplies to the Uptown crowd. Though its once impeccable alternative credentials are increasingly tarnished these days, the paper's "Choices" listing remains top-drawer, if at times awfully predictable.

The *New York Press* combines a poverty-stricken slacker sensibility with a larder of gallivanting sarcasm. The "Movie Clock" section supplies compressed versions of Godfrey Cheshire's dandy film critiques, and the paper features a very reliable cluster of neighborhood-by-neighborhood restaurant reviews. Best of all, the paper is free, dispensed from green street-corner boxes throughout Downtown.

New York magazine covers more ground than *The New Yorker*, but culture-scarred Gothamites tend to view the publication as a very expensively produced newsletter for inhabitants of the Upper East and West Sides. The back-of-the-book rundown of weekly events is not only *The New Yorker*'s main competition, but may have surpassed it as the most colorful and *au courant* available.

The New York *Observer* runs a weekly calendar of stuff worth seeing or, better yet, crashing ("The Eight-Day Week"), but be careful: the rag is wry and snooty, which makes for great reading but doesn't always transmit the most straightforward summary of what's hot and what's not. The *Observer* notices every smarmy detail of city life in haute muckraking fashion, providing salty comments peppered with spicy gossip. *HX* and *Next*, ostensibly dedicated to the gay/lesbian/bisexual/transgendered/aren't we P.C.? scene, are also superb sources for cabaret listings, club lowdowns and highlights, and anything with a whiff of decadence.

Getting Tickets

The swiftest way to get tickets to major theatrical events is by hitting the **TKTS** booth in Duffy Square (at 47th and Broadway) or the one in the World Trade Center, where discounted tickets go on sale the day of performances. Lines can be long, so your best bet is to show up early. Wednesday and Saturday matinees are on sale from 10am to 2; tickets to evening performances sell from 3 to 8; and Sunday performances, both matinee and evening, are offered from noon to 8. What's available is posted on a digital bulletin board that's updated as ticket supplies dwindle. Remember, TKTS accepts only cash or traveler's checks, no credit cards. And you never know what Broadway troupes will be on hand to boost flagging ticket sales.

To secure seats in advance, the surest plan of attack is to phone the theater's box office. It's sensible to call several weeks in advance for big-time Broadway musicals, but off- and off-off-Broadway theaters and performance venues often have tickets right up till show time. A lot of box offices will first steer you toward **Ticketmaster** (tel 307–7171), **Telecharge** (tel 239–6200), or **Centercharge** (tel 721–6500), which smack you with surcharges and limited seating choices.

For eleventh-hour enthusiasts, the concierge at your hotel is a better bet than any overpriced ticket agency. **Ticket scalpers** are always an option, too. Look for forlorn types hanging around in front of the theater or concert hall with their tickets raised. Expect to cough up some serious cash for this last-resort technique. It doesn't hurt to visit the box office first, either, particularly at Lincoln Center, to ask if there are any last-minute **returns**. Don't bet on scoring anything if Yo-Yo Ma is playing Carnegie Hall, but for a spontaneous night out, this is often a way to luck into an interesting evening.

The Lowdown

All that jazz... All roads lead to the **Village Vanguard**, which cannot really be trumped by any other of the city's many jazz meccas. This underground former speakeasy oozes credibility from every nicotinic pore. Listeners really listen, with an intensity that often verges on the pathological. For catching the next Wynton Marsalis or Joshua Redman, the Vanguard can't be beat. **Iridium**, with its Dr. Seuss-meets-Gaudí decor, looked like it was going to suffer the usual Uptown-seeks-Downtown audience identity crisis, but the deeply weird downstairs space has established a reputation for booking the best of the best and the sharpest of the up-and-coming. The **Blue Note** sports a history that most other clubs would give up a year's worth of door receipts to borrow, and it shows both in the gargantuan ticket prices and the gift shop. The place is a shrine, and no one's going to knock it—everyone who still is anyone, from Dave Brubeck to the Modern Jazz Quartet, has the Blue Note slotted as their venue of choice in Gotham. The **Café Carlyle** in the Carlyle Hotel books in other performers, but the one who keeps well-heeled connoisseurs of American pop standards coming back is Bobby Short, an Uptown institution at the hotel's grand piano. Short plays and sings his songbook like it was meant to be, with unparalleled urbanity and sophistication (he looks devilishly comfortable in a tux); looking devilishly uncomfortable and sweaty is Woody Allen—yeah, the Woodman himself—playing here on Monday nights, now that his long-time haunt Michael's Pub has closed. Absolutely fabulous cabaret divas like Georgia Brown and Barbara Cook also spell Short at the Carlyle. **Sweet Basil**, which outwardly resembles a glorified coffee shop, has a split personality: By night, the talent on stage is often so high caliber that the appropriate response is to fawn; by day (on weekends, at any rate) it's home to 90-year-old Doc Cheatham, who performs a jazz brunch loaded with peerlessly performed Dixieland chestnuts and episodes of somewhat windy storytelling.

If old-style jazz is getting you down, the **Knitting Factory** puts on occasional off-the-wall jazz festivals that feature the likes of Cecil Taylor and John Zorn. **Visiones**—a club that features young, less expensive players—possesses limited chic but rarely fails to draw in the knowledgeable jazz buffs who understand that money isn't everything. Standards are indeed high at **The Jazz Standard**, which presents purists and iconoclasts like Vincent Herring and Eric Alexander.

If Sinatra's your style... The **Rainbow Room**, perhaps Gotham's most famous bar, possesses one of the city's grandest views, taking in the whole sweep of the island in four directions from its windowed home atop Midtown's Rockefeller Center. Revolving dance floor, big-band music, the works; top cabaret acts perform at the attached **Rainbow & Stars**. **Tavern on the Green**, Central Park's twinkle-lit restaurant, attracts jazz luminaries like Margaret Whiting and Lionel Hampton to its Chestnut Room; in summer, you can dance cheek-to-cheek outside in the garden, under glowing chintz-covered lanterns. The legendary **Algonquin** hotel, once home to the scabrous wit of Dorothy Parker and the Round Table's clutch of literary regulars (among them humorist Robert

Benchley and *New Yorker* founder Harold Ross), still offers clubby charm, and its Oak Room books superb pop- and jazz-standard vocalists on the order of Andrea Marcovicci and Michael Feinstein. If you can't get into the Rainbow Room, the swank **Supper Club** is the high-priced ticket for touch-dancing (black tie optional) to pop vocalists and neo-swing bands.

Cheap jazz and cabaret... There's always room for cheap jazz and cabaret, most of which is clustered around Sheridan Square in a neighborhood famous for its large gay population. Anchoring the scene is **The Duplex,** a glittery, garish, gloriously tasteless club with a piano bar downstairs and various camp, comedy, and performance acts upstairs in the Game Room. Out of favor in recent years, but lately staging a comeback thanks to several critically-acclaimed young talents. On nearby Grove Street, **Arthur's Tavern** books in less-than-serious jazz from semi-vanished musicians—which doesn't mean that the blowing isn't good; it's just cheaper than at the haughtier joints. Next door, **Marie's Crisis Cafe** could be rightly accused of suffering from a crisis of decor (the color scheme is wood and red), but it's a genial and casual place to hang out by the piano for a few hours. Keep your eye open for the beloved Diva Arthur, a waiter at Marie's for years—a 300-lb. number who could vanquish any Valkyrie and slaughter Siegfried. **Eighty Eights** and **Don't Tell Mama** both book more conventional acts by up-and-coming chorus boys and girls; you can get a free taste in their front rooms when the bit players take to the mike with a vengeance. **Smalls,** on West 10th Street, has reintroduced the jazz marathon to budget-conscious aficianados. For $10 you get ten hours of music, from 10pm to 8am every night, plus free food and drinks.

Men in tights... In the past decade, New York has conceded some of its dominance of the dance world to Seattle and San Francisco, but Gotham still has more venues where the absolute best and brightest perform regularly. The perfect place to start is at **Lincoln Center**, where the **New York City Ballet** holds two seasons a year at the New York State Theater. This is classical dance with a strong modernist edge, the product of ballet master George Balanchine's longtime creative influence and

ENTERTAINMENT | THE LOWDOWN

Lincoln Kirstein's intellectual enthusiasm for the art form. Nowadays, Peter Martins runs the show, but Balanchine's chosen successor is not without his troubles: several prominent dance critics have been calling for his head. Despite the politics and critical opinions about the corruption of the Balanchine legacy, the company soldiers on, and December belongs to *The Nutcracker*, a New York holiday institution. During the summer, when NYCB retires to its off-season home in Saratoga, the State Theater's stage is turned over to the likes of the Mark Morris Dance Company and Barishnikov's White Oaks Project.

American Ballet Theater (ABT) also holds court at Lincoln Center, but in the Metropolitan Opera House, for two short seasons at the beginning of summer and fall. What City Ballet is to modernist severity and innovation, ABT is to reliable, melodramatic gush like *Giselle* and *Swan Lake:* a romantic museum for *la danse classique*. Mikhail Barishnikov presided over the company for a while, but since his departure ABT has been struggling to build an identity, recently reanimated by several promising young dancers.

City Center, a gloomy Spanish baroque pile (fast by Carnegie Hall) that was City Ballet's home long ago, now most often plays host to New York's great post-Balanchine experimental companies, such as Merce Cunningham, Paul Taylor, and Alvin Ailey.

Downtown, the **Joyce Theater**, with its unpretentious architecture, intimate scale, and unobstructed views, may be the best place in town to catch a performance. A constant stream of local, regional, and international talent crosses the Joyce's stage, everyone from Garth Fagen and Bill T. Jones to Eliot Feld and a gaggle of Native American and European companies. Right around the corner is **Dance Theater Workshop** (DTW), the liveliest of the city's alternative dance spaces, where the critics go to check the pulse of postmodern choreography and performance. Farther downtown, **St. Mark's Church-in-the-Bowery**, a converted church, opens its iron gates to a variety of innovative young companies, as does Soho's **Ohio Theater**. **P.S. 122**, a central venue for the alternative East Village theater and arts scene, often features performances that involve dance, though that could as easily mean someone writhing on the floor as something more upstanding.

The **Brooklyn Academy of Music** (BAM) plays host each year to the vaunted Next Wave Festival, a smorgasbord of avant-garde performances that never fails to include the work of some inventive new choreographer; Mark Morris first began to capture critical attention here.

What's opera, doc?... Most New Yorkers are too intimidated by the hopelessly garish Metropolitan Opera House to be properly Italian in their passions toward the city's largest opera company, the **Metropolitan Opera**. The Big House, as some have less-than-affectionately dubbed it, instead seems like a high-art cathedral for corporate sponsors and wealthy expatriate Eurotrash, a sorry state of affairs borne out by bloated ticket prices and overblown staging. Still, this is grand opera on a vast scale, the only house in America with the wherewithal to stage Wagner's compete Ring Cycle on consecutive nights and provide a home for one of the world's finest opera orchestras. The ultra-cheap seats are miles from the action, but if you have $30 and a powerful set of binoculars, you can hang out with the opera queens and longtime devotees, some of whom whip themselves into a scary lather of "bravos" for curtain calls. All operas are sung in the original language, but the Met projects supertitles on the backs of each row of seats. Since its inception, the audience even laughs at the jokes in Verdi (but, tellingly, a beat or two *before* the joke is sung).

A pleasant alternative is provided by the perennially strapped **New York City Opera**, where supertitles accompany a more dynamic series of seasonal offerings at Lincoln Center's New York State Theater. Culture-watchers have been hailing City Opera as the more interesting option for years, but the institution-in-waiting has yet to catch on with the public. The quality of the performances is high, however, and radically eclectic, recently showcasing classic Broadway musicals and new work such as an opera about slain San Francisco gay activist Harvey Milk.

The truly intrepid will board the subway or cross the Brooklyn Bridge and visit the **Brooklyn Academy of Music** (BAM), whose lushly renovated opera house combines starkly experimental offerings and an occasional tidbit from the canon. The building itself is a jewel, a remnant from the days when Brooklyn competed with Manhattan in a interborough contest to rule the city's cultural roost.

Miscellaneous operatic treats are available on a catch-as-catch-can basis at **Carnegie Hall**, where opera's living legends sometimes sing solo gigs, and at several smaller venues around town, including the Bowery's tiny **Amato Opera Company**.

Comedy tonight... Comedy in New York is hit-or-miss: amateur nights are more common than headliner-thick extravaganzas. As a rule, it's not one of the less-expensive entertainment options in town, but clubs like **ReBar** and **Stand-up New York** have begun to reverse the upwardly-mobile trend established by glossy venues such as **Caroline's**, where many popular current comics got their big breaks.

The theatah... Theater courses through the veins of New York. No other city in the world, except perhaps London, can match Manhattan for sheer volume of nightly offerings, and Wednesdays, Saturdays and Sundays add matinees as well. The scene separates somewhat uncertainly into three groups, with ticket prices falling accordingly. Broadway means large-scale musical productions, à la Andrew Lloyd Webber's *Phantom of the Opera* and the recent revival hits *Chicago* and *1776*, as well as beloved dramas featuring big Hollywood names, like Kathleen Turner in Tennessee Williams' *Cat on a Hot Tin Roof* or Ralph Fiennes in a touring British production of *Hamlet*. Most Broadway theaters are clustered around Times Square. Off-Broadway is quirkier and more artistically aloof, though not immune to booking goofy acts like magicians Penn & Teller, acrobat/jugglers like the Flying Karamazov Brothers, and mime Bill Irwin. The line between the two has become increasingly blurred, with numerous transfers from smaller houses to Broadway theaters. You're more likely to find plays here rather than musicals. Off-off Broadway is anything-goes territory, with theaters scattered all over town, largely in Greenwich Village, the East Village, SoHo, and Tribeca. For alternative performances and the avant-garde, this is where you'll want to focus your energies. On Broadway, *Cats* has been at the **Winter Garden** forever, playing to unsophisticated outsiders who don't realize what a local joke it has become. Theaters like the **Shubert** and the **Martin Beck** continue to host full-scale events even though their physical spaces are somewhat cramped (most common comment from first-time

New York theatergoers: "I had no idea they'd be so small…"). Bigger theaters like the cavernous **Gershwin Theater** present just the opposite problem; if you sit in back you can't see anything without binoculars, or hear anything except the reverberations of over-amplified dialogue—that lip-synching feeling. (Hardly a show on Broadway these days isn't miked—actors have practically forgotten how to project.) Broadway has absorbed plenty of criticism over the past 15 years for sacrificing the great American musical (*Oklahoma!*) for overblown production extravaganzas imported from London, but a recent resurgence of native talent, notably from legendary director Hal Prince, has raised local temperatures. Mammoth, ambitious SRO shows like *Rent*, *Titanic*, and the Disney Organization's gorgeously surreal *The Lion King* at the newly restored **New Amsterdam Theater** demonstrate the Yanks can razzle dazzle as well as any Brit import. Good thing, too, with orchestra seats now going at $75 for the big shows. At Lincoln Center, tucked behind the Metropolitan Opera House, discriminating theatergoers will find the **Vivian Beaumont Theatre**, where recent years have seen formidable plays on the order of *Arcadia* and *Six Degrees of Separation*. The Lincoln Center Theater Company also presents top revivals like *The Heiress* and *A Delicate Balance*.

Off-Broadway, more a state of mind than an address, begins on Ninth Avenue and stretches to Tenth along 42nd Street's Theater Row, a neighborhood of houses with smaller seating capacities (and occasionally grander artistic ambitions) than the Broadway houses. Hailing a cab Downtown will extend your off-Broadway excursion; theaters that specialize in the serious work of sustaining American drama down here include **Circle Rep**, the **Cherry Lane Theater**, **Ohio Theater**, and the **Orpheum**. Farther uptown and off Broadway's beaten path reside the **Manhattan Theater Club**, the **Roundabout** (specializing in star-studded revivals), **Playwrights Horizons**, and the **Promenade/Second Stage**. For the denizens of Downtown, Joe Papp's legendary **Public Theatre**, now under George Wolfe's direction, presents some of the finest contemporary drama available to New Yorkers, including the likes of Sam Shepard and David Henry Hwang. It also presents the New York Shakespeare Festival at Central Park's

Delacorte Theater and develops the occasional Broadway mega-hit like *Bring in Da Noise, Bring in Da Funk.*

Off-off Broadway experiments can be found far from the Theater District's madding throngs; catching satirist David Sedaris' latest zany ensemble exercise or the debut by a previously unheard-of playwright at a Downtown venue can add up to lotsa hipster cachet. **P.S. 122** and the fabled **LaMama** fall into this camp. In another category, performance art (ridiculed by some stodgy critics as being neither), along with some pretty respectable satires of contemporary mores, regularly take over spaces (not theaters, kiddo, performance spaces) like the **Kitchen**, **Franklin Furnace**, and the **Brooklyn Academy of Music** (BAM). These are the folks who cause furors over NEA grants; in extremis you may be splattered with bodily secretions, but generally the (out)rage is confined to the stage.

Classical sounds... Lincoln Center's **Avery Fisher Hall** boasts the New York Philharmonic, considered by many in the know as the best band in America. Unfortunately, the hall has never provided acoustics to match the Philharmonic's world-class reputation, but new maestro Kurt Masur has assured the public that something is being done. In recent years, programming at the Philharmonic has fallen into a bit of a rut, at the expense of forays into dense and complicated 20th–century music. Still a great place to hear Beethoven and Mahler, however. During the summer, be sure to catch the Mostly Mozart Festival, when classical-music greats most certainly do not limit themselves to the output of Austria's boy *wunderkind.*

Adjoining Avery Fisher is the more intimate (and acoustically satisfying) **Alice Tully Hall**, a cube into which are squeezed devotees of the Chamber Society of Lincoln Center and the assorted groups affiliated with the **Juilliard School**.

Ten or so blocks from Lincoln Center is the forever glorious **Carnegie Hall,** which to out-of-towners remains synonymous with American music and the tradition of classical performances in New York. The interior is sturdy and patriotic, the sound extraordinary and irreplaceable, even after its successful 1986 renovation. Upstairs, its Weill Recital Hall hosts smaller recitals and chamber groups.

The cerebral modern-music crowd hangs out at **Merkin Concert Hall,** just north of Lincoln Center, where they discuss music matters in hushed and reverent whispers. Make no mistake: this stuff is not for everybody, and the likelihood is slim that you'll meet someone at intermission whose specialty is light banter. But the chance that you'll find yourself sitting next to the composer is pretty good, and even if you know nothing of 12-tone architectures or sound-poems, eavesdropping on post-performance conversations can be entertaining as well as instructional.

Way Uptown, at City College's **Aaron Davis Hall**, the World Music Institute lures string-and-reed junkies from around Manhattan to listen to the unusual performances that regularly crop up on its schedule. Downtown, **Grace Church** puts together occasional performances of classical and sacred music. Church-concert enthusiasts will want to make the long subway trek Uptown to the **Cathedral of St. John the Divine**, a vast superterranean cavern—still unfinished—where the fare runs from New Age acts, such as the Paul Winter Consort, to performances of Native American music and dance, to AIDS benefit concerts. Back in Midtown, the **Museum of Modern Art**'s sculpture garden plays host to a variety of free "Summergarden" concerts that often feature dense, cerebral 20th-century music. At **Lincoln Center**, students at the Julliard School also give frequent free recitals.

In concert... The really happening music happens in the clubs—see the Nightlife chapter for the dirt on that scene. Larger venues such as the **Bottom Line**, and the **Beacon Theater**, can be depended upon to bring in somebody you've heard of before, probably someone with piles of CDs on the racks at Tower Records, probably someone slogging through a multi-record deal. Of these, the Beacon has the healthiest attitude toward juicy live performances. Not a hopeless option if you'd prefer to catch an act in a venue where your feet won't stick to the floor and where mosh pits are rare. **Town Hall** is a mid-sized space whose eclecticism ranges from bluegrass or jazz quintets to staged readings of Broadway musical revivals. **Irving Plaza** books the latest new-wave musical acts, with an almost psychic ability to select performers who are about to break out mainstream. The crowd is barely legal and enthusiastic as hell. Major-label bands explore their arena potential at New York's larger locations, including **Giants Stadium** in East Rutherford, NJ.

The big acts also put in appearances at **Madison Square Garden** and the **Brendan Byrne Arena** at the Meadowlands, in the same complex as Giants Stadium. The **Paramount**, which is within the Madison Square Garden building, also offers plenty of room to stretch out and rock, but if the likes of Bette Midler and Barbra Streisand are more your taste, make tracks for **Radio City Music Hall** at Rockefeller Center, still home to the fabulous, leggy Rockettes.

Spoken word... A neo-Beatnik revival of "spoken word" or "performance" poetry has been invigorating New York's literary life. Used to be that almost none of the poets who took the stage at the **Nuyorican Poets Café** had published anything, but that's all changing now with limber-lyricked wordsmiths like Paul Beatty, Reg E. Gaines, Sapphire, and Carl Hancock Rux. The scene is much, much less whitebread than it was in the good old Beat days.

For traditional poetry, there are the Academy of American Poets' seasonal readings at **The New School** and the **92nd St. Y**'s continuing series of readings. This is the place to hear old white male poets. The Y also seems to snag every *New Yorker* writer, whitebeards (i.e., Peter Matthiessen) in particular, and offers numerous intriguing lecture series, like Lyrics and Lyricists. The **Dia Center for the Arts**, on West 22nd Street, also offers a reading series that features noted poets on the order of Richard Howard and Thom Gunn. **St. Mark's Church-in-the-Bowery** has hosted readings since Kerouac and Ginsberg made it a favored hangout, and the beat, from rap-poetry to all-too-free verse, goes on. That bastion of civility, the **Algonquin Hotel**, has returned to its literary roasts, uh, roots, hoping to resurrect the spirit of the Round Table with regular readings (no poisoned quills or barbs yet, alas). **A Different Light** features not only often-hilarious gay, lesbian, bisexual, and transgendered authors, but even mainstream heteros, like George Plimpton (well, okay, he was reading from his oral history of uber-fag Truman Capote). At the gazillion **Barnes and Noble** and **Borders** bookstores you can repair for a latte, then hear anyone from Emeril Lagasse to Don De Lillo. Check out the monthly Poetry Calendar, available at **B. Dalton** in the Village and at **St. Mark's Book Shop**, to scan all of the poetic offerings.

The big game... With everything else there is to do in New York, watching sports could be confined to sports bars. Good spots for sports bar potatoes are: **Boomer's** (349 Amsterdam Ave., tel 212/362–5400), **Mickey Mantle's**, 42 Central Park S., tel 212/688–7777), **Rusty Staub's** (575 Fifth Ave., tel 212/682–1000), and the **Sporting Club** (99 Hudson St., tel 212/219–0900), and in a post-season where a local club is still in the running, virtually any neighborhood bar with a television.

Of course, if that strikes you as a pale substitute for the real thing, you can mosey up to **Yankee Stadium** in the Bronx or **Shea Stadium** in Queens to watch, respectively, the storied Yankees and the upstart Mets. Tickets are easy to come by right now for both. For football fans, the Giants and Jets knock heads with their NFL rivals at **Giants Stadium** in the Meadowlands; tickets are hard to find for Jets games and impossible for the Giants. The hockey puck flies at **Madison Square Garden**, where the 1994 Stanley Cup champion Rangers slap it around. The 1995 champs, the New Jersey Devils, play at the **Brendan Byrne Arena** across the Hudson, while the New York Islanders can be found at the **Nassau Coliseum** in Uniondale, Long Island. The Rangers are the toughest ticket out of the three. During basketball season the New York Knicks share the Garden with the Rangers, and their Jersey counterparts, the Nets, alternate with the Devils at Byrne Arena. Knicks' tickets have been hard to come by the last few years, but lackadaisical play and Patrick Ewing's career-threatening knee injury may change that. The **U.S.T.A. National Tennis Center** in Flushing, Queens, plays host each year to the US Open Tennis Championships (tickets cost a mint and must be secured a year in advance), a grueling two-week affair around Labor Day that showcases the best the sport has to offer in a brilliantly redesigned space including a newer, larger stadium with superb sightlines. Later each fall, the New York City Marathon is run in November on a 26-mile course that winds through each of Manhattan's five boroughs. There's thoroughbred horseracing at **Aqueduct Racetrack** and at **Belmont Park**, home to the hotly followed last race in the Triple Crown, the Belmont Stakes. But for the truly urbane, the spectator sport of choice is billiards; rack 'em up for a languid game of eight-ball or a swift game of nine-ball at **Julian's Famous Poolroom**, the city's best-known pool hall.

The silver screen... At $8.75-$9 a seat, it's expensive by some standards, but film in New York is also thorough, with major Hollywood flicks premiering at the same time as cerebral art-house releases. The **Film Forum** maintains an untrammeled reputation for uncovering independent gems as well as for scheduling festivals and revivals of classics. **Anthology Film Archives** monitors the avant-garde, presenting documentary shorts and experimental celluloid from indy legends such as Stan Brackidge. The **Angelika Film Center** brings in an endless supply of minor European films and small-budget American stuff, all as lively and eclectic as possible; enjoy a muffin and espresso prior to the show at their inviting upstairs cafe. The **Public Theater** puts together well-curated festivals, as well as short-run re-releases and experimental gallery projects, such as video artist Matthew Barney's *Cremaster 4*. Uptown and for the more retrospectively inclined, there's the **Museum of Modern Art**, which screens stuff from its archives; it doesn't shy away from the controversial—half the audience once walked out on a screening of Werner Herzog's *Even Dwarfs Started Small*. The **Whitney Museum of American Art** has a respectable interest in films by gay, lesbian, ethnic, and African-American movie- and videomakers (PixleVision maven Sadie Benning first achieved notice at the Whitney's Biennial show, which features a film and video program alongside more traditional artworks). Lincoln Center's **Walter Reade Theater** gives film buffs the New York Film Festival, and during the rest of the year puts together ambitious surveys of whole directorial careers. An excellent place to spot Susan Sontag with a huge tub of popcorn, if that strikes your fancy. In Queens, the **American Museum of the Moving Image** attempts to do for film what the Metropolitan Museum has done for oil and canvas. A strong foreign-film diet can be cultivated at **Lincoln Plaza**, where the Muzak between showings is as sophisticated as the well-heeled crowd. If what you desire is a maximum-large, good old-fashioned cinematic experience, the giant screen at the **Ziegfeld** provides a grand alternative to the suburban-mall multiplex. Midtown's **Bryant Park**, home to the chic-at-lunch Bryant Park Grill, takes Manhattan to the drive-in with a series of free summer screenings that start at dusk. Arrive early and pack a picnic. If the dorky IMAX is your thing, check out the hilariously kitschy **Lincoln Square** mondoplex.

The Index

Aaron Davis Hall (at City College). Venture far uptown for a varied tasting of concert offerings.... *Tel 212/650–7100. W. 134th St. at Convent Ave., 1/9 train to 137th St.*
(see p. 200)

A Different Light. New York's preeminent queer bookstore, with performers and film screenings.... *Tel 212/989–4950. 151 West 19th St., 1/9 train to West 18th.* **(see p. 201)**

Algonquin. See Accommodations.

Alice Tully Hall. Avery Fisher's younger sister, a smaller venue that comfortably contains the Chamber Music Society of Lincoln Center.... *Tel 212/875–5050. 65 W. 65th St., 1/9 train to 66th St./Lincoln Center.* **(see p. 199)**

Amato Opera Company. Where young opera talent cut their chops on the Bowery.... *Tel 212/228–8200. 319 Bowery, B/D/Q/F train to Broadway/Lafayette or F to Second Ave.*
(see p. 197)

American Ballet Theater (ABT). Where the classics thrive, performed by some outstanding younger dancers.... *Tel 212/477–3030. Lincoln Center, 1/9 train to 66th St./Lincoln Center.* **(see p. 195)**

American Museum of the Moving Image. see Diversions.

Angelika Film Center. As the hippest multiplex in this hipper-than-thou neighborhood, it can be offputtingly crowded on weekends.... *Tel 212/995–2000. 18 W. Houston St., B/D/Q/F train to Broadway/Lafayette.* **(see p. 203)**

Anthology Film Archives. Even if you're a film junkie, this small East Village theater will show something you've never heard of.... *Tel 212/505–5110. 32–34 Second Ave., B/D/ Q/F train to Broadway/Lafayette.* **(see p. 203)**

Aqueduct Racetrack. Thoroughbred racing here runs from late October or early November to early May.... *Tel 718/641– 4700. Rockaway Beach, Queens; A train to North Conduit. Closed Mon and Tue.* **(see p. 202)**

Arthur's Tavern. Low-rent jazz for fans with flexible standards....*Tel 212/675–6879. 57 Grove St., 1/9 train to Christopher St.* **(see p. 194)**

Avery Fisher Hall. The posh crowd shouldn't ruin an evening with the generally fabulous, if rarely provocative, New York Philharmonic.... *Tel 212/875–5030. Lincoln Center, 1/9 train to 66th St./Lincoln Center.* **(see p. 199)**

Barnes and Noble. These book superstores are thick as flies on honey in Manhattan, but all provide the usual cafe (yes, it IS the same mural at each location) and frequent readings. Call the Events Line, tel 212/727–4810, for daily events and locations. **(see p. 201)**

B Dalton. A multi-level west village literary hub with readings and excellent window designs.... *Tel 212/674–8780. 396 Avenue of the Americas, take B/D/Q/F or A/C/E to West 4th Street. Call 212/633–3300 for other locations.* **(see p. 201)**

Beacon Theater. A decent-sized house that books in a wide variety of mainstream and semi-mainstream acts.... *Tel 212/ 496–7070. 2124 Broadway, 1/9 or 2/3 train to 72nd St.* **(see p. 200)**

Belmont Park. Whenever the horses don't run at Aqueduct (see above), they're racing here. Season May to mid-July and late August or early September to October.... *Tel 718/ 641–4700. Hempstead Ave., Elmont, Long Island, LIRR Belmont Express from Penn Station or Flatbush Ave. Closed Mon and Tue.* **(see p. 202)**

Blue Note. Expensive tickets and too damn much merchandise, but also the place for live performances by jazz's giants like Herbie Hancock and Chick Corea... *Tel 212/475–8592. 131 W. 3rd St., A/C/E or B/D/Q/F train to W. 4th St.* **(see p. 192)**

Borders. Huge bookstores with all of the usual suspects: cafe, large children's section, and lots of helpful salespeople.... *Tel 212/839–8049. 5 World Trade Plaza, take 1/9, A/C/E to the World Trade Center, and 212/980–6785, 57th Street and Park Avenue, take 4/5/6 or N/R to 59th Street and Lexington.*
(see p. 201)

Bottom Line. No surprises, at this club, which is more likely to bring in an easy-listening heartthrob than a guitar-slashing punkster. Still, a groovy standby.... *Tel 212/228–6300. 15 W. 4th St., A/C/E or B/D/Q/F train to W. 4th St.* **(see p. 200)**

Brendan Byrne Arena. Cavernous arena across the Hudson in New Jersey where NHL's Devils and NBA's Nets compete.... *Tel 201/935–3900. The Meadowlands, East Rutherford, NJ, Buses from Port Authority.* **(see pp. 201, 202)**

Brooklyn Academy of Music (BAM). Where the avant-garde hangs its beret.... *Tel 718/636–4100. 30 Lafayette Ave., Brooklyn; D/Q, 2/3, or 4/5 train to Atlantic Ave. or B, M, or N/R to Pacific St.* **(see pp. 196, 199)**

Bryant Park. Pleasant oasis next to the Public Library offers free outdoor films in warm weather.... *No tel. 42nd St. between 5th and 6th Avenues, 1/9/2/3/N/R trains to Times Square.* **(see p. 203)**

Café Carlyle. Two words: Bobby Short. When he is elsewhere, look for the likes of Julie Wilson and Barbara Cook.... *Tel 212/570-7189. 981 Madison Ave., 6 train to 77th St.*
(see p. 193)

Carnegie Hall. The most celebrated performance space for live music in New York. The air is thick with the ghosts of greats.... *Tel 212/247–7800. 156 W. 57th St., N/R train to 57th St.* **(see pp. 197, 199)**

Caroline's. An essential space for stand-up in Manhattan. The room is huge, but surprisingly intimate.... *Tel 212/757–4100. 1626 Broadway, 1/9 train to 50th St. or N/R to 49th St.* **(see p. 197)**

Cathedral of St. John the Divine. So vast you wouldn't think it would be much fun, but it's actually one of the city's most free-spirited concert spaces... *Tel 212/*

316–7400. 1047 Amsterdam Ave., 1/9 train to 110th St./Cathedral Parkway. **(see p. 200)**

Cherry Lane Theater. This small and picturesque off-Broadway theater in a hidden-away corner of the West Village near Sheridan Square usually books lower-key artistically substantial shows... *Tel 212/989–2020. 38 Commerce St., 1/9 train to Christopher St.* **(see p. 198)**

Circle Rep. Low-key Downtown theater that maintains an experimental program without going off the deep end. Playwright Lanford Wilson and other notables got some early attention here.... *Tel 212/254–6330. 159 Bleecker St., A/C/E or B/D/Q/F train to W. 4th St.* **(see p. 198)**

City Center. Before Lincoln Center took over its sprawling expanse, this was one of New York's performance mansions. Nowadays, it hosts a mix of dance and music.... *Tel 212/581–7907. 131 W. 55th St., N/R or B/Q to 57th St.* **(see p. 195)**

Dance Theater Workshop (DTW). Chelsea's crucible for developing and spotting new choreographic and dance talent.... *Tel 212/924–0077. 219 W. 19th St., C/E train to 23rd St.* **(see p. 195)**

Dia Center for the Arts. A Chelsea Gallery that provides an excellent space for a variety of artistic media... *Tel 212/989–5566. 548 W. 22nd St., E/C train to 23rd St.* **(see p. 201)**

Don't Tell Mama. Big Great White Way hangout afterwork for chorus members, with some fine cabaret stylings.... *Tel 212/757–0788. 343 W. 46th St., A/C/E to 42nd St., N/R or 1/9/2/3 train to Times Square.* **(see p. 194)**

The Duplex. First stop for a variety of cabaret and comedy acts, along with the obligatory piano bars.... *Tel 212/255–5438. Corner of Christopher St. and Seventh Ave., 1/9 train to Christopher St.* **(see p. 194)**

Eighty Eights. A raucous place where show tunes are belted and egos punctured nightly.... *Tel 212/924–0088. 228 West 10th St., 1/9 train to Christopher St.* **(see p. 194)**

ENTERTAINMENT | THE INDEX

Film Forum. The jewel in New York's cinema crown, almost single-handedly feeding the Big Apple's voracious appetite for avant-garde cinema.... *Tel 212/727–8110. 209 W. Houston St., 1/9 train to Houston St.* **(see p. 203)**

Franklin Furnace. Some of the best and most extreme, not to mention unwatchable, performance artists have passed through this Tribeca space.... *Tel 212/925–4671. 112 Franklin St., 1/9 to Franklin St.* **(see p. 199)**

Giants Stadium. Arena rock acts, football's Jets and Giants. A long way to go to spend a lot of money for a crummy view of the Stones, but it's a great place to watch football.... *Tel 201/935–3900. The Meadowlands, East Rutherford, NJ; buses from Port Authority.* **(see pp. 200, 202)**

Grace Church. Beloved old gothic church that sits on the border between the West and East Villages. Frequent classical music concerts... *Tel 212/254–2000. 802 Broadway, 6 train to Astor Place.* **(see p. 200)**

Iridium. Where knowledgeable jazz junkies gather to score a glimpse at this or that giant. The surreal decor might prompt an acid flashback.... *Tel 212/582–2121. 44 W. 63rd St., 1/9 train to 66th St./Lincoln Center.*
(see p. 192)

Irving Plaza. Huge, former cabaret hosts alternative bands and performers.... *Tel 212/249–8870. 17 Irving Place, 4/5/6 or N/R train to Union Square.* **(see p. 200)**

The Jazz Standard. Presents some of the idiom's finest young talents in comfy surroundings.... *Tel 212/576–2232. 116 East 27th St., 6 train to 28th St.* **(see p. 193)**

Joyce Theater. The best theater in New York for contemporary dance, it's also home to Eliot Feld's company, The Feld Ballet.... *Tel 212/242–0800. 175 Eighth Ave., C/E train to 23rd St. or 1/9 to 18th St.* **(see p. 195)**

Juilliard School. The famous school for the performing arts schedules numerous concerts by its students. Price is usually low to nil.... *Tel 212/799–5000, ext. 235. Lincoln Center, 1/9 train to 66th St./Lincoln Center.*
(see p. 199)

Julian's Famous Poolroom. This E. 14th Street landmark remains the place to rack 'em up.... *Tel 212/598–9884. 138 E. 14th St., 4/5/6 or N/R to Union Square.*

(see p. 202)

Kitchen. Performance art space extraordinaire.... *Tel 212/255–5793. 512 W. 19th St., A/C/E train to 14th St.*

(see p. 199)

Knitting Factory. Ensconced in fancier environs, this former celebrant of the rock-bottom cover charge has gotten posher and more expensive.... *Tel 212/219–3055. 74 Leonard St., 1/9 train to Franklin St.* **(see p. 193)**

Lincoln Square Cinemas. The decor's gimmicky with deliriously tacky recreations of famous old movie palaces.... *Tel 212/336–5000. 1900 Broadway, 1/9 train to 66th St./Lincoln Center.* **(see p. 203)**

Lincoln Plaza. If it's up for "Best Foreign Film" at the Oscars, it probably played here.... *Tel 212/757–2280. Broadway and 62nd St., 1/9 to 59th St./Columbus Circle.* **(see p. 203)**

Madison Square Garden. Home to the Rangers and the Knicks, this arena built in the 1960s on the site of the razed Pennsylvania Station.... *Tel 212/465–6741. 4 Pennsylvania Plaza, 1/9 or 2/3 train to Penn Station.* **(see pp. 201, 202)**

La Mama. Venerable East Village performance space with years of showcasing new talent under its belt.... *Tel 212/475–7710. 74 E. 4th St., B/D/Q/F train to Broadway/Lafayette or 6 to Astor Place.* **(see p. 199)**

Manhattan Theater Club. Seminal new theater is offered a first chance here... *Tel 212/645–5590. 453 W. 16th St., F train to 14th St.* **(see p. 198)**

Marie's Crisis Cafe. Nowhere near the height of style, but plenty friendly. Piano bar opens at 8.... *Tel 212/243–9323. 59 Grove St., 1/9 train to Christopher St.* **(see p. 194)**

Merkin Concert Hall. Contemporary classical's NYC home, so brush up on those obscure composers.... *Tel 212/362–8719. 129 W. 67th St. (Abraham Goodman House), 1/9 train to 66th St./Lincoln Center* **(see p. 199)**

ENTERTAINMENT | THE INDEX

Metropolitan Opera. Where fur-bearing dames of the culture circuit drag their investment-banker husbands to hear the fat lady sing.... *Tel 212/362–6000. Lincoln Center, 1/9 train to 66th St./Lincoln Center.* **(see p. 196)**

Museum of Modern Art. See Diversions.

Nassau Coliseum. This stadium could use some serious sprucing up, but if you're looking for a chance to watch NHL hockey, this is your place.... *Tel 800/888-9000. Uniondale, NY; LIRR to Hempstead Station, then N70, N71 or N72 bus.* **(see p. 202)**

New School. If reedy poets in carefully chosen tweeds floats your versifying boat, then the Academy of American Poets seasonal readings here are just what Dr. Johnson ordered.... *Tel 212/229–5600. 66 W. 12th St., F train to 14th St.* **(see p. 201)**

New York City Ballet. Unabashed beauty, with a trust of ballets so good that you'll want to see most of them over and over.... *Tel 212/870–5570. Lincoln Center, 1/9 train to 66th St./Lincoln Center.* **(see p. 194)**

New York City Opera. The little opera that could—maybe. Much cheaper and much more fun than the Met's grander offerings across the plaza.... *Tel 212/870–5570. Lincoln Center, 1/9 train to 66th St./Lincoln Center.* **(see p. 196)**

92nd St. Y. Uptown home to the Ecco Press and *Paris Review* crowd, where poetry is read mainly by white guys who still wear khakis.... *Tel 212/415–5440. 1395 Lexington Ave., 4/5/6 train to 96th St.* **(see p. 201)**

Nuyorican Poets Café. This East Village haunt practically invented the notorious Poetry Slam and continues to be the vanguard of the spoken word scene..... *Tel 212/ 505–8183. 236 E. 3rd St., F train to Second Ave.* **(see p. 201)**

Ohio Theater. Small SoHo theater that frequently presents experimental choreography.... *Tel 212/966–4844. 66 Wooster St., C/E train to Spring St. or N/R to Prince St.* **(see pp. 195, 198)**

Orpheum. This off-Broadway space has recently hosted long-run *Stomp*, a frenzy of Brits with nearly shaved heads banging on all sorts of industrial detritus.... *Tel 212/307–4100. 126 Second Ave., 6 train to Astor Place or N/R to 8th St.*
(see p. 198)

Playwrights Horizons. If you're feeling bold, this is an excellent venue for freshly minted drama... *Tel 212/279–4200. 416 W. 42nd St., A/C/E train to Times Square.* **(see p. 198)**

Promenade/Second Stage. The former hosts Broadway-caliber shows; the latter is a home to second runs of quality shows and increasingly, new works by hot young dramatists.... *Tel 212/580–1313. 2162 Broadway, 1/9 train to 79th St.* **(see p. 198)**

P.S. 122. Mabou Mines in the back, as well as whatever/whoever's in the main space, consistently push the extremes of Downtown performance.... *Tel 212/477–5288. 150 First Ave., 6 train to Astor Place.* **(see pp. 195, 199)**

Public Theater. Joe Papp, the übermensch of New York theater, transformed this limited operation into a world leader in theatrical experimentation.... *Tel 212/260–2400. 425 Lafayette St., 6 train to Astor Place or N/R to 8th St.*
(see pp. 198, 203)

Radio City Music Hall. An Art-Deco cathedral with erratic booking and always the high-kicking Rockettes.... *Tel 212/247–4777. 1260 Sixth Ave., B/D/F/Q train to Rockefeller Center.* **(see p. 201)**

Rainbow Room/Rainbow and Stars. The view's the thing, of course, as well as playing Fred and Ginger in the glam Art Deco Room. Fab cabaret acts and revues.... *Tel 212/632–5100. 30 Rockefeller Plaza, B/D/Q/F train to Rockefeller Center.* **(see p. 193)**

ReBar. A new haven for young comics.... *Tel 212/627–1680. 127 Eighth Ave., A/C/E train to 14th St.* **(see p. 197)**

Roundabout. Broadway theater that insists on resisting the big-production currents that rule Broadway.... *Tel 212/869–8400. 1520 Broadway, 1/9, 2/3, or N/R train to Times Square.* **(see p. 198)**

ENTERTAINMENT | THE INDEX

St. Mark's Bookshop. Excellent collection of modern fiction, poetry, and alternative publications.... *Tel 212/260–7853. 31 Third Avenue, 6 train to Astor Place.* **(see p. 201)**

St. Mark's Church-in-the-Bowery. Wonderful performance space on the edge of the East Village.... *Tel 212/674–8194 (Danspace Project); 212/533–4650 (Ontological Theater); 212/674–0910 (Poetry Project). 131 E. 10th St., 6 train to Astor Place.* **(see pp. 195, 201)**

Shea Stadium. Fairly generic, early Sixties-style ballyard at the end of the number 7 subway line, is home to the Mets.... *Tel 718/507–8499. 126th St. at Roosevelt Ave., Queens; 7 train to Willets Point/Shea Stadium.* **(see p. 202)**

Smalls. Great programming, great price, open practically all hours. The ten-hour $10 jazz marathon gets going at 10.... *Tel 212/929–7565. 183 W. 10th St. at Seventh Ave., 1/9 train to Christopher St.* **(see p. 194)**

Stand-up New York. The Upper West Side's answer to the comedy craze mixes amateur nights with more established acts.... *Tel 212/595–0850. 236 W. 78th St., 1/9 train to 79th St.* **(see p. 197)**

The Supper Club. Where would-be, not-so-well-bred, well-off swells put on the ritz and glitz to old-style crooners.... *Tel 212/921–1940. 240 West 47th St., N/R/1/9/2/3 train to Times Square.* **(see p. 194)**

Sweet Basil. Nighttime gigs usually start at 9 and 11 and Dixieland trumpet legend Doc Cheetham holds a jazz brunch here on weekends.... *Tel 212/242–1785. 88 Seventh Ave. S., 1/9 train to Christopher St.* **(see p. 193)**

Tavern on the Green. Central Park's stunningly lovely, tourist-gawking eatery books top jazz artists into the Chestnut Room and offers summertime dancing in the garden.... *Tel 212/873–3200. Central Park West at 67th St., B/C train to 72nd St. No music or dancing Mon.* **(see p. 193)**

Town Hall. A fine, mid-sized venue featuring a wide variety of musical acts.... *Tel 212/840–2824. 123 W. 43rd St., B/D/Q/F train to 42nd St., N/R or 1/9/2/3/7 train to Times Square.* **(see p. 200)**

U.S.T.A. National Tennis Center. Tennis' finest do battle on the hard courts here each year at the U.S. Open championships.... *Tel 718/760–6200. Flushing Meadows, Queens; 7 train to Willets Point/Shea Stadium.* **(see p. 202)**

Village Vanguard. The Downtown jazz joint for the truly devoted. Always an intense, 'round-midnight scene. Music charge around $15.... *Tel 212/255–4037. 178 Seventh Ave. S., 1/9 train to Christopher St.* **(see p. 192)**

Visiones. Affordable Spanish food and live jazz.... *Tel 212/673–5576. 125 MacDougal Street, take B/D/Q/F or A/C/E to West 4th Street.* **(see p. 193)**

Vivian Beaumont. Lincoln Center's main theater space... *Tel 212/362–6000. Lincoln Center, 1/9 train to 68th St./ Lincoln Center.* **(see p. 198)**

Walter Reade Theater. Home to the annual New York Film Festival. At other times, a great program of art-house revivals and essential cinema.... *Tel 212/875–5600. 65 W. 65th St., above Alice Tully Hall, 1/9 train to 66th St./Lincoln Center.* **(see p. 203)**

Whitney Museum of American Art. See Diversions.

Yankee Stadium. The House that Ruth Built, itself still splendid, sits in a crummy neighborhood that freaks out the baseball crowds about limited parking.... *Tel 718/293–6000. 161st St. and River Ave., Bronx, 4 train to 161st St.* **(see p. 202)**

The Ziegfeld. The biggest of New York's big screens. Gotham's antidote to the postage-stamps at the multiplex. Sit close.... *Tel 212/505-CINE#602, 141 W. 54th St., F train to 53rd and Third.* **(see p. 203)**

ENTERTAINMENT | THE INDEX

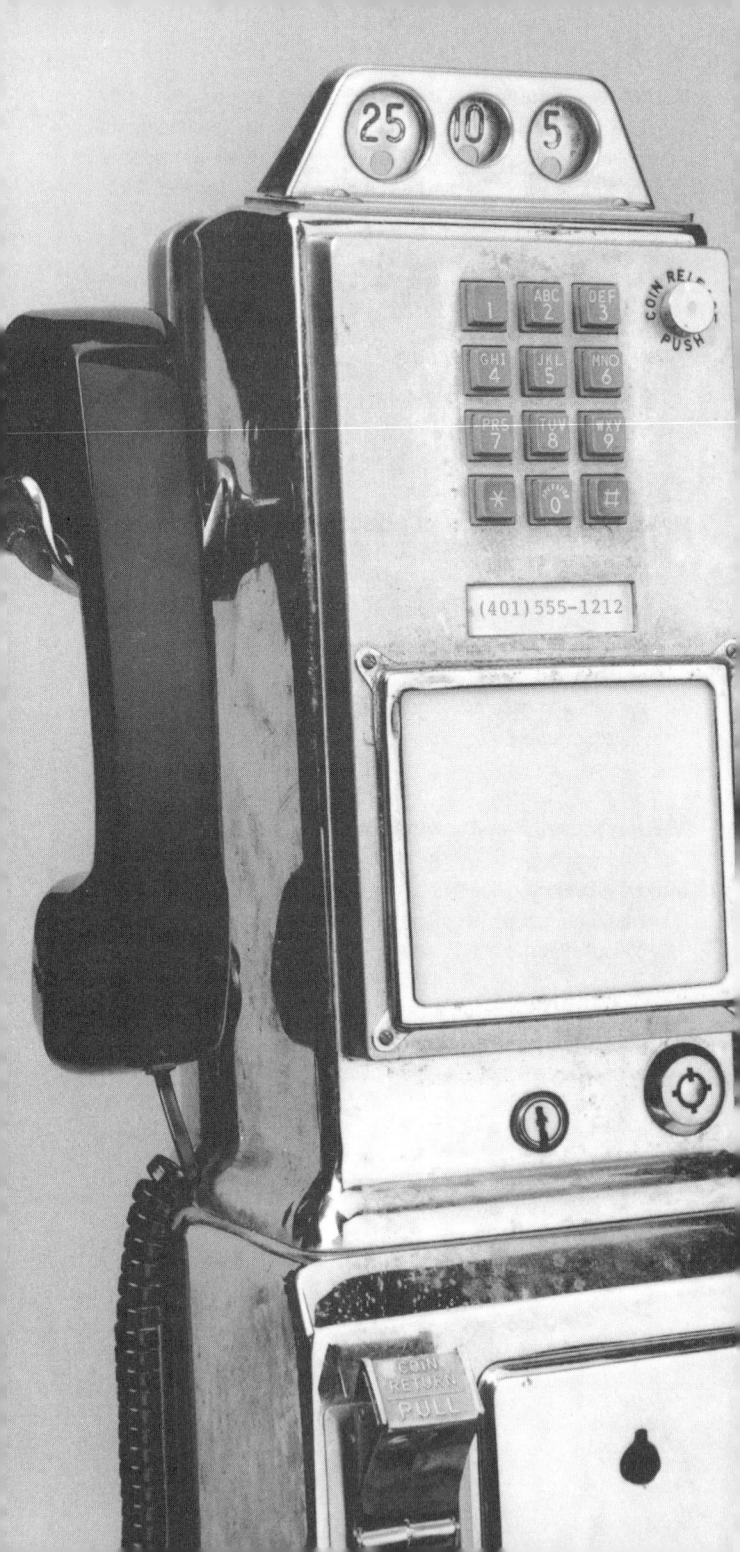

hotlines & other basics

Airports... New York City is served by three major airports—
La Guardia Airport (tel 718/533–3400), **John F. Kennedy
(JFK) International Airport** (tel 718/244–4444), and
Newark International Airport (tel 973/961–6000) in New
Jersey. JFK, in southeastern Queens, is the major international airport for the entire East Coast, and serves both
international and domestic travelers. Domestic passengers
usually prefer LaGuardia Airport, also in Queens, but a
shorter ride and cheaper cab or bus fare to Manhattan. More
and more travelers, both domestic and international, are
switching to Newark Airport, whose new terminals are less
crowded and more relaxed. **Carey Airport Express** buses
(tel 718/632–0500) connect LaGuardia and JFK, and
Airporter (tel 800/385–4000) links Newark with JFK—so
if you miss a flight at one airport you may be able to catch a
plane at another.

Airport transportation to the city... The cheapest way
to get into the city from **JFK** is via the free **Port Authority
Shuttle Bus** to the Howard Beach **subway** station, where
you can catch an "A" train into Manhattan (subway fare
$1.50). Subway transport is possible from **LaGuardia** by
taking a **Q33 bus** (fare $1.50, exact change, Metro Card,
or token) to the subway's Roosevelt Avenue station, where

for another $1.50 token you can ride the number 7 train to Midtown. Just as cheap, and more scenic, is the new **M60 bus** from **LaGuardia** (fare $1.50, MetroCard, token, or exact change). You cross the Triboro Bridge and see Harlem's 125th Street on your way to Broadway and 106th Street, where you can transfer free to a Midtown-bound **M104** bus. Or you can catch a **Carey Airport Express Bus** from either JFK or LaGuardia to Manhattan. Buses leave every 20 to 30 minutes: the trip in from JFK costs $13 and takes about an hour; from La Guardia it's $10 and takes 45 minutes. Carey buses stop at the Port Authority Bus Terminal (42nd St. and 8th Ave.) and Grand Central Terminal (42nd St. and Park Ave.). Leaving **Newark Airport**, catch the **Olympia Trails Airport Express** (tel 212/964–6233) for a $7, 30-minute ride to Penn Station (34th St. and 8th Ave.), Grand Central, or the World Trade Center downtown. Buses leave every 20 to 30 minutes. **Gray Line Air Shuttle** (tel 212/315–3006) operates a minibus service between all three airports and a number of Manhattan hotels for $16 from JFK, $13 from LaGuardia, and $18 from Newark. Those who prefer a cab ride into the city should ignore the tempting offers of freelance limousine drivers and march straight to the taxi stand, where a uniformed dispatcher ushers passengers into licensed cabs. JFK and LaGuardia now have a flat fare of $30 to Manhattan, but you must have an officially dispatched cab (and the fare doesn't include tolls and tip). The estimated fare from Newark is between $34 and $55; the dispatcher will give you the fare when you let them know where in town you're going. Legitimate limousine pickup is available at all three airports from such private companies as **Carmel Limousine Service** (tel 212/666–6666). The cost is $17 from LaGuardia, $27 from JFK, and $28 from Newark, plus tolls and tip.

All-night pharmacies... A must in the city that never sleeps, 24-hour drug stores include **Duane Reade Drugs** at Broadway and 57th Street (tel 212/541–9708), Broadway and 91st Street (tel 212/799–3172), Third Avenue and 74th Street (tel 212/744–2668), and Lexington Avenue and 47th Street (tel 212/682–5338); and the absurdly overpriced **Kaufman Pharmacy** (tel 212/755–2266) at Lexington Avenue and 50th Street.

Buses... MTA-New York City Transit (tel 718/330–1234) operates the world's largest fleet of public buses, running round the clock. The best way to pay your $1.50 fare is with the new electronic **MetroCard**, sold in subway stations and many retail stores. It allows you a free transfer to another bus *or* to the subway. If you pay with a token or exact change, you have to request a transfer when you pay your fare, and it's good only for another bus. Each bus's destination appears above its front windshield; routes are posted at most bus stops. Children under 44 inches tall ride free. The **Port Authority Bus Terminal** (tel 212/564–8484, 8th Ave. at 42nd St.) serves **Greyhound**, **Trailways**, and other long-distance bus lines.

Car rentals... Cars are the least efficient way to get around town, but if you must drive, modest economy- or mid-sized cars are more likely to survive parallel parking, taxi-cab-bumping, and other everyday urban experiences. Try **Budget** (tel 800/527–0700, all three airports plus three NYC locations); **Avis** (tel 800/331–1212, all three airports plus 10 NYC locations); **Hertz** (tel 800/654–3131, all airports plus 9 Manhattan locations); or **Village Rent A Car** (tel 212/243–9200, 19 E. 12th St.), which rents nearly new compacts for $40 per day, mid-sized cars for $50—both with 100 free miles. Since the least attractive car is the least likely to be vandalized or stolen, your best bet for city driving might actually be **Rent-A-Wreck** (tel 718/784–3302), which charges an average of $125 for a weekend, though this involves a subway ride to Queens, where someone from the office will pick you up. On the other hand, if you feel a sudden urge to take off for the Hamptons for the weekend, consider a Mercedes 500 SL convertible from **Vogel's Eurocars, Inc.** (tel 914/968–8200), for only $495 per day plus pick-up and delivery charges.

Child care services... Many New York hotels provide baby-sitting services, or keep a list of reliable sitters. If your hotel isn't among them, call **The Baby Sitters Guild** (tel 212/682–0227) or the **Frances Stewart Agency** (tel 212/439–9222). Both services provide in-room child care as well as on-request trips to the playground, the Central Park Zoo, etc., for children of all ages, with licensed, bonded, insured sitters (baby nurses are trained in CPR). Parents who want to keep their young children with them can lighten their child care load at **Playspace** (tel 212/769–2300), an all–available–options indoor playground at 2473 Broadway at 92nd Street. Admission is $5.50 per person, with the second parent free.

Cultural-events hotlines... For information on theater, music, and dance performances, call **NYC On Stage** (tel 212/768–1818). The **City Parks Special Events Hotline** (tel 212/360–3456) provides news of outdoor concerts and performances and New York Roadrunner Club events. If you have Web access, point your browser to **www.sidewalk.com**, Bill Gates' internet project, for a continuously updated listing of music, theater, museum, and other events.

Dentists... You can get a list of dentists near you by calling **Dental Emergency Service** (tel 212/679–3966). Emergency dental service is also available from **ABC Dental Care** (tel 212/888–0015).

Disability services... Alexander Wood of **Big Apple Greeters** (tel 212/669–3602) specializes in advising disabled visitors on how to get around and enjoy the city. Note that the subway system remains largely inaccessible to the disabled, but 95% of the city's buses are equipped to carry wheelchairs.

Doctors... **Dial-A-Doctor** (tel 212/971–9692) sends physicians on house- or hotel calls 24 hours a day, as does **Doctors On Call** (tel 718/238–2100).

Driving around... In Midtown, and other spots where the police feel it's vital to keep traffic flowing, your illegally parked car will be towed in minutes, so don't even think of violating parking laws there. Elsewhere, officers are required to complete any parking ticket they've begun filling out, so begging or threatening will do no good. To find out where your car has been towed, call the **Borough Tow Pound** (tel 212/971–0770). For information on parking regulations currently in effect, call the **New York City Department of Transportation** (tel 212/442–7080). (See also Parking, below.)

Emergencies... The number to know is **911**, for police, fire, and ambulance service. Other emergency numbers include **AIDS Hotline** (tel 212/447–8200); **Animal Bites** (tel 212/676–2483); **Deaf Emergencies** (tel 212/777–3900, Voice/TTY); **Poison Control** (tel 212/340–4494); **Suicide Prevention** (tel 212/532–2400); **Traveler's Aid** (tel 212/944–0013); and **Victim Services Hotline** (tel 212/577–7777).

Ferries... The **Staten Island Ferry** (tel 718/727–2508) at Battery Park remains the best way to enjoy views of the Manhattan skyline, New York Harbor, and the Statue of Liberty. Best of all, it's now free. Still, other ferries work the harbor as well: the **Ellis Island and Statue of Liberty Ferry** (tel 212/269–5755) leaves Battery Park every 15–30 minutes for two of the city's most popular tourist destinations, for $7 round-trip. The **New York Waterway Ferry and Bus System** (tel 201/902–8700) has instituted a spiffy new service between New Jersey and Manhattan for $4.50 each way.

Festivals and special events... New York thrives on festivals, and the best way to find out about them is to pick up a copy of *The Big Apple Visitors Guide* at your hotel, or call the **The New York Convention & Visitors Bureau** (tel 800/NYC–VISIT or 212/484–1222, 224 W. 42nd Street). The guide lists a year's worth of art exhibits, walking tours, children's entertainment, ethnic festivals, and performances. Some events draw such a crowd that you'll want to reserve your hotel room, plane tickets, and events tickets well in advance. These include: **New Year's Eve** in Times Square; the **St. Patrick's Day Parade** down Fifth Avenue in March; the **Gay Pride Parade** on the last Sunday in June; **Macy's July 4th Fireworks Extravaganza**; the **U.S. Open Tennis Championships** in Flushing Meadows, Queens, in September; the **New York Film Festival** in late September/early October; the **Macy's Thanksgiving Day Parade**; and the **Christmas Tree Lighting** at Rockefeller Center in early December.

Foreign currency exchange... **American Express Travel Agencies** (tel 800/528–4800) will exchange currency at offices in the World Financial Center, at Macy's department store, and in half a dozen other locations. The offices of **Thomas Cook Currency Services** (tel 800/287–7362) are open from 9–5 in Times Square, Grand Central Station, Herald Square, Wall Street, and on Madison Avenue at 53rd Street. **Chase Manhattan Bank** (tel 800/287–4054) exchanges currency in all its branch banks or will deliver foreign currency to your home or office.

Gay and lesbian resources... New York boasts a gay and lesbian population large enough to support such organizations as the **Gay and Lesbian Anti-Violence Project** (tel 212/807–0197) and the **Gay Men's Health Crisis** (tel 212/807–6664), and institutions including **A Different Light Bookstore and Cafe** (tel 212/989–4850, 151 W. 19th St.) and **Three Lives Bookstore** (tel 212/741–2069, Waverly Place and W. 10th St.). *The Village Voice* remains a dependable source of gay-related news and entertainment listings. There is also a new free newspaper in town called the *New York City Blade* which boasts the largest (50,000) circulation of any gay weekly. It is available in maroon-colored stands that line the streets of Chelsea and the West Village.

Limousine and car services... Gotham Limousine, **Inc.**'s (tel 718/361–2401) rates range from $40 per hour for a chauffeured four-passenger sedan to $100 per hour for a 10-passenger stretch limousine; Rates for **Capricorn Limousine Service** at the Regency Hotel (tel 212/688–5530) run from $45 to $60 per hour; and **Promenade Car Service** (tel 718/858–6666) offers non-luxury cars with a driver for $25 per hour, and individual pickups and deliveries for slightly lower than yellow cab rates.

Newspapers... Manhattan newsstands offer a blizzard of political, professional, academic, alternative, business, and foreign language periodicals. Where to begin? Perhaps with the three major English-language dailies: *The New York Times*, *The Daily News*, and *The New York Post*. Briefly, the *Times* is the "official" paper, the *News* is the boroughs' favorite, and the *Post* is a tabloid owned by Mr. Murdoch. *The New York Observer*, a brash weekly printed on salmon-colored newsprint, focuses on fads, fashion, and gossip, particularly within the media. *The Wall Street Journal* is also edited here. *The Village Voice* offers liberal politics, entertainment listings, and the biggest personal ad section in New York.

Parking... Garages dot Manhattan streets every two blocks or so, with rates averaging about $5 for less than two hours, $12 for half a day, and $30 overnight. Prices are sometimes lower at night in business districts and during the day in residential areas; outdoor lots are less expensive, when you can find them. Our advice: find a hotel that offers free parking, such as the **Franklin** or the **Algonquin** (see Accommodations). Most Midtown hotels provide valet parking at about $35 per night. A partial list of garages: **Kinney System, Inc.** (tel 800/KNY–PARK), with over 150 garages; **Rapid Park** (tel 800/804–7275), with over 30 locations; **GMC** (tel 212/888–7400), with 55 locations.

Personal services... The Intrepid New Yorker (tel 212/534–5071) is available 24 hours a day to help visitors find personal shoppers, get around town, and otherwise cope with New York, for $25 per request. Their new emphasis is on helping those who are relocating to New York.

Phone facts... The area code for Manhattan is 212. To call Brooklyn, Queens, Staten Island, or the Bronx (at no extra charge), dial 1, then area code 718, then the phone number. For directory assistance, dial 411. There are public phones on every other street corner in Manhattan, and there, directory assistance calls are free. Some take coins; others require calling cards. A local call costs 25 cents. For fax service, a private booth, or TDDs, try the **AT&T Public Calling Center** (tel 800/CALL–ATT) at Grand Central Terminal at 42nd Street and Lexington Avenue.

Post offices... The **Main Post Office** at 8th Avenue and 33rd Street (tel 212/967–8585) is open 24 hours a day, seven days a week. Call the **Postal Answer Line** (tel 800/725–2161) for other information.

Radio stations... On the FM dial, **WPLJ (95.5)** concentrates on Top 40 hits; **WBLS (107.5)** plays soul and R&B; **WFMU (91.1)** offers alternative, eclectic fare; **HOT 97** does urban contemporary; **WRKS (KISS-FM, 98.7)** has soul classics; **Z100** specializes in rock; and **WKCR (89.9)** offers jazz. Tune in to **WNYC (93.9)** for classical music, and **WXRK (92.3)** for Howard Stern. AM stations include **WNYC (820)**, the National Public Radio affiliate; **WFAN (660)** for sports; and **WCBS (880)** and **WINS (1010)** for continual news.

Restrooms... Freud himself was reputedly scandalized by New York's lack of public restrooms, and the situation has not changed much since then. Restrooms do exist in **Central Park** across from the Delacorte Theater, mid-park at 79th Street; **Bryant Park**, at 42nd Street and 6th Avenue behind the New York Public Library, now offers clean, guarded restrooms free of charge. The library itself has nice, large bathrooms that are easy to duck into, as do most of the branch libraries throughout the city. If you can't find a public facility, do what the natives do: stride into the nearest hotel lobby or cafe and back to the ladies' or gents' like you own the place. No one is likely to stop you.

Smoking... New York's stringent smoking regulations forbid smoking in all but the smallest restaurants (though you can light up at bars) and in workplaces—you'll see office workers madly puffing just outside lobby entrances at buildings all over town. Forget smoking on buses and subway trains, or in taxis. Taxi drivers are not allowed to smoke, either.

Subways... Operated by the **New York City Metropolitan Transit Authority** (tel 718/330–1234), the subway transports three-and-a-half-million people per day from 469 stations in Manhattan, Brooklyn, Queens, and the Bronx—so give the MTA a break if some stations are a tad grimy or the trains a little noisy. Even mildly adventurous visitors should feel comfortable underground from 7am–10pm. Tokens, sold at booths in each station, are $1.50 each. The new electronic **MetroCards** are available at $6 and $15. You can put as much as $80 on one, if you like. With a token, you can ride the rails as long and as far as you like but you can't leave the system. With a MetroCard, you can also transfer free to a bus. If you put more than one fare at a time on a MetroCard, it somehow remembers and gives you that number of free transfers, provided you use them all at the same time. Also, if you put more than $15 on a card, you get a free ride. Children under 44 inches ride free. Maps are posted inside stations and in most cars.

Taxes... Sales tax is 8.25%, charged on everything except groceries and take-out food. Hotels add a 13.25% hotel tax to room rates.

Taxis... The only taxis authorized to pick up passengers hailing them on the street are **yellow cabs**, which have an official taxi medallion screwed onto the hood. So-called "gypsy cabs," working for car services, sometimes stop illegally for passengers on the street, but since they have no meter, you'll have to negotiate your own fare with the driver, and you'll have no legal recourse if there's a problem. To know whether a yellow taxi is free, look for the lit-up sign on the roof of the cab; off-duty cabs (side sections of the roof sign lit) may pick up passengers at their own discretion. Taxi meters calculate the fare: $2.00 when you get in, plus 30 cents for each 1/5th of a mile or 90 seconds of waiting time in traffic. There's an extra 50-cent charge, 8pm–6am. Passengers pay any bridge or tunnel tolls. A 15–20% tip is expected. Complaints concerning limousines, car services, or cabs should be directed to the **NYC Taxi and Limousine Commission** (tel 212/692–8294).

Ticket charge lines... Telecharge (tel 212/239–6200); Ticketmaster (tel 212/307–7171).

Tipping... When calculating a restaurant tip, many New Yorkers simply double the tax amount on their check (2 x 8.25% = 16.5%, a reasonable tip). But New York waitpeople work hard for their money, so round it up to 20% if you can. At top restaurants, give the waiter 15%

and the captain 5%. Tip hotel doormen $1 per taxi, and bellhops and airport porters $1 per bag.

Trains... There are two major railway terminals in Manhattan: **Grand Central Terminal** at 42nd Street and Lexington Avenue, and **Pennsylvania (Penn) Station** at 33rd Street and 7th Avenue. **Amtrak** trains (tel 800/872–7245) depart Penn Station for points across the country. Among them are Amtrak's Metroliner, an hourly express train to Washington, D.C. Also operating out of Penn Station are the **New Jersey Transit** (tel 201/762–5100) and **Long Island Railroad** (tel 718/217–5477) commuter lines. The **Metro-North Commuter Railroad** (212/532–4900) serves Connecticut and New York State from Grand Central.

TV stations... CBS plays on Channel 2; **NBC** is 4; the **Fox** network is 5; **ABC** is 7; 13 is reserved for **PBS** (two other PBS stations are at 21 and 31 on the dial). The other channels reel with foreign-language, public access, sports, news, and additional networks.

Visitor information... The **New York Convention & Visitors Bureau's Visitors Information Center** (see "Festivals and Special Events," above) is open seven days a week, providing maps and advice, along with "two-fers" for savings on Broadway and Off-Broadway plays. The Visitors Bureau's toll-free, 24-hour **information hotline** (tel 800-NYC–VISIT or 212/397–8222 outside the U.S.) offers similar information by phone.

Taxi Fair

Despite the enduring re-run success of the TV series "Taxi", New York cabbies these days are more like the Andy Kaufman character, Latka, than like Judd Hirsch's Alex. Gone is the shrewd cabbie of legend, replaced by recent immigrants who speak little English and don't care how the Yankees are playing. Drivers are required to take you anywhere within the five boroughs, Westchester and Nassau Counties, and should ask you to specify the route. They're supposed to be pros, so I often leave it up to them; but don't be shy about telling the driver to change his course if he (or she) gets caught in traffic or road construction. From Newark Airport and LaGuardia the routes to Midtown are fairly straightforward. JFK is another story—I suggest telling the driver to take the Long Island Expressway and Midtown Tunnel. Cab fares to Midtown from JFK and Newark should run about $40, including tolls and tip; $35 from LaGuardia.

MANHATTAN | HOTLINES & OTHER BASICS